DATE DUE

NOV 1 6 1993	MAR 2 5 1999
JAN 3 1 1994	APR 0 4 2000
FEB 1 1 1994	OCT 2 4 2003
MAR - 7 1994	NOV 1 3 2000
MAR 2 1 1994	
SEP 2 0 1994	
SEP 3 0 1994	
OCT 2 0 1994	
MAR 1 3 1995	
MAR 2 2 1995	
APR 1 1 1995	
NOV 2 1 1996	
DEC 1 1 1996	
MAR 1 0 1997	
MAR 2 6 1997	
FEB 2 7 1998	
MAR 0 4 2000	

CHIEFLY FEASTS

The Enduring Kwakiutl Potlatch

CHIEFLY FEASTS

contributions by

Stacy Alyn Marcus

Judith Ostrowitz

and special editorial help by

Peter L. Macnair

color photographs by

Lynton Gardiner

American Museum of Natural History   *New York*

The Enduring Kwakiutl Potlatch

Edited by

ALDONA JONAITIS

with essays by

Douglas Cole

Ira Jacknis

Aldona Jonaitis

Wayne Suttles

Gloria Cranmer Webster

University of Washington Press *Seattle & London*

To the Kwakwa̱ka̱'wakw people,
with respect and admiration

Copyright © 1991 by the American Museum of Natural History
Composition by Typeworks, Vancouver
Typesetting by Antoinette Warren
Printed and bound by Dai Nippon Printing Company, Tokyo
Designed by Audrey Meyer

Published simultaneously in Canada by
Douglas & McIntyre Ltd.
1615 Venables Street
Vancouver, British Columbia   V5L 2H1

Library of Congress Cataloging-in-Publication Data

Chiefly Feasts : the enduring Kwakiutl potlatch / edited by Aldona
    Jonaitis : with essays by Douglas Cole ... [et al.] ; and special edito-
    rial help by Peter Macnair.
        p.   cm.
    Includes bibliographical references and index.
    ISBN 0-295-97114-2 (cloth : alk. paper). -- ISBN 0-295-97115-0
        (pbk. : alk. paper)
    1. Kwakiutl Indians--Rites and ceremonies. 2. Potlatch--British
Columbia. 3. Kwakiutl Indians--Art. I. Jonaitis, Aldona, 1948- . II.
Cole, Douglas, 1938- . III. American Museum of Natural History.
E99.K9C45   1991
971.1'004979--dc20   91-16778
                                                              CIP

The paper used in this publication meets the minimum requirements of American National Standard for Information Sciences—Permanence of Paper for Printed Library Materials, ANSI A39.48-1984.

Itinerary of the Exhibition

American Museum of Natural History, New York,
October–February 1992

Royal British Columbia Museum, Victoria, *June–November 1992*

California Academy of Sciences, San Francisco, *January–August 1993*

National Museum of Natural History, Smithsonian Institution,
Washington, D.C., *October 1993–March 1994*

Seattle Art Museum, *May–September 1994*

Contents

Illustrations

All objects, unless otherwise noted, are nineteenth century. All objects and all black and white photographs, unless otherwise noted, are in the collection of the American Museum of Natural History (AMNH). Other objects and black and white photographs are illustrated courtesy of the Royal British Columbia Museum (RBCM), Victoria; the U'mista Cultural Centre (UCC), Alert Bay; the Burke Museum, Seattle; the Campbell River Museum; the Chicago Historical Society (CHS); the Milwaukee Public Museum (MPM); and the Provincial Archives of British Columbia (PABC).

The extended captions accompanying the color illustrations were prepared by Judith Ostrowitz (JO), Stacy Alyn Marcus (SAM), and Gloria Cranmer Webster (GCW).

All color photographs, unless otherwise noted, are by Lynton Gardiner.

Foreword

THE TWO KEYS TO A GREAT ETHNOGRAPHIC EXHI-bition are a magnificent collection that fully represents a culture or a particular activity and a scholar intensely interested in the subject and committed to transforming a collection of exotic objects into a vibrant, informative exhibit. *Chiefly Feasts* is blessed on both scores. At its heart is one of the finest, most comprehensive collections ever assembled for a North American Indian tribe: the Kwakiutl collection of the American Museum of Natural History. Aldona Jonaitis, who conceived the exhibition, brought expertise and tremendous enthusiasm to the project.

Franz Boas and George Hunt assembled the Kwakiutl collection for the American Museum in the course of the Jesup North Pacific Expedition (1897–1902). Boas became interested in Northwest Coast culture when, as a young man in the 1880s, he worked with some Northwest Coast Indians then visiting Berlin and found their culture and art irresistible. A native of Germany, he came to the United States, eventually settling at the American Museum where he became assistant curator in the Department of Anthropology. He lost no time in seeking the financial support of museum president Morris K. Jesup for a research project of extensive scope in his favorite region.

George Hunt was Boas's colleague on the Northwest Coast. Hunt's mother was a Tlingit noblewoman, and his English father was a factor for the Hudson's Bay Company. Hunt was raised in Fort Rupert as a Kwakiutl, spoke Kwakwala fluently, and was literate in English. He was Boas's principal collector on the Northwest Coast, and much of Boas's research depended on his. The close collaboration of Boas and Hunt was basic to their classic ethnographic studies and to the formation of a great collection. This cooperative tradition reappears in *Chiefly Feasts*, where the Kwakiutl worked closely with museum personnel to create the exhibition.

The Kwakiutl, the larger society, and scholarship have come a long way since the time of Hunt and Boas. People like Hunt, who were more or less comfortable in two cultures, were rare in his day, and great museums competed for his services during the heyday of museum collecting on the Northwest Coast. Today, well-educated Kwakiutl who know both the Kwakiutl and Canadian cultures are the rule. A group of Kwakiutl, rather than one person, worked with the American Museum, and one of them, Gloria Cranmer Webster, curated a major part of the exhibition.

Boas too was a rarity, a man in advance of his time. He fought an ultimately successful battle to win the respect of the larger society for Indian art and culture, but at the beginning it was not easy. The potlatch was central to Kwakiutl culture, so Boas focused on it in press interviews, only to find that one popular account misrepresented the ceremony in the most lurid prose imaginable. Boas was embarrassed, and the Kwakiutl were angry, but they accepted his explanation, knowing that he was a friend. The larger society has today generally abandoned sensationalism in dealing with Native peoples. Anthropology has played a major role in the development of more accurate accounts and humane interpretations.

Although the work of Boas and Hunt is still basic to Kwakiutl studies, continuing research has followed the history of the Kwakiutl and their potlatch to modern times. The present volume is a case in point. The 120 or so objects that make up the exhibit are beautifully illustrated and intensively researched. Each of the essays is a significant scholarly contribution. Douglas Cole's account of the history of the potlatch is a balanced treatment, noteworthy for its understanding of the positions both of the Kwakiutl and of Canadian officials. Ira Jacknis offers a detailed study of George Hunt and his relationship with Boas. The paper by Wayne Suttles on the traditional potlatch is descriptive ethnography and analysis at their best. The "Postscript" by Judith Ostrowitz and Aldona Jonaitis is a fine example of the discoveries that can be made when experts and collections are brought together. Jonaitis writes revealingly of her first encounter with the Kwakiutl and outlines the gradual development of the exhibit. Gloria Webster's delightful essay brings the potlatch down to the present. She wonders how ancestral Kwakiutl would view the contemporary potlatch and believes that "we are not doing too badly." Were old museum hand Franz Boas to visit *Chiefly Feasts* and read this volume, I think that he would agree that Jonaitis and her colleagues have not done too badly either.

STANLEY A. FREED
Curator, American Museum of Natural History

Preface

THE KWAKIUTL LIVE ON THE NORTHERN AND eastern side of Vancouver Island as far south as Campbell River and on the mainland opposite. They are sometimes called the Southern Kwakiutl in the literature, to distinguish them from the Haisla, the Heiltsuk, and the Oowekeeno, once improperly called the Northern Kwakiutl. Their potlatch, in this exhibit celebrated as an uninterrupted tradition from precontact times until the present, is the occasion on which a noble family invites guests who witness the display of the host's status. In the late nineteenth and early twentieth centuries, various grades of potlatches were given, ranging from relatively minor events for children at various times in their life cycle, through the more significant festivals celebrating the assumption of dance privileges, to the most important, called "Doing a Great Thing." This last type of potlatch could celebrate several different activities: the assumption of a chiefly name and position, the exchange of coppers (objects of greatest value to these people), marriages, the erection of totem poles, and the building of houses. On each of these occasions, guests received payment from the host for their service as witnesses; their acceptance of these payments signified their validation of the host's claims of status.

At the end of the nineteenth century, most Euro-Canadians misunderstood the potlatch. The singular feature of nineteenth century potlatches, which caught the attention of non-Natives, was the host's extravagant distribution of gifts to his guests and the occasional deliberate distribution of valuable property, acts intended to display his great wealth and high status. Another feature of some potlatches was ritual cannibalism, either simulated or occurring in the token form of superficial biting. This "cannibalism" inflamed Euro-Canadian opinion against the potlatch. At the behest of missionaries and in accord with general sentiment, the government of Canada passed a law in 1884 prohibiting the potlatch ceremony. Although potlatching became less and less frequent among some of the other Northwest Coast peoples, the Kwakiutl resisted the law and actually appear to have put on more and more lavish affairs during the late nineteenth and early twentieth centuries.

These people, defiant in their resistance to oppression and tenaciously adhering to their traditions, fascinated anthropologist Franz Boas. Boas carried out his research with George Hunt, a half-English, half-Tlingit collaborator, who had been raised in a Kwakiutl village and who was integrated into that culture. Like many of his contemporaries, Boas believed that the Kwakiutl would soon vanish. It was the responsibility of anthropology to save whatever could be recorded in books and displayed in museums. Hunt played a pivotal role in acquiring considerable amounts of information on what Boas assumed to be a "dying culture."

In actuality, neither the Kwakiutl nor their traditions died, as a visit to their thriving communities in British Columbia will clearly testify. Despite the anti-potlatch law, they continued to potlatch, albeit furtively, throughout the first half of the twentieth century. After the prohibition was dropped in the 1950s (it was never formally rescinded), the Kwakiutl potlatch, lavish and impressive as ever, became public once again. New art by excellently trained artists continues to be created for these events, which by any account are dazzling affairs.

This catalogue was conceived to accompany the exhibition that describes the continuity of this extraordinary tradition, *Chiefly Feasts: The Enduring Kwakiutl Potlatch*. Its five essays provide an extensive background on the meaning and history of the potlatch. In "Streams of Property, Armor of Wealth: The Traditional Potlatch," Wayne Suttles analyzes the nature of the nineteenth century manifestation of this ceremonial. Douglas Cole's "The History of the Kwakiutl Potlatch" details white responses to the potlatch as well as Native responses to the government's attempt to eradicate it. In "George Hunt, Collector of Indian Specimens," Ira Jacknis describes the manner by which information about the Kwakiutl as well as their artifacts were collected. Framing these pieces are somewhat more personal narratives, "The Contemporary Potlatch" by Gloria Cranmer Webster, a Kwakiutl great-granddaughter of George Hunt, and my own "Chiefly Feasts: The Creation of an Exhibition." The postscript, by Judith Ostrowitz and me, describes our discovery that an extraordinary array of artifacts were connected to one particular legend.

Illustrating these essays are color pictures of objects in the exhibition and black-and-white archival and contemporary photographs. The largest number of objects are nineteenth century artifacts, almost all from the collection of the American Museum of Natural History; a smaller group includes twentieth century and contemporary pieces as well as some older objects from U'mista Cultural Centre in Alert Bay, British Columbia, the Royal British Columbia Museum in Victoria, the Campbell River Museum in Campbell River, British Columbia, and the Thomas Burke Museum in Seattle.

The Kwakiutl potlatch was and continues to be a complex ceremonial during which the host family communicates its status by displaying inherited privileges embodied in lavishly decorated artworks and dances as well as by making eloquent speeches detailing those privileges. The guests are treated to sumptuous cuisine and, at the end, receive gifts as payment for having witnessed these displays.

When we were designing *Chiefly Feasts*, we decided not to arrange the pieces according to type of object, such as masks, figures, and bowls, but instead to express several major themes that reveal the significance of the potlatch to the Kwakiutl people. The first such theme is the chief. The embodiment of the prestige and history of his extended family as well as the host of the potlatch, the chief had associated with himself elaborate and elegant art replete with imagery, usually of animals, that represented family histories and signified privileges. Among such artworks were colorful button blankets, carved headdresses with trains of ermine, settees, masks, and an assortment of sculptures that depicted ancestors, animals, chiefs, and their orators or speakers. Perhaps the most impressive of all is the 289-cm-high speaker's post (fig. 4.26) that depicts the ancestors of the family who owned it. It was through the open mouth of the uppermost figure that the chief's speaker welcomed visitors to the potlatch and proudly orated his family's traditions. Closely connected to the theme of the chief is that of marriage, for it was from his wife that the Kwakiutl male acquired ceremonial privileges so central to his social standing.

The most central symbol of wealth, power, and prestige is the copper, a shield-shaped plate of beaten copper that usually has a painted or engraved representation of a crest animal on its surface (fig. 1.16). The section on wealth includes not only these plates, but also carvings of individuals holding these significant artifacts as well as posing the most formidable challenge, namely, "breaking" a copper. To break a copper, the chief cut off a section of this precious possession and handed it, in a gesture of retaliation, to a rival whom he believed had insulted his family. The recipient had to reciprocate at a larger potlatch to avoid losing face. This section also discusses the significance of the Hudson's Bay Company blanket as a nineteenth century version of the furs and skins that in precontact time were the measure of the value of a copper and also served as major potlatch gifts.

The next section involves food and feasting. Because feasting played such an important role in the Kwakiutl potlatch, the preparation and presentation of food was of considerable interest to hosts and guests alike. The artistry and grandeur of the serving vessels had to match the elaborate cuisine, and much effort went into creating food bowls and serving implements for ceremonial purposes. Some of these vessels were quite large, such as the 270-cm-long bowl depicting the Wild Woman of the Woods and the 188-cm-long bowl representing the face of the mythic devilfish (figs. 4.16, 2.42).

The potlatch dances, the theme of the next section, are divided into two categories, *tseḵa* and *tła'saḻa*. An extremely important privilege that needed validation at potlatches was the right to perform these dances and display associated ritual paraphernalia. The *tseḵa*, which some anthropologists call Winter Ceremonials, is a complex of ranked privileges that an individual inherits; the performance constitutes an initiation. The dances of the *tseḵa*, which embody the powers of supernatural beings, dramatically reenact the interaction of an initiate with one of several mythic beings whose contact in legendary times with the initiate's ancestors gave his or her family the dance privilege. One specific example of this is the Siwidi masquerade, which reenacts the voyage to the undersea kingdom by the hero Siwidi. Separate from the *tseḵa* dances, and somewhat lower in status, were the *tła'saḻa* performances, which displayed the inherited crest privileges. In the nineteenth century, *tseḵa* and *tła'saḻa* dances were never performed at the same time and in the same house, and active participants in one of these types of dances could not attend the other during the same season. In the twentieth century, the *tła'saḻa* is performed after the *tseḵa*, on the same day, in the same house, and by the same people.

The final sections of *Chiefly Feasts* bring the potlatch into the twentieth century. The section on suppression and resistance describes the Kwakiutl's defiance of the anti-potlatch legislation and the eventual rescinding of it in 1951. The section on contemporary potlatch illustrates the art made today for celebrations in the various villages of northern Vancouver Island. In these two sections are pieces made by earlier modern masters such as Willie Seaweed and Mungo Martin, as well as more recent artists such as Henry Hunt, Tony Hunt, Tony Hunt, Jr., Richard Hunt, Doug Cranmer, Beau Dick, and Shirley Ford. These materials will testify with clarity to the remarkable persistence of a great ceremonial and artistic tradition.

The captions in this catalogue are longer than most. When I asked Stacy Marcus and Judith Ostrowitz, my assistants on this project, to research the objects and write up the captions, none of us knew really what that would entail. With the help of Peter Macnair, they discovered that the information we had on many of these pieces was located in a variety of places. Marcus and Ostrowitz first researched each object in the department catalogue, which provided information on what it was, and when and where it was found. They then scrutinized the Boas-Hunt correspondence, both in the Museum's Anthropology Archives and in the Boas Professional Papers at the American Philosophical Society in Philadelphia, to record what, if anything, Hunt said about the piece in his letters to Boas. When Hunt collected artworks, he often recorded stories associated with the objects. Many of these stories were published in Boas and Hunt 1905, 1906. Unfortunately, only a field list handwritten by Hunt correlated the objects to the stories, by indicating where they appeared in the handwritten manuscripts. Gloria Cranmer Webster and Wayne Suttles assisted in the translation of the Kwak̓wala words in these documents. Marcus and Ostrowitz then found a key in the American Philosophical Society in Philadelphia provided by Boas that correlated the page numbers of some of the Hunt manuscripts to the pagination of Boas and Hunt 1905 and 1906. All this information was drawn on for the captions. (It was this process that resulted in our discovery of our Siwidi treasures—see Ostrowitz and Jonaitis, this volume.)

As one of the themes of *Chiefly Feasts* is the representation of Kwakiutl traditions, it was imperative that we consult the elder members of the community about the objects selected for this exhibition so that we could include invaluable information only they could provide. Marcus and Ostrowitz traveled to Alert Bay in March 1990 to discuss the objects with Agnes Cranmer, Margaret Cook, Doug Cranmer, as well as Gloria Cranmer Webster. Then in May 1990, they worked closely with the old people who visited the museum (chapter 1) to record

their comments on the pieces. This information, as well as information provided by Bill Holm, Peter Macnair, and Wayne Suttles, is also incorporated into these extended captions.

I would like to thank those who have helped make this exhibition and this catalogue a reality. First of all, of course, I wish to express my respect and admiration for the Kwakiutl people whose culture we are celebrating. Individuals who have been of great help include the older members of the community who shared their memories: Ethel Alfred, Margaret Cook, Agnes Cranmer, Adam Dick, Emma Hunt, William Hunt, Helen Knox, Alice Peters, Alice Smith, Peter Smith (d.), Thomas Willie, James Wilson, Sr., and Elsie Williams.

Special thanks go to my good friends in Alert Bay, who were always warm and gracious when I visited their magical community. Without Gloria Cranmer Webster's help this entire project could not possibly have become a reality. She has worked as a consultant on the exhibition, read all the essays and captions for this publication, curated the section on the contemporary potlatch, and wrote a moving piece in this catalogue about the experiences of a modern Kwakiutl at one of these celebrations. I have learned an immense amount from Gloria and deeply appreciate everything she has done for this exhibition.

Davina Hunt of Alert Bay was always available for warm conversations over good cups of coffee. Bill and Denise Cranmer were also helpful and took good care of me on my visits. I remember with special pleasure my conversations with Doug Cranmer, not only a fine artist but also a fascinating intellectual. Bill Wasden took time from his schedule to take me to the other Kwakiutl villages.

It is necessary to acknowledge the important role the artists played in this project. Tony Hunt played a most important role as an advisor, consultant, and guide in Kwakiutl ways. Calvin Hunt replicated the screen and *sisiyuɫ* board magnificently. Other fine artists that helped include Bruce Alfred, Tony Hunt, Jr., Kevin Cranmer, Richard Hunt, and Wayne Alfred.

Other Kwakiutl were exceedingly gracious and helpful: Harry Assu, Dora Sewid Cook, Peter Cook, David Dawson, Flora Dawson, Robert Joseph, Irene Hunt Hayman, David Hunt, George Hunt, Marie Hunt, Harry James, Henry Seaweed, Beatrice Smith, Albert Wilson, Jr., and James Wilson, Jr.

Peter Macnair of the Royal British Columbia Museum has been instrumental in making this project a reality. An extraordinary wellspring of information, Peter assisted me in every phase of the conceptualization, planning, and design of the show. He was particularly helpful in introducing me to members of the community. I am deeply grateful for the time and effort he spent on *Chiefly Feasts*; in a very real way this is as much Peter Macnair's exhibition as it is mine. He also worked very closely with Stacy Marcus and Judith Ostrowitz, by assisting them in researching the artworks illustrated here and writing the captions.

In addition to Gloria Cranmer Webster, the other authors of the catalogue essays deserve special thanks for submitting their essays on time and being so agreeable during the editing process: Douglas Cole, Ira Jacknis, and Wayne Suttles. Stacey Marcus and Judith Ostrowitz worked hard on all aspects of the exhibition, particularly on the captions. Gloria Cranmer Webster, Wayne Suttles, Bill Holm, and Peter Macnair deserve special thanks for their careful reading of the entire manuscript.

Others who assisted me in my trips to northern Vancouver Island were Bill and Donna Mackay and Jim and Ann Borrowman of Stubbs Island Charters. They were all extremely generous and gracious to me. Jay Stewart and Estelle Inman of the Campbell River Museum and Laurie Jones of the Cape Mudge Kwagiulth Museum also assisted me in many ways, as did Jay Powell of the University of British Columbia and Vickie Jensen. Michael Ames of the University of British Columbia's Museum of Anthropology offered very sound advice on the project. And thanks go to James Haggarty, Alan Hoover, and Richard Inglis of the Royal British Columbia Museum, who shared generously in their time, expertise, and warmth. Thanks also to Shelley Reid, John Veillette, Andrew Niemann, and Eric Peterson.

I have many people to thank for the photographs in this book. First of course is Lynton Gardiner, who has made photographic artworks from the Kwakiutl artworks illustrated here. Thanks as well go to Denis Finnin, Jackie Beckett, and Kerry Perkins of the American Museum of Natural History photographic archives and photography studio. Dan Savard of the Royal British Columbia Museum was exceptionally helpful in our efforts to obtain historic photographs of the Kwakiutl potlatch. Thanks also go to Leni Hoover of the same institution. Bill McLennan of the University of British Columbia Museum of Anthropology was most generous with his infrared photograph of the settee. Susan Otto of the Milwaukee Public Museum was also very helpful. Thanks as well to Phillip Yampolsky.

The staff at the American Museum of Natural History have been wonderfully supportive. Stanley Freed, Curator of North American Ethnology, merits special mention as a collaborator on this entire project. Others in the Anthropology Department who have helped greatly are Paul Beelitz, Barbara Conklin, John Hansen, Belinda Kaye, Bill Weinstein, Judith Levinson, Marian Kaminitz, Sasha Stollman, Linda Nieuwenhuizen, Geraldine Santoro, Anibal Rodriguez, Laila Williamson. Others I would like to acknowledge are Rose Wadsworth, Adele Meyer, Barbara Mathé, Sarah Granato, Alec Madoff, Gene Bergman, and Kevin Coffee. Scarlett Lovell and Elizabeth Streeter were a tremendous help in the production of this book. Many people at the museum helped make the visit of the Kwakiutl a success: Fran Dunleavy, Alfredo Guererro, Don Kossar, Charles Urban, Charles Miles, Sankar Gokool, Rebecca Moore, Elda Luisi, Amy Rudnick, and Jerome Williams deserve thanks.

I wish to express my special appreciation to Geralyn Abinader, my assistant at the American Museum of Natural History, who worked very hard at organizing the many activities that went into the creation of this book and the exhibition.

We also benefited very much from the help of Robin Wright of the University of Washington, Beth Carroll-Horrocks of the American Philosophical Society, and Helen Codere.

As always, the professionals at the University of Washington Press should be thanked for producing a beautiful book. I especially appreciate the support of Naomi Pascal and Donald Ellegood and the help of Audrey Meyer, Julidta Tarver and Lorna Price, Kathleen Pike Timko, and Bronwyn Echols.

I would like to thank the National Endowment for the Humanities, the New York State Council on the Arts, and The John Ben Snow Memorial Trust for assisting in the publication of this book.

In appreciation for the help of so many Kwakiutl of northern Vancouver Island, the editor's royalties for this catalogue are going to the U'mista Cultural Centre in Alert Bay.

ALDONA JONAITIS
February 1991

The Spelling of Kwakwala

Wayne Suttles

KWAKWALA, LIKE ALL THE LANGUAGES SPOKEN by the Native peoples of northwestern North America, uses a good many sounds that do not occur in English. In fact, over half of the consonant sounds of Kwakwala have no counterparts in English, and when first heard by an English-speaking person, they are likely to be hard to distinguish from each other, or mistaken for other, more familiar sounds. But these different sounds make the distinction between one word and another, and therefore if Kwakwala is to be written so that it can be read easily, its different sounds must be differentiated and represented in a consistent system of spelling.

Throughout this volume (except in quotes from previously published material), words in Kwakwala are spelled according to the system used by the U'mista Cultural Centre. The U'mista system was developed by Jay Powell and Gloria Cranmer Webster in the mid-1970s. In this system the letters represent sounds as follows:

P, b, t, d, s, m, n, l, y, and w are pronounced much as in English. Ts and dz are as in English "pets" and "adz," but they represent unitary sounds that can occur initially as well as elsewhere in a word (as in *dzoli*, cockle), while English ts or dz can occur only after a vowel.

K and g, except when followed by w, are pronounced with the tongue pressed forward so that they are accompanied by a y sound; what are written ka and ga are pronounced like kya and gya. Kw and gw are pronounced as in English, but kw can occur at the end of a word (as in *kwikw*, eagle), while English kw (or qu) can occur only before a vowel. K̲ and g̲ are pronounced farther back in the mouth than English k and g; the root of the tongue is pulled back against the uvula.

Like English, Kwakwala has a set of voiceless plosive consonants (p, t, ts, etc.) and a set of voiced plosives (b, d, dz, etc.), but unlike English it has a third set, a set of glottalized or ejective plosives. Glottalization is represented by a raised apostrophe or comma over the letter. Thus ṗ is a glottalized p, t̓ a glottalized t, and so on. A glottalized p is produced by closing the vocal chords (pretend you are going to cough and hold your breath) and then letting the ṗ pop out.

The letter ł represents a sound made by putting the tongue in the position for l and, without any voicing, forcing the air out. Some speakers of English hear it as "lth" and pronounce *Kwaguł* "kwagiulth." Tł represents a kind of t (some speakers of English hear it as a kind of k) released with a ł sound. Dł and t̓ł are its voiced and glottalized counterparts.

The letter x, except when followed by w, is pronounced like the h in "huge" or the ch of German "ich." Like k and g, it is accompanied by a y sound. Xw is the fricative counterpart of kw. X̲ and x̲w are made with the tongue farther back; they are the fricative counterparts of k̲ and k̲w.

The apostrophe ' represents a glottal stop, the catch in the throat heard in "Hawai'i." In Kwakwala it can occur preceding m, n, l, y, and w as well as following a vowel.

Kwakwala has six vowels: i generally sounds like the i of machine, but when adjacent to a back consonant (k̲, etc.) it may be more like the a of rate; u is as in rule, a as in father, and e as in met; o is like the aw of raw or the o of shore; and a̲ is generally like the u of run, but following y, k, g, or x it can sound like the i of bit, and preceding kw or xw it can sound like the u of put.

A Kwakwala word is usually stressed on the first syllable, but if the first vowel is a̲ followed by a consonant other than m, n, l, y, or w, the stress is usually on the second syllable. Exceptions are marked with an acute accent (á, í, etc.). The stress is light, and subsequent syllables are all given equal weight.

Until the 1880s, attempts to record names and words in the Native languages of the Northwest Coast were woefully inadequate. Some writers recognized that the languages had sounds unlike any they had ever heard before, but few tried to represent these sounds consistently, and none successfully. Consequently, it is usually difficult and sometimes impossible to identify an early spelling with the actual Native name or word.

This situation began to change with the arrival of Franz

Boas. In his earliest work, Boas's transcriptions of Native names were very inaccurate, but it is clear that he was beginning to understand what he had to listen for. In his "Social Organization and Secret Societies of the Kwakiutl Indians" (1897), his spelling of Kwakwala was still faulty. In particular, he often confused a voiced sound for its unvoiced or its glottal- ized counterpart. But by around 1900, he had become much more accurate and had worked out the system that he changed only slightly through his later publications. In fact, his post-1900 spelling is phonetically more accurate than necessary, showing qualities of vowels that are not significant to speakers of the language.

The following table shows a few names and terms as spelled in Boas's early system, in his later system, in the U'mista orthography, and by linguists working with Northwest Coast languages today.

Boas 1897	Boas 1900 +	U'mista	Linguistic
Kwakiutl	Kwā/g·uł	kwaguł, kwagu'ł	kʷaguł, kʷagu?ł
Lau'itsis	Ła'wits!es	Ławitsis	ławičis
Nemqic	ᵋnɛ'mgis	'Namgis	ṅəmǧis
Lēkwiltôq	Lē'gwiłdaᵋxᵘ	Ligwiłda'xw	liǧʷiłda?x̌ʷ
Qāniqilakᵘ	Q!ā'neqeᵋlakᵘ	Ḵaniḵi'lakw	q̇aniqiḻakʷ
Ts'ō'noqoa	Dzō'noq!wa	dzunuḵwa	ʒunuq̇ʷa
	Bɛk!u's	baḵwas	bək̓ʷəs
sī'siuL	sī'siyuL	sisiyutł, sisiyuł	sisiyux̌, sisiyuł
BaxbakuālanuXsī'waē	Baxᵘbakwalanuxᵘsīwē	baxwbakwalanuxwsiwe'	Baxʷbakʷalanuxʷsiwe?
hā'mats'a	hā'mats!a	hamatsa	hamača
hō'Xhok	hō'xᵘhok	huxwhukw	huxʷhukʷ
ha'mshamtsɛs	hă'mhămts!ɛs	hamshamtsas	həmshəmčəs
nū'LmaL	nū'łɛmał	nuḻamał	nuləmał
matɛm	ma'dɛm	madam	madəm
Winā'lag·ilis	Winā'lag·ilis	Winalagalis	winalagəlis
t'ō'X'uit	tō'xᵋwid	tuxw'id	tuxʷẇid
xoā'ēxoē	xwē'xwe	xwixwi	x̌ʷix̌ʷi

16

Gloria Cranmer Webster has provided the following list of locales referred to in the book, with the village names and tribes given in U'mista orthography:

Locale	Village Name	Tribe
Fort Rupert	Tsax̱is	Kwagu'ł
Village Island	'Mi'mkwam̱lis	Mamaliliḵala
Alert Bay	'Yalis	'Nam̱gis
Turnour Island	Ḵalugwis	Ławitsis (earlier Kwagu'ł)
Knight Inlet	Dzawadi	A'wa'etłala
New Vancouver	Tsadzis'nukwaame'	Da'naxda'x̱w
Kingcome	Gwa'yi	Dzawada'enux̱w
Gilford Island	Gwa'yasd̲ams	K̲wik̲wasutinex̱w
Hopetown	Heg̱ams	Gwawa'enux̱w
Wakeman Sound	Ałatx̱u	Ḵaxwa'mis
Blunden Harbour	Ba'a's	'Nakwaxda'x̱w
Quatsino	X̱watis	Gusgimax̱w
Winter Harbour	Oyag̱am'la	Gwatsinuxw
Hope Island	X̱wamdasbe'	Tłatłasikwala
Smith Inlet	Ta̱kus	Gwa'sa̱la

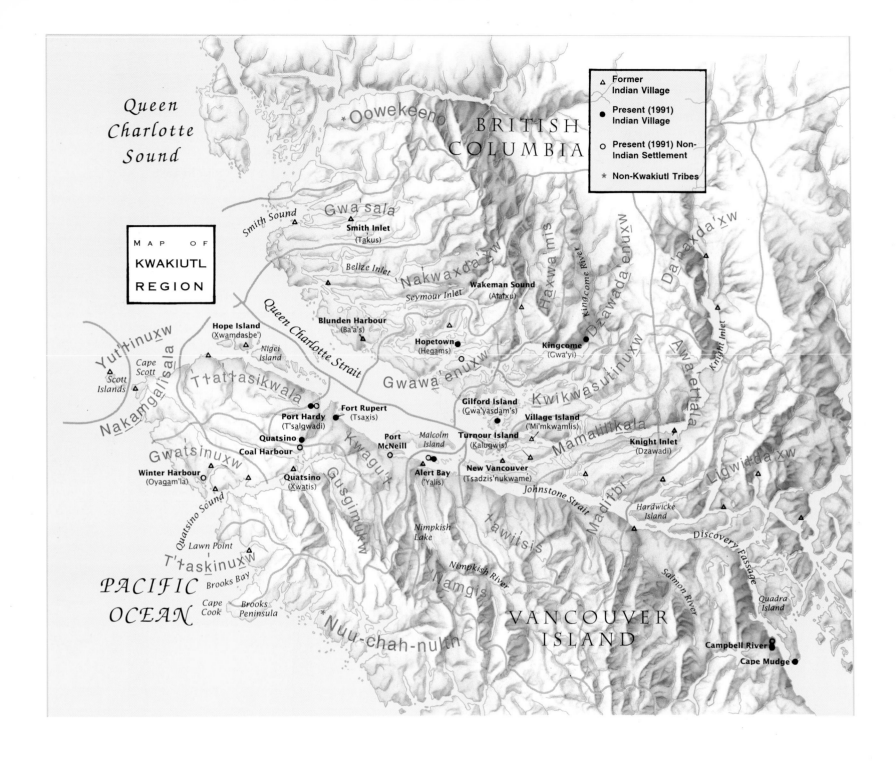

Queen
Charlotte
Sound

*Oowekeeno   BRITISH
                COLUMBIA

MAP OF
KWAKIUTL
REGION

Former
Indian Village

Present (1991)
Indian Village

Present (1991) Non-
Indian Settlement

Non-Kwakiutl Tribes

Smith Sound

Gwa'sala
Smith Inlet
(Takus)

Belize Inlet

'Nakwaxda'xw

Seymour Inlet

Wakeman Sound
(Atatxu)

Haxwa'mis

Kingcome River

Dzawada'enuxw

Da'naxda'xw

Hope Island
(Xwamdasbe')

Nigei
Island

Queen Charlotte Strait

Blunden Harbour
(Ba'a's)

Hopetown
(Hegams)

Kingcome
(Gwa'yi)

Knight Inlet

Yuttinuxw

Cape
Scott

Scott
Islands

Nakamgalisala

T'łatłasikwala

Gwawa'enuxw

Kwikwasutinuxw

Awa'etlala

Port Hardy
(T'salgwadi)

Fort Rupert
(Tsaxis)

Gilford Island
(Gwa'yasdam's)

Village Island
('Mi'mkwamlis)

Mamalilikala

Knight Inlet
(Dzawadi)

Quatsino
Coal Harbour

Port
McNeill

Malcolm
Island

Turnour Island
(Kalugwis)

Kwagu'ł

Ligwiłda'xw

Gwat'sinuxw

Winter Harbour
(Oyagam'la)

Quatsino
(Xwatis)

Gusgimukw

Alert Bay
('Yalis)

New Vancouver
(Tsadzis'nukwame)

Johnstone Strait

Madiłbi

Hardwicke
Island

Discovery Passage

Nimpkish
Lake

Xa'witsis

Quadra
Island

Lawn Point

T'łatskinuxw

Brooks Bay

'Namgis

Nimpkish River

Salmon River

Campbell River

PACIFIC
OCEAN

Cape
Cook

Brooks
Peninsula

*Nuu-chah-nulth

VANCOUVER
ISLAND

Cape Mudge

CHIEFLY FEASTS

The Enduring Kwakiutl Potlatch

1.1 'Nak̓waxda'x̱w chief Tuⱡⱡidi giving away a copper in honor of
his son, Fort Rupert, 1894. *Photo by O.C. Hastings.* AMNH 106707

1 / Chiefly Feasts: The Creation of an Exhibition

Aldona Jonaitis

AS A RESULT OF WORKING ON THIS EXHIBITION, I have undergone a transformation of both mind and soul. Mine is not a unique story, for virtually every person who has had the opportunity to work with a Native community returns to her own deeply touched by the experience and profoundly changed.[1] Since 1988, I have worked with the people commonly known as Kwakiutl, who would prefer to be called Kwakwaka'wakw, a name that means speakers of Kwakwala. They have welcomed me into their homes, fed me fine food, and shared their lives with me.

My first introduction to the Kwakiutl was years ago, when, in graduate school, I read Boas's ethnographies. Written in an objective and authoritative voice, these provided a wealth of information, but offered little sense of the people whose culture was being described. Like so many other anthropological texts, these monographs gave one a thorough picture of the social organization, ceremonialism, belief systems, and art of these Native peoples, but said virtually nothing about the individuals who voiced the speeches, wore the extraordinary masks, or prepared the sumptuous food at potlatches. Captions on illustrations in these books, such as "Chief holding copper" (Boas 1897: fig. 11) (fig. 1.1), were no more revealing. The texts hardly ever referred to specific individuals; in the lengthy accounts of ceremonials, it was often difficult to discern exactly who was participating (although, as Wayne Suttles will show in his essay in this volume, it was not impossible). This kind of anthropological writing, although very much in keeping with the paradigm of the time, tends to dehumanize the human beings who constitute the culture being described.

What is true of ethnographies is also, to a certain extent, true of objects in museums, such as the Kwakiutl pieces at the American Museum of Natural History's Northwest Coast Hall. They, too, are exhibited without reference to the individuals who owned and displayed them. As an art historian, I tend to concentrate on art as a vehicle for understanding a culture. Thus, for years I saw the Kwakiutl through the lens of their superb deeply carved poles, vividly painted masks (fig. 1.2), and elegantly finished feast dishes (fig. 1.3); my understanding, I have come to realize, was limited by the information available about these exquisite creations. When George Hunt collected these treasures for Franz Boas at the turn of the century, he rarely said anything about their owners, or how they were used in specific ceremonials. And when he did, he often included this information not with the pieces themselves in the Museum acquisition records, but in manuscripts that ended up in the Boas archives in the American Philosophical Society in Philadelphia and the Columbia University Rare Books and Manuscript Collection. The task of collating the story with the artifact is formidable.[2]

The kind of nonindividualistic descriptions that result from published texts and museum collections would have been fine for a turn-of-the-century anthropologist like Boas, who was trying desperately to describe a culture he thought would soon succumb to the forces of acculturation. He and his colleagues were primarily interested in the broader anthropological questions to which these cultures offered some answers.[3] Over the years, these texts have also proved adequate for the purposes of publications describing the culture of the Kwakiutl as well as those that attempt to interpret their myths, symbolism, and art from a theoretical perspective.[4] In the process of working on this exhibition, I have learned that the texts, the artifacts, and the theories, valuable as they may be for gaining certain insights to Kwakiutl culture, offer a limited picture of these people. What changed my life was the discovery of the real people behind the books and artworks, the real Kwakiutl, who live in one of the most spectacular parts of Canada, and who have welcomed me into their community.

To an urban academic like me, participating in this community, with its shared values and sense of real identity, is most seductive. So is the more leisurely pace, the opportunities for sitting over cup after cup of coffee or tea, just talking, being together. As a high-energy New Yorker accustomed to con-

1.2 **Octopus mask**. Gilford Island. Wood, bark, cord, H 30.6 cm, W 27.5 cm. *Collected by George Hunt, 1899. 16/6874, AMNH 1899–50*

THE KWAKIUTL ARTIST WAS A MASTER OF ILLUSION. The carver of this mask went to considerable lengths to create a depiction of a living octopus or devilfish. He rigged the tentacles in such a way that when the dancer manipulated the cord that controls them, the octopus's arms would pulsate in rhythms suggestive of its underwater movement. To add to this dynamism, the hinged jaws of this mask could open and close. In the firelight, the cords that enabled the dancer to set this mask into motion would have been virtually invisible, adding to the drama of the representation.

Hunt tells us that the name of this octopus is X̱aʼniyus. In the accession ledger, he associates this mask with the history of Tsekame', Head-Winter-Dancer (Dept. of Anthropology, AMNH). In this account, Stone-Body, one of Head-Winter-Dancer's sons, makes war around the world to acquire great wealth for his tribe. Among the prerogatives given him by Head-Winter-Dancer is the *sisiyutł* (see fig. 2.18). Among those he attains for himself is the octopus mask. This privilege is actually transferred to Stone-Body from the Oowekeeno chief Wisest-One through Stone-Body's marriage to the princess of Wisest-One:

Wisest-One at once went and called his princess, and she was married to Stone-Body. Then [Wisest-One] also took a large box, and took out many masks. There were the devil-fish [octopus] mask, the mask of the fisher of devil-fish, and the mask of the second fisher of devil-fish, and the mask of the attendant, and the mask of Wisest-One himself. . . . The name of the devil-fish mask is Xa'nius, and the name of the fisher of the devil-fish is Nanudze. (Boas and Hunt 1905:225–26)

This mask probably came to the people of Gilford Island as part of the *tła'sala* ceremony (Tom Willie: personal communication, 1990). The mention in the history of the existence of an octopus fisher suggests that when this mask performed, it did not dance alone but interacted with another being, the fisher, possibly to re-enact a scene from the history (Peter Macnair: personal communication, 1990). SAM

stantly pushing to get things done, my being compelled to just slow down was initially frustrating. It soon, however, became intoxicating. I came to anticipate with pleasure visiting an older member of the community with my envelope full of pictures of the artworks we were planning on displaying in *Chiefly Feasts*. Instead of setting to work discussing these objects, we often began by discussing her family. She first introduced me to *her* photographic treasures in picture albums with images of weddings, potlatches, family gatherings, children, grandchildren, even great-grandchildren. I came to luxuriate in these precious moments. And I came to appreciate the lesson I learned: that the business of my visits was not so much to acquire information about the artifacts for the exhibition, but instead to stop, to listen, and to appreciate this sharing of a world at once similar to mine and very different.

It took three years to prepare for *Chiefly Feasts*. Now, whenever I return to New York from the coast of British Columbia, I cannot stop thinking about these men and women who live thousands of miles away. They are not the anonymous descendants of a once-great culture, but real people with a rich ceremonial life that continues to support the creation of masks, costumes, and other ritual objects.

Working with the Kwakiutl has also taught me something important about the meaning of scholarship. Often, as academics, we address an audience of other academics; if our thoughts have any impact at all (an often-unlikely scenario), it is for a small coterie of fellow scholars. Not so when writing about Native peoples. I have learned that we bear a profound responsibility in trying to communicate to the public the culture of the Kwakiutl. I know people in Alert Bay, in Fort Rupert, in Kingcome, in Hopetown, in Gilford Island, in Campbell River and Cape Mudge, in the urban centers of Victoria and Vancouver, who are very concerned about how they are represented in scholarship. Works on Native people do not exist in an intellectual vacuum but instead have an impact on and among those people. As a white woman from New York from a culture with different rules and different values, it is not surprising that I have made mistakes in the past, and doubtless I will make more in the future; I take full responsibility for them. It is my one hope that these Kwakiutl will accept this book and the exhibition it accompanies as a celebration of their culture, its rich past, and its impressive present. I dedicate them both, with deep respect and profound appreciation, to the Kwakwaka'wakw people. They allowed me to see a different world from the one I knew.

1.3 **Seal dish**. Quatsino. Wood, L 127 cm. *Collected by George Hunt, 1898. 16/4687, AMNH 1898–41*

Too great is, what you are doing, our chief. Who equals our chief! He is giving feasts to the whole world. (Boas 1966:100)

GEORGE HUNT'S FIRST WIFE, LUCY HO'MISKA'NIS, who was credited by Boas as the source for much of her husband's writings on "cookery" (1921:45), described far more than the recipes for scorched salmon and salal berry cakes. The meals prepared by a Kwakiutl husband and wife were choreographed from the time of the fishing or gathering expedition, through the cleaning, preparation, and presentation of the food, the seating of guests, and ceremonies and protocols of the meal and its completion (Boas 1921:305–601, and 1909:427–43). As Hunt recorded, even breakfast might include the entertainment of guests:

When the man invites six friends, as soon as he comes home, he tells his wife about having invited his six friends. His wife at once takes a mat and spreads it out in the rear of the fireplace. As soon as she has done so, the man goes again [to call] his friends; but he does not stay long before his friends come in. The woman leads them up to their seats, to the place where the mat has been spread. Immediately they sit down on the mat. Now, six men are enough to sing. Immediately the host takes the drum, and he puts it down on the righthand side of his six guests. One of them begins to sing the songs of their ancestors. As soon as they begin to sing, the woman takes the kettle and puts it down near the place where she is sitting and her husband takes a bucket and goes to draw water. (Boas 1909:431)

This emphasis on correct procedure was applied alike to ordinary meals and opulent feasts sponsored by high-ranking chiefs. Acts that publicly demonstrated the relative social position of each member of the community, such as the right of noble individuals to eat and drink before others, were an important component of the public dining experience (ibid.:439, 442, 443).

The dishes, spoons, and ladles used on these occasions were carefully conceived in support of fundamental notions about rank and family identity. The carved serving pieces were therefore outstanding works of art, produced for a discerning audience. The small, "ordinary" dishes were graceful containers that may suggest the form of canoes. They might have been used by one person or perhaps shared by a husband and wife (Boas 1909:421).

The more elaborate "house dishes," with forms both human and animal, were treasured heirlooms, which families brought out for the great feasts (Boas 1921:756). The use of these house dishes was an inherited privilege of old, aristocratic families. They were acquired by ancestral heroes in the course of legendary encounters with various supernatural benefactors, along with the exclusive rights to other architectural embellishments such as painted house fronts and carved house posts (ibid.:805–20). In the course of marriage transactions, however, feast dishes might travel from one village to another as a dowry portion (see Suttles, this volume).

Hunt recorded that, at least on the occasion of the viburnum berry (high-bush cranberry) feast, the house dishes were put down first in front of the highest-ranking numaym present. Chiefs would then seat themselves around the large dishes and eat with spoons of wood, mountain goat horn, or shell, while the common people ate from small vessels (Boas 1921:758–59). Large spoons were used by men and the smaller, pointed spoons by high-born girls, who were admonished not to open their mouths too wide, a sign of bad manners (see fig. 1.14). Larger implements, such as ladles, sometimes with elaborately carved handles, were used to serve food from the house dishes into the smaller containers.

Viburnum berry feasts were second in greatness only to grease feasts (ibid.:755), during which significant prestige might be gained by a chief who disbursed extravagant amounts of expensive oil rendered from the eulachon. His actions and songs were designed to ridicule his rival, who was supposedly unable to match the host's generosity and sheer wastefulness:

Now my feast! Go to him, the poor one who wants to be fed from the son of the chief whose name is "Full of Smoke" and "Greatest Smoke" [referring to the smoke of the oil-fueled fire]. Never mind; give him plenty to eat, make him drink until he will be qualmish and vomits. My feast steps over the fire right up to the [rival] chief. (Boas 1966:97–98)

The oil was poured directly onto the central fire and, although the resulting flames leapt up in a dramatic show of bravado, subjecting the guests to unbearable heat and threatening to burn down the entire house, no form of protest was acceptable. A complaint about the heat might stand for the guests' capitulation, an admission of their inferiority (ibid.:96).

Other feasts were given in anger, as a challenge to rival chiefs. The salal berry and crabapple feast, for example, was designed to make the guests squeamish because these foods were completely drenched in oil. Hunt wrote that both chief and commoner were "afraid" of this feast, but etiquette demanded that they take up the challenge and attend the festivities or be laughed at by the numaym of the host (Boas 1921:770).

The carvings associated with the consumption of food far exceed their function as mere containers or useful implements. This heirloom dish is carved as a full-bodied seal, poised and energetic, its mouth slightly open. The conventionalized profile of a raven and the form of a steelhead have been carefully painted on both sides of the body. Boas wrote that the form of dishes (made to look like seals and sea lions) was linked with their function as vessels for plentiful food and not with the crest privileges of any particular family. JO

Inception of the Project

My first real involvement with Kwakiutl art and culture began in 1985 when I did research at the American Museum of Natural History in New York City for a book on that institution's Northwest Coast Indian art collection (Jonaitis 1988). Although during the course of this research I discovered many treasures previously hidden in storerooms and closets, particularly extraordinary to me were the boldly sculpted and brightly painted artworks of the Kwakiutl.

Franz Boas (fig. 1.5) had the most to do with bringing this collection to the American Museum. A German-Jewish immigrant, he literally transformed American anthropology from a discipline that supported a hierarchical view on races to a relativistic science premised on the equality of all humankind. In my research for *From the Land of the Totem Poles* I found myself fascinated by this committed, sensitive, and passionate man who served as curator of anthropology at the American Museum from 1895–1905. Equally intriguing to me was Boas's chief collaborator, George Hunt (fig. 1.6), who made investigations and collected among the Kwakiutl of Vancouver Island. The son of a Hudson's Bay Company official and a Tlingit noblewoman, Hunt was raised in the Kwakiutl community of Fort Rupert, where he participated actively in Kwakiutl culture (see Jacknis, this volume). Under Boas's guidance, Hunt collected an extraordinary array of Kwakiutl art for the American Museum, from naturalistic statues depicting the proud nobility of chiefs and vividly painted masks (fig. 1.7) to masterfully carved food bowls representing wolves, bears, seals, and other animals. I found myself compelled as much by this art as by the two remarkable men responsible for bringing it to New York.

The correspondence between Boas and Hunt on these pieces revealed a wealth of information about the ceremonial contexts of Kwakiutl material culture. During his earliest trips to the Northwest Coast, Boas attended potlatches where the host chief, in order to validate his status, staged masquerades, offered lavish feasts, and gave away large quantities of goods (fig. 1.8) (see Suttles, this volume). As a high-ranking Native person, Hunt comfortably participated in these rituals, which he described in detail for Boas's publications. It would be wonderful, I thought, if these splendid artworks could be assembled into a temporary exhibit. Although the American Museum did have a large and impressive permanent Northwest Coast Indian Hall, there was so much more that could be shown, and such interesting history that could be told. I decided to propose to the museum administration (I was at that

1.4 Stacks of blankets, frontlets, and hats to be given away at a potlatch, Alert Bay. Anthropomorphic carving at left wears a blanket. *RBCM PN 1078*

time at a university) a temporary exhibit on one particular facet of Kwakiutl art and culture, namely potlatch feasting.

I selected this theme because of a common ground between the Kwakiutl Indians and the urban audience that would come to the museum to see this show in New York. Experience had taught me that Kwakiutl, in Boas's time as well as today, and New Yorkers share a deep interest in fine food elegantly served. At their potlatches, Kwakiutl hosts presented to their guests lavish food in extraordinary bowls. Other items for food presentation included carved dishes, large ladles, and elegant spoons (figs. 1.9–14). We also know what food the Kwakiutl served, for George Hunt acquired from his wife an exceptional collection of over 150 recipes of Kwakiutl cuisine: recipes for every possible way to roast, steam, or boil every single part of salmon and halibut, as well as for octopus served with fish oil, mountain goat brisket, steamed seal, and for a variety of preparations of currants, huckleberries, crabapples, and gooseberries (Boas 1921:305–602).

As I spent pleasurable hours in the storerooms selecting objects for the exhibition and the accompanying catalogue, it became clear that to limit the show's theme to feasting would tell only part of a story, for the potlatch has a variety of other important features for which many artworks are created. There are statues, such as the Kwakiutl chief holding on his lap an infant who represented the relative size of all the other chiefs, that communicates the theme of chiefly power (fig. 1.15). Central to Kwakiutl myth, ritual, and life is the copper, a shield-shaped plaque of beaten metal emblazoned with an animal crest (figs. 1.16, 1.17). Somewhat more familiar are their dazzling masks. Some depict cannibal birds with snapping beaks, others, known as transformation masks, are a nest of supernatural representations, the outer one snapping open to reveal another being behind it (fig. 1.18). As I found more and more extraordinary carvings and paintings, it became clear to me that the exhibition would have to expand beyond its initial narrow focus to include the entire array of art associated with Kwakiutl ceremonialism.

Authenticity and Tradition

While the objects themselves inspired me to plan a more diverse exhibition, current trends in anthropological research motivated me to reconsider a basic premise of the show. In the 1970s, when I received my academic training in what was then called "primitive art," we were taught to describe and to analyze the art of Native Americans in its "traditional" context, preferably as we believed it to have been before whites came along. Much of our writing presented the culture of Native peoples in the "ethnographic present," describing art, society, and ceremonialism in the present tense, even if what we were describing had changed considerably since the nineteenth century. As Boas had encouraged Hunt to do, we were trained to seek out the oldest, the most authentic elements of the artistic culture we studied. By focusing on the nineteenth century Kwakiutl potlatches as Boas and Hunt described, I was following a practice that was increasingly challenged in modern anthropology.

The primacy of the pristine, the seeking after the unacculturated, was part of an ethnographic legacy established at the turn of the century. Concerned that the Native peoples were "disappearing" as influences from the dominant society destroyed much of the traditional culture, Boas and his generation tried both to salvage what remained, and also to reconstruct what had existed in the past. The publications informed by this paradigm ended up describing not so much what Franz Boas, George Hunt, and others actually observed among the Native peoples of British Columbia (and elsewhere), but instead represented reconstructed cultures as the authors believed they existed prior to white intrusion. As Johannes Fabian has pointed out, such representations place Native peoples into a timeless and ahistoric era, separating them cleanly from western cultures with their sense of historical change (Fabian 1983; see also Wolf 1982, Clifford 1986, 1987, Mason 1990, Torgovnick 1990). In our western society, so smitten by progress and conscious of history, a people stuck in being, incapable of becoming, is at best to be pitied, and at worst to be disdained. Moreover, this society was destined, we believed, to be modernized and acculturated, processes that by their very nature signified corruption and decay of the pure "primitive" culture (Clifford 1987:122).

The salvage paradigm, which pervaded American and Canadian anthropology for much of the twentieth century, resulted in ethnographic texts and museum displays that represented unchanged Native peoples captured at the moment they were "really" Indians. In the life group (fig. 1.19) Franz Boas designed for the American Museum of Natural History in 1895 are models of several Kwakiutl men and women, dressed in "traditional" cedar bark clothing (Jacknis 1985). The museum visitor would certainly assume, seeing this display, either that this was how the Kwakiutl Indians still dressed, or, perhaps accepting the common notion of a "dying race," that this was the way these soon-to-be-extinct peoples used to appear. The

who cuts eyebrows in such a beautiful manner. The stout woman then reveals herself as a *dzunukwa*. They soon depart for the house of the princess's father. When they arrive, Ḱodi tricks the *dzunukwa* by calling his warrior, who kills her. She-Who-Will-Be-a-Princess takes her father to the *dzunukwa*'s house and they take all her privileges, including this mask:

Red cedar-bark was twisted all around the face of the mask, [which represented] a man, and on it revolved the nest of an eagle which was sitting in the nest. Then She-Who-Will-Be-a-Princess called her father, and her father took it, and he named the mask at once Nightmare-Bringer-Nest-Mask. (Boas and Hunt 1905:92)

This description of the mask corresponds very closely with the mask Hunt collected. The twisted bands of red and white cedar bark appear as a border surrounding the human face. The nest, made of thin slats of wood, encircles an eagle that sits atop the head.

A later version of this mask was used at Kingcome Inlet in the early fifties. Somewhat smaller in size, that mask was rigged so that the nest opened like a flower and the eagle rose from the head and turned (Adam Dick: personal communication, 1990). The privilege of using it in a *tła'sala* performance may have been originally acquired from the 'Nakwaxda'xw people of Blunden Harbour (Tom Willie: personal communication, 1990). SAM

1.5 Franz Boas, New York, 1887. *Photo courtesy of Philip Yampolsky*

1.6 George Hunt and his wife Francine, Fort Rupert, 1930. *Photo by J.B. Scott.* AMNH 32734

1.7 **Nightmare-Bringer-Nest mask**. Kingcome. Wood, H 87 cm, W 45.5 cm. *Collected by George Hunt, 1899. 16/6771.* AMNH 1899–48

THIS MASK IS ASSOCIATED WITH A DZAWADA'ENUXW tradition concerning a princess's encounter with a *dzunukwa*, the wild woman of the woods (acc. 1899–48, AMNH). The tradition tells of She-Who-Will-Be-Made-a-Princess, who has just reached maturity. After following the requisite taboos, she has her eyebrows cut in the way women wear them and returns to her father's house with her new adult appearance. Ḱodi, her father, welcomes her home (Boas and Hunt 1905:86–93).

After some time has passed, She-Who-Will-Be-Made-a-Princess begins to take walks in the woods. Her father, worried that she will encounter a *dzunukwa*, warns her not to go, yet she persists. Soon she meets a stout woman who is envious of the young princess's beautiful eyebrows. The strange woman indicates she would like to have hers cut the same way. The princess is hesitant but agrees to accept gifts of yellow cedar bark and abalone from the stout woman in exchange for an introduction to the person

1.8 Alert Bay potlatch, c. 1902–5. *Photo by George Hunt.*
AMNH 104471

truth is, of course, that on a daily basis the Kwakiutl encountered by Boas had worn western clothing for decades. Photographs such as that of the chief shown in 1873 on the steamer *Boxer* (fig. 1.20) demonstrate this quite clearly, for under his blanket this man wears a purchased suit. Moreover, his button blanket, indicative of his high status, was made from a purchased Hudson's Bay Company blanket. Despite his genuine good will, Boas, who met many such "modern" people who nonetheless participated in a distinct and thriving "Kwakiutl" culture, reinforced the notion of a stereotyped Indian who lived entirely in a world extremely foreign to our own, a world soon to be destroyed by the forces of progress.

Our own recent disenchantment with many of the fruits of progress and the abatement of our Eurocentrism has permitted ethnographers to realize that they can no longer describe their subjects as remote and timeless. Instead of contributing to the myth of a people without history, the ethnographer must acknowledge the relation between these people and the peoples with whom they share the world and interrelate (Marcus 1986). As Clifford Geertz (1988:132) has said, "One of the major assumptions upon which anthropological writing rested until only yesterday, that its subjects and its audience were not only separable but morally disconnected, that the first were to be described but not addressed, the second informed but not implicated, has fairly well dissolved. The world has compartments still, but the passages between them are much more numerous and much less well secured" (see also Tyler 1986).

Today, we realize that museum displays representing Native peoples must be particularly sensitive to the pitfalls of an ahistoric approach; indeed, much recent literature has addressed this very issue. As Dean MacCannell has noted (1989:83), the process of preserving the "authentic" primitive serves actually to position modern culture above that of the represented society. This is not, MacCannell correctly observes, an intentional act, but the logical consequence of the structure inherent in such representations. An extension of the quest for authenticity can be seen in the "particularistic and empirical" bias of museum exhibits in which the cultures being depicted are represented as isolated from the larger society (Durrans 1988:156). In recent years museum professionals themselves have begun questioning how their institutions ought to represent Native peoples; conferences, publications, and new museological practices all give evidence of a major change in the ways the lives of Native people are displayed.[5]

Within the last ten years, the emphasis of Native American scholarship has shifted from salvage ethnography, with its implication of ahistoricity and decline, to a recognition, and for many a celebration, of the persistence of Native cultures as they respond to outside influences. In the past, many Native arts that manifested clear signs of acculturation, such as the Haida argillite carvings made to sell to whites, or the red yarn sometimes substituted for shredded cedar bark in Kwakiutl rituals, would have been deemed inauthentic, not "really" Indian.[6] We now realize that such romanticizing of the "genuine" Native person immune to historical forces, coupled with the refusal to accept as "Indian" cultural features that draw some elements from the dominant society, is tantamount to separating Native peoples from the common experience of all humanity, in effect, to dehumanizing them. Although there is no question that much has been lost over the past century, some traditions have been retained and/or transformed in accommodations to the modern world, resulting in developments that are often novel and ingenious.[7]

Today young Kwakiutl children in Alert Bay learn about their heritage by listening to their elders, by practicing songs and dances in the U'mista Cultural Centre, and from attending the potlatches that occur on a regular basis in their communities. Complementing these more traditional methods of educating young people are means appropriated from white society. The Kwakiutl have insisted that their culture become part of the school curriculum. They have also produced a series of Kwakwala workbooks written to educate children about their culture and language. One of these books, *Yaxwatłan's* (We Will Dance; Powell et al., n.d.) employs text, photographs, and drawings to communicate to the youth of this culture the continuity of their traditions. It complements and supplements the living education the children receive at potlatches. In a sense, the Kwakiutl have appropriated an artifact of the western educational system to help educate their children about a tradition central to their culture. The words they use to convey the significance of their rituals to the youth are compelling and poetic:

Dancing is not only a right and a privilege for us. It is an obligation. As the chiefs said to Franz Boas when he first came to see their ceremonies at Fort Rupert, "It is a strict law that bids us to dance." Performing our dances is not just a chance to show off. It is one of the ways that we carry on our responsibilities as Kwakwaka'wakw. (Powell et al., n.d.:6)

The contemporary Kwakiutl, with their potlatching, their art production, and their deep sense of ethnic pride present serious problems to those concerned with preserving "traditional Indian culture." J. C. H. King (1986:69–70), in an essay on

1.9 **Feast dish**. Fort Rupert. Wood, L 57 cm, W 36.5 cm, H 40.5 cm. *Collected by George Hunt, 1901. 16/8573, AMNH 1901–32*

BOAS ORIGINALLY DESIGNATED THIS VESSEL AS A grizzly bear and eagle dish when he recorded it in his ledger. Later he published an illustration of it, calling it a wolf and eagle dish (1909:519). The face of a ferocious-looking animal, whose identity is therefore open to some question, is the focal point of this cylindrical bowl.

The exaggerated twist of the neck and asymmetrical presentation of the head create a sense of great animation. The teeth are bared in a threatening snarl, and light glints from the metallic eyes. The tail doubles as the head and neck of an eagle with rounded eyes and a hooked beak.

The Kwakiutl used opercula, the "trap doors" of the red turban sea snail, on various works of art. Here, they stud the rim of the bowl, where they have become encrusted with a greasy residue, accumulated after years of use as a food vessel. JO

1.10 **Dish**. Fort Rupert. Wood, L 30 cm. *Collected by George Hunt, 1897. 16/2253, AMNH 1897–73*

THIS DISH FOR ORDINARY USE, ITS ELEGANT FORM reminiscent of some water craft, has been simply carved from a single block of wood (Boas 1909:420–21). True "canoe dishes" do exist (see for instance ibid., fig. 102b), and Boas referred to both these vessels and seal-shaped dishes as examples of symbolic carving, which should be distinguished from totemic or crest representations among the Kwakiutl. Hunt had informed him that a small, well-washed canoe was actually used as a container for serving salal berries and crabapples at a feast (Boas 1921:768). Perhaps serving food in such a vessel might represent the abundance of resources, a "canoe-load" of food offered to guests (Boas 1896:101–102). JO

1.11 **Dish**. Quatsino. Wood, L 40 cm, W 25.5 cm. *Collected by George Hunt, 1900. 16/8178, AMNH 1900–73*

B OAS NOTED IN HIS LEDGER THAT THIS DISH WAS used for "good food." Indeed, all meals must have included some interesting fare, as the flat bottom, sweeping sides, and arched "bow" and "stern" identify this dish as an ordinary vessel for everyday use. This type of dish might have been used by one person, or it could have been shared by as many as three (Boas 1909:421). JO

1.12 **Ladle**. Kingcome. Wood, L 139.2 cm, W 35.5 cm. *Collected by George Hunt, 1901. 16/8426, AMNH 1901–32*

LARGE LADLES WITH ELABORATELY CARVED HANDLES were used to serve food at great feasts (Boas 1909:424), as well as to pour oil over food (Boas 1921:757; see fig. 2.6).

This ladle has a long, bifurcated handle that terminates in the form of two hands carved in shallow relief and positioned on either side of the bowl-like portion of the ladle. The hands appear to offer the contents of the bowl, which is darkened with use. At the tip of the handle another, shallower bowl has been carved, which suggests the "head" of this anthropomorphic utensil. JO

1.13 **Spoons**. Fort Rupert. *Collected by George Hunt, 1897.* AMNH *1897–43.* Left: Mountain sheep horn, L 18.5 cm; *16/2289.* Center: Mountain sheep horn, L 27 cm; *16/2287.* Right: Wood, L 24.5 cm; *16/2294*

THE TIP OF THE TYPICAL KWAKIUTL WOODEN SPOON shown on the right is sharply angled away from the continuous sweep of the bowl and handle (Boas 1909:432). Bill Holm has aptly compared this shape to a long-necked swimming bird (1987:90).

It is not surprising, in view of the elaborate dining etiquette favored by the Kwakiutl, that a particular posture was prescribed when eating with a spoon. One was supposed to squat, with the right elbow resting on the right knee, and sip carefully from the tip (see fig. 1.14). Boas noted that afterwards the spoon might be dipped in water to prevent its further use in witchcraft (1909:427), perhaps because saliva might be used in contagious magic.

Horn spoons may be recognized by certain qualities specific to the material. Horn is translucent unless very much darkened by age and use (e.g., the spoon on the left, as well as many Columbia River bowls and spoons). Mountain sheep horn usually shows characteristic lines of growth across the bowl (Holm: personal communication, 1990). The spoon in the center has a small hole in its handle, which may have been made to mount a brass stud; the other retains its stud. JO

1.14 Fort Rupert woman demonstrating spoon etiquette, 1894. *Photo by O.C. Hastings.* AMNH *11607*

Native American art, points out that scholars and museum professionals typically describe as "traditional" artworks made and collected between 1860 and 1930, a period of considerable social change for Indians.[8]

Native peoples today are objecting to the attempts by whites to impose alien notions of tradition and authenticity upon their cultures. At a conference sponsored by the Assembly of First Nations, National Indian Brotherhood, in Ottawa in November 1988, entitled "Preserving Our Heritage: A Working Conference for Museums and First People," Indian speakers urged museums not to "museumify" their culture. They want to be shown as they live today, as well as how they lived in the past. The notion that prior to white contact Indians were pure, and afterwards they became "less Indian" is not only untrue, it is unacceptable to Native peoples. As Tom Hill (1988), Iroquois Curator of the Woodland Culture Centre, stated:

A prominent bureaucrat, here in Ottawa, was tired of Indians coming to his office with designer watches. And I thought, what is the problem, we can wear designer watches if we can earn them. He did not know how to respond, he had a problem, he could not envision what Indians should be. And museums prevent that in a way. We like to take the past, freeze it in time and marvel at it. . . . An Indian cannot be an intellectual, he can only do x number of things as the ethnography says he is supposed to do, he cannot think about the present, about politics. . . . The time is right, we have to move forward, we have to look to the twenty-first century.

It is clearly time to reassess what whites perceive as "traditional" Indian art. One of the pieces in this exhibit is an apron made of red cloth and a flour sack (fig. 1.22). Because it is made from materials acquired in trade with whites rather than the shredded cedar bark or skins of pre-contact times, one might negatively characterize this apron as acculturated. This would not have made sense to the Kwakiutl chief who wore this apron, because for him the garment, regardless of its materials, operated effectively in the Kwakiutl world as an indication of his rank and status. Nowadays much of the art that has been called acculturated and impure is being evaluated as an imaginative response of a people to the disruptive forces of contact with whites. And, as has been pointed out on many occasions, the nineteenth century flourishing of the potlatch which had a great deal to do with white contact, coupled with the trade goods acquired from whites, such as iron tools and commercial paints, were at the heart of what we characterize as "traditional Northwest Coast culture and art."

Virginia Dominguez (1986) has suggested that it was collec-

1.15 Chief figure. Fort Rupert. Wood, hair, iron, H 103 cm. *Collected by George Hunt, 1879. 16/2395, AMNH 1897–43*

CHIEFS DISPLAYED ANTHROPOMORPHIC FIGURES such as this either inside the house or outside on the beach, depending on where the business of the potlatch was taking place. Those placed out of doors faced the water and thus would confront those arriving at the potlatch house by canoe. Although some of these figures communicated the chief's immensely high standing in the community, others served to insult his rivals.

This particular carving communicated the greatness of the host chief at the expense of all the other nobility. Boas describes this (1909:pl. 47):

A figure used in a potlatch, symbolizing the Greatness of the Chief, the Child in the Arms of the Figure representing the Size of other Chiefs as compared to the One who gives the feast.

It is of interest to note that when George Hunt purchased this figure, he described it as female:

The chief in her arm is to show that she is true chief daughter that the other chiefs is like a little baby under her and she is carrying one of them in her arms to show that she is great and they are small under her. (Acc. 1897–43, AMNH)

While this statement makes clear that the statue communicates the relative stature of the two individuals depicted, Hunt is clearly wrong about the sex of the larger one. Without further documentation, it is not possible to know the reason for this particular attribution, which Boas corrected for his 1909 publication.

Several features of this sculpture convey the supreme status of the host who displays it. The most obvious manifestation of this is the relative size of the large host chief as compared to the infantile size of the other chiefs. Because the baby actually sits on his lap, the smaller chief is represented as part of the host's vast wealth; the host literally dominates his rival here. Another portrayal of wealth appears on the chest of the larger chief. A painted upside-down T most likely signifies the raised ribs of a copper, the most valued object for the Kwakiutl (see figure 1.16). Although the great chief's face is carved naturalistically, the face of the baby is distorted. SAM

tors and ethnographers (such as Franz Boas and George Hunt) who established "tradition" and "heritage" as models for the acquisition, the categorization, and the coherent representation to whites of Native art; the Indians who made the carvings, pottery, textiles, and paintings certainly never concerned themselves with such issues. It was Hunt, not the Kwakiutl from whom he was collecting, who was most concerned about acquiring the really old pieces; and it was Boas who informed Hunt that these artworks constituted the genuine, traditional objects that embodied Kwakiutl heritage.[9]

It was clear to me that I could not tell the story of the Kwakiutl artworks in the museum's storerooms as if they were artifacts frozen in time. Thus, this exhibition had to expand well beyond the art of feasting at the end of the nineteenth century to become a story of the ongoing vitality of the Kwakiutl people. We ended up displaying the potlatch of the 1890s and the potlatch of the 1990s. To tell this story, we needed to refer to all those who participated in the history of this ceremony. Although the Kwakiutl are of course central, whites play roles as well; these include missionaries and government officials who tried to deny the Kwakiutl the right to their ceremonies, agents who arrested potlatch participants and confiscated artworks, merchants whose goods enabled increasingly lavish potlatches to be hosted and more impressive art to be made, and, of course, the participant-observer cum collector George Hunt, and the sympathetic supporter of the potlatch, Franz Boas. As it turned out, by allowing the Kwakiutl their history, *Chiefly Feasts* tells a far richer, more complex, and, ultimately, a more optimistic story.

The History of the Kwakiutl and Their Potlatch

The first record of contacts between the Kwakiutl and Europeans is in 1786 when the British trader James Strange traveled in Queen Charlotte Strait; later a series of American, Spanish, and British boats visited the region, bringing in metal tools, guns, and trade paints, among many other items of western manufacture. The Hudson's Bay Company began to play an active role in Native-white contact on the Northwest Coast after it established trading posts at Forts Langley on the Fraser River (1827), McLaughlin on Milbanke Sound (1833), and Victoria at the southern end of Vancouver Island (1843). Like many other Northwest Coast peoples, the Kwakiutl visited these posts and would travel considerable distances to trade goods.

When the Hudson's Bay Company established a trading post in Kwakiutl territory in 1849, several villages that had their traditional sites elsewhere moved to the newly established village of Fort Rupert on Beaver Harbour (see Suttles, this volume). As a center of commerce and ceremonial activity and the home of a confederacy of several very high-ranking tribes, Fort Rupert (fig. 1.24) became the most prominent Kwakiutl village for the rest of the nineteenth century. It is worth remembering that this village, the location for numerous descriptions of Kwakiutl culture in Franz Boas's texts, did not exist before 1849. Alert Bay (figs. 1.25–26), the other principal Kwakiutl community that Boas and Hunt studied, had been established only in 1870 when two whites opened a cannery there; this attracted people from other villages who moved from the mainland of Vancouver Island to this small sheltered island at the end of Queen Charlotte Strait. Alert Bay became especially prominent after 1900, having become the site of the governmental Kwawkewlth Agency and a residential school. Even though these were major communities, other Kwakiutl villages such as those on Hope Island, Gilford Island, and Village Island, and at Kingcome, Blunden Harbour, and Quatsino (figs. 1.23, 1.27–29) maintained populations into the twentieth century.

There are good indications that the Kwakiutl potlatch changed considerably after the establishment of the Hudson's Bay Company store and Fort Rupert. Before that time the potlatch seems to have been a relatively modest affair compared to what it later became. Like other Northwest Coast groups before white contact, the Kwakiutl gave away such presents as food, furs, skins, and wooden boxes and bowls, but in relatively fewer numbers than they would later. This expansion was owed in part to the movement of tribes into confederacies such as that at Fort Rupert, where they could potlatch more actively with other tribes. As well, throughout the late nineteenth century, the Kwakiutl participated in the white economy by working for wages as fishermen and in canneries, and in the process acquired considerable expendable wealth that was distributed at potlatches. Kwakiutl social structure was also affected by the decline in their population due to infectious diseases, creating an uncertain ranking order, and making necessary the more competitive potlatches, at which hosts literally destroyed vast amounts of goods in order to be seen as the most prosperous and thus the highest ranking (Codere 1950).

Creative responses to all this white contact are illustrated by the adoption of the Hudson's Bay blanket as the dominant gift distributed at potlatches and the standard against which the value of other gifts was measured (fig. 1.30). The most valuable

1.16 **Copper**. 68 cm x 23 cm. *Private Collection. Photo by Andrew Niemann*

THE PARTICULAR HISTORY OF A COPPER, IF IT COULD be recalled by living people, might serve to document some of the most important events and transactions engaged in during the life of its owner and perhaps his or her descendants as well. Wilson Duff's moving history of Mungo Martin's copper Max'inuxwadzi (Great Killer Whale), for instance, is the thorough and unique account of the life of a twentieth century copper (1961).

Some information concerning the copper illustrated here, once the property of Willie Seaweed, is still available to us and provides some sense of the continuity of the copper tradition as it operates among contemporary Kwakiutl. Known as Galgatu (Long Top), this copper has been reconstructed at least two times around the T-shaped raised ridge of a very old, broken copper. Perhaps this ridge (*ga'las*) was a part of the old copper, also called Long Top, referred to in the course of a family history, recounted by Tłatłakwasila, a Gwa'sala woman, to George Hunt.

Upon the birth of his grandson, a chief by the name of Yakałanlis gave this copper to his son-in-law. When the grandson reached maturity, he sold the copper for an impressive 9,000 woolen blankets (Boas 1921:883).

The surface of this work has been painted in the unique black and silvery grey color combination favored by Willie Seaweed. The drawn lines are scratched through the paint, revealing the copper beneath it (Holm 1983:62). Coppers have traditionally been engraved on a black ground in the form of a conventionalized face representing the crest animal of the original owner (Boas 1897:344). Here, an animal with a unique combination of stylized features suggests both human and bird. A firm identification of this creature is not possible given the limited information about this work.

A chief might break a copper, destroying the integrity of the crest design. He would then offer the broken pieces to his rival, who then had to break a copper of equal or higher value. A rival unable to do so would be humiliated before the community. In an even grander gesture, chiefs have thrown the pieces or even the entire copper into the sea (Boas 1897:354).

A piece has been broken off from the upper left corner of this copper, and the entire right half of the face has been removed. Bill Holm has been able to postulate the chronology of these excisions by examining several old photographs. The copper was still whole when displayed, probably in 1939, at Village Island. In a 1955 photo, the right section is missing, and since then the small square section from the upper left-hand corner has been lost (1983:62).

Although the incidents that attended the breaking of this copper are not recorded, we do know that Seaweed's main potlatch rival was a chief from Xwamdasbe' (Hope Island). Apparently Seaweed did break coppers for this chief during the 1940s and 1950s.

In 1953, at a potlatch held at Gilford Island, Willie Seaweed was known to have broken one of his coppers, perhaps the right side of this one, for this particular rival (Duff n.d.).

This copper was not broken according to the pattern that Boas reported as being customary; the prescribed pattern began with a section removed from the upper right, then the lower left, followed by the upper left and finally the lower right side (1897:354).

The copper still plays a significant role in the life of the contemporary Kwakiutl, but the rivalries played out through these works of art may not be so fierce as those of the past. Seaweed's adversarial relationship with the chief from Hope Island was characterized as "friendly rivalry" by the contesting chiefs late in their careers (Duff n.d.). Furthermore, the breaking of coppers is not permitted at all within the ceremonial house at Alert Bay, because it would be considered a hostile act comparable to "wishing someone dead" (Gloria Webster: personal communication, 1990).

Contemporary coppers as well as older ones frequently bear animal names–Sea Lion, Beaver Face, Bear Face–probably referring to the crests of their original owners. Other names, such as All-Other-Coppers-Are-Ashamed-to-Look-at-It, Making-the-House-Empty-of-Blankets, and About-Whose-Possession-All-Are-Quarreling, were named in connection with the economic transactions that involved the copper (Boas 1897:344).

The wealth exchanged in connection with contemporary coppers is now in the form of cash, not blankets. Nonetheless, values such as the prestige of the family and the proper use of a copper in ceremony have been maintained. Furthermore, Long Top was valued not only for the price most recently paid for it, but for its title as well (ibid.:156).

The progress of this copper, as it has been displayed by the Seaweed family on significant social occasions, has punctuated the life-cycles of its various members. Long Top was brought out at Henry Seaweed's *hamatsa* initiation and was presumably a part of various weddings, cradle ceremonies, and other occasions. JO

1.17 Willie Seaweed with coppers, 1955. *Photo by Wilson Duff.* *RBCM SN 2933*

1.18 **Transformation mask**. Alert Bay. Wood, feathers, rope, L 58 cm, W 33 cm. *Collected by George Hunt, 1899. 16/6770AB, AMNH 1899–50*

ONE OF THE MOST DRAMATIC CARVINGS OF THE Kwakiutl is the transformation mask, which depicts two different beings. The dancer would first appear wearing a mask representing one creature; then, by manipulating strings and other devices, he would snap the mask open to reveal another being.

This particular transformation mask was probably danced in one of the *tła'sala* ceremonies. In his accession ledger, Boas documents it as belonging to Tsitsaɫwalagame', a numaym of the 'Namgis (acc. 1899–50, AMNH). The privilege of dancing with this mask was probably brought to the 'Namgis by marriage.

The mask demonstrates an old rigging technique. It is held on the dancer's face with a wickerwork construction strung together with sinew (Macnair: personal communication, May 1990). The two bars extending from either side of the eagle's head supply the leverage to pull open its beak. As the external beak opened, the two sides were pulled backwards and the bottom "chin" lowered, revealing a central visage surrounded by the eagle's profile on either side. The central image depicts an anthropomorphic face with a hooked nose. This portrayal was a relatively common one at the turn of the century when Hunt collected this piece (ibid.). SAM

1.19 American Museum of Natural History life group depicting the uses of cedar. *AMNH 384*

1.20 Chief photographed on the steamer *Boxer* at Cape Caution in 1873. *Photo by R. Maynard. RBCM 2209*

1.21 **Drinking bucket for a chief's wife**. Quatsino. Wood, L 13 cm, W 15.8 cm, H 18.5 cm. *Collected by George Hunt, 1900. 16/8232, AMNH 1900–73*

THE KWAKIUTL PRODUCED DRINKING BUCKETS THAT looked like small bent-corner boxes (Boas 1909:422–23); water was drunk from one of the corners (ibid.:427). This one was constructed of a flat board, kerfed and bent with one joint pegged together. Both the curved and completely rectilinear sides of the box are decorated with a series of carved striations, parallel lines organized to form a border. A gracefully arched handle surmounts this restrained and functional object.

Etiquette demanded that high-ranking individuals of some delicacy did not take food and water together at mealtime. For this reason, adult members of the nobility avoided eating roasted salmon backs, a food much enjoyed by young men who did not as yet concern themselves with the cultivation of a public image. This brittle food was known to cause choking, requiring that water be drunk to wash it down. If a grown man of some standing displayed such bad manners he would immediately have had to promise to give a potlatch in order to maintain his high image. Such a man would rather choke to death (ibid.: 427–28). JO

gift, a famous copper, was worth thousands of blankets. The Hudson's Bay Company store was at the center of the action, and the standard company blanket was the most popular gift item. Photographs from great potlatches held around 1900 show many piles of blankets, waiting to be given away.[10]

The most negative feature of white contact was the legislation of 1884, when the Canadian government declared potlatching and the associated Winter Ceremonials illegal (see Cole, this volume). Despite the law, the Kwakiutl continued to hold potlatches more or less openly for decades. But in 1922, government agent William Halliday arrested many participants in Dan Cranmer's great potlatch. Halliday coerced them: if they would sell their potlatch masks and coppers, they would not go to jail. Being imprisoned was shameful for a Kwakiutl, and many Indians agreed to sell their precious objects, particularly the coppers, for considerably less than their owners thought they were worth. (Most of them went to the Museum of Man in Ottawa, now the Canadian Museum of Civilization in Hull, some to the Royal Ontario Museum in Toronto, and a few to the Museum of the American Indian in New York.)

Kwakiutl potlatching became far more secretive after the 1922 episode, but never ceased entirely. Carvers like Willie Seaweed (fig. 1.31) and Mungo Martin (fig. 1.32) continued producing masks and other ceremonial paraphernalia, albeit quietly.[11] After the Canadian government dropped the anti-potlatch law in 1951, several Kwakiutl asked the Museum of Man to return the artifacts from the 1922 confiscation, arguing that they had been acquired under coercion. The Ottawa institution agreed on the condition that the Kwakiutl build a museum to house the artifacts, which would be returned to the community but not to individuals. By the early 1980s, two Native museums had been built to receive these pieces, the U'mista Cultural Centre in Alert Bay and the Kwagiulth Museum at Cape Mudge near Campbell River (Webster 1989). The Toronto pieces were returned in 1988 to the museums in Cape Mudge and Alert Bay. As this publication goes to press, the Museum of the American Indian, which has now become the National Museum of the American Indian and is part of the Smithsonian Institution, is reviewing the Kwakiutl request to return its part of confiscated materials.

It was most important for *Chiefly Feasts* to describe the entire story of the potlatch by including information on the role of whites in suppressing the potlatch, the admirable and successful resistance by the Kwakiutl to this suppression, and the creative responses of these people to the situation they found themselves in vis-à-vis white society. I was especially pleased

1.22 **Dance apron**. Fort Rupert. Cloth, puffin beaks, beads, L 69 cm, W 51 cm. *Collected by George Hunt, 1897. 16/2356, AMNH 1897–43*

AT A KWAKIUTL POTLATCH, HOSTS AND GUESTS alike dressed as elegantly as possible. Although in the time before contact the Kwakiutl dressed in skins, furs, and cedar bark costumes, once they had access to western trade goods they rapidly assimilated them into their clothing. This apron is an example of how the Kwakiutl transformed materials from another culture in order to create a costume distinctly their own.

This apron was made from a patchwork of flour sacking and pieces of a Hudson's Bay Company blanket. The assembled cloth rectangle is divided horizontally in four blue bands. The divisions are further emphasized by the outline of red piping. Rows of puffin beaks are sewn into the bottom three bands. Tassels made from four strands of string finished with trade beads are suspended across the bottom of the apron in a colorful fringe. Such aprons were worn on ceremonial occasions to enhance prestige. SAM

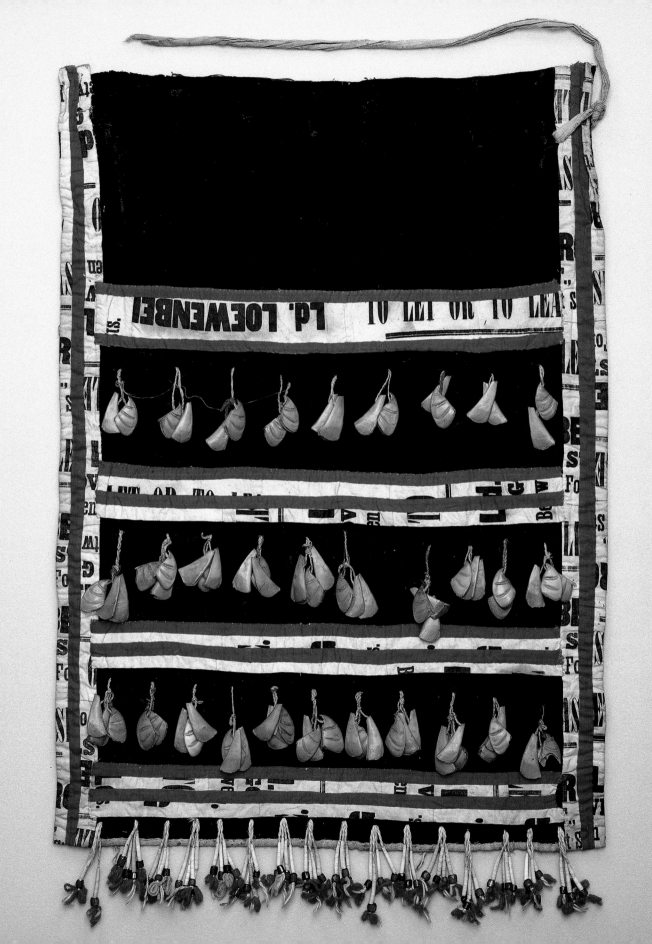

1.23 Blunden Harbour. *RBCM PN 228*

1.24 Fort Rupert, 1894. *Photo by O.C. Hastings.* AMNH 336058

1.25 Alert Bay, 1881. *Photo by Edward Dossetter.* AMNH 42271

1.26 Alert Bay, 1898. *Photo by H.I. Smith.* AMNH 411790

1.27 Hope Island, 1881. *Photo by Edward Dossetter.* AMNH 42298

1.28 Blunden Harbour, c. 1900. *Photo by C.F. Newcombe.*
RBCM PN 257

1.30 (*left*) Piles of Hudson's Bay Company blankets, Fort Rupert,
1894. *Photo by O.C. Hastings.* AMNH 411813

1.29 Gilford Island, c. 1900. John Scow's house, Sea Monster
House, with painted front; house to left has carved representation
of the *sisiyutł*, or double-headed serpent. *Photo by C.F. Newcombe.*
RBCM PN 235

that the U'mista Cultural Centre agreed to loan to this exhibition one of the returned treasures from the 1922 confiscation, an elegant raven and ermine headdress owned by the Wakas family (fig. 1.33). In the context of this exhibition, this piece signifies the tragic suppression of the potlatch by whites, the rectification of a wrong by the Canadian government, and the celebratory reunification of a people with their alienated heritage. It also tells an optimistic story of the continuation of a tradition under adverse conditions.

Today the Kwakiutl potlatch is still going strong. Master carvers make spectacular masks for dances, young people learn songs in Kwakwala, and feasting and gift-giving retain an important place in the lives of these people. Over the century since Boas and Hunt collected the American Museum's treasures, the Kwakiutl have certainly changed and their potlatches have changed as well. Their art, surely one of the most splendid and impressive features of their traditions, also has changed, but continues to be created in impressive quantities. This dynamic culture has become part of the modern world.

In the creation of this exhibition, questions of what is traditional and authentic became relevant in terms of the conservation of the objects we selected for display. Although many of the artifacts are well preserved and in excellent shape, a few pieces are in poor condition. Two in particular, one a 511-cm-long depiction of the double-headed serpent, or *sisiyutł* (fig. 1.34), and the other a 523-cm-long muslin screen associated with another of equal length (fig. 1.36), were so remarkable that they had to be included in the show. Knowing that neither work could tolerate the processing necessary to be displayed and then moved to the exhibition's several other venues, I decided to ask one of the contemporary Kwakiutl artists, Calvin Hunt, to create new versions of both pieces (pls. 1.35, 1.37, 1.38). These recreations of traditional pieces will be presented in the exhibition alongside other nineteenth century objects as authentic Kwakiutl artworks. I expect some visitors to be jarred by what they might consider a dissonance between the old objects and these new creations; this reaction will, I hope, turn into respect for the long and unbroken artistic tradition that Calvin Hunt represents. In this exhibition, the old and the new together communicate the great cultural legacy of the Kwakiutl people.

Women in Kwakiutl Ceremonialism

Contemporary observers of museology point out that displays are not simply representations of another culture, but also re-

1.31 **Crooked-Beak mask by Willie Seaweed**. Wood, red cedar bark, feathers, cord, fabric, 103 cm x 90 cm. 20th century. *17377, RBCM 1983–0224*

WILLIE SEAWEED (1873–1967), A 'NAK̓WAXDA'X̱W chief from Blunden Harbour, was born just eleven years before the passage of the anti-potlatch law. Despite living most of his life under this repressive legislation, Seaweed created some of the most remarkable art used for potlatches. This Crooked-Beak mask was using during the *hamatsa* ceremony.

The name 'Seaweed' is an anglicization of the Kwakwala 'Siwid,' which can be translated as 'Paddling owner,' 'Recipient of paddling,' or 'Paddled to,' all metaphors for a great chief who sponsors potlatches to which guests come from far off (Holm 1983). Seaweed was an exceptional artist and also a great chief, a talented orator and singer, and a keeper of traditions. Along with other artists and people of courage and conviction, he kept the potlatch going for all the years of the twentieth century when it was illegal.

This mask, depicting one of the avian associates of the *hamatsa* spirit, is called Crooked-Beak because of the dramatic curving arch of the upper beak; below the lower bill is a similar arch. The dancer wears this mask at an upward-reaching angle, slowly moving around the dance floor in a counter-clockwise motion. The rhythm of the music changes four times during his dance; at each change, the dancer squats on the floor and snaps the articulated beak open and shut, then resumes his dance (Macnair et al. 1980:149).

The bright enamel paint and the flamboyant carving style are twentieth century innovations. Earlier Crooked-Beak masks tended to be smaller, simpler, and cruder; only after 1910 did artists start carving in this more baroque style that has become the hallmark of twentieth century Kwakiutl art.

1.32 **Cannibal Bird, Raven, and Crooked-Beak mask by Mungo Martin**. Wood, cedar bark, feathers, 138 cm x 57 cm. 1953. *RBCM 9201*

Franz Boas met Mungo Martin (1881–1962) in 1894, when he visited Fort Rupert on one of his first field trips to the Northwest Coast. Member of a noble family, Martin was apprenticed to his artist-stepfather Charlie James and became a carver of considerable talent. This complex mask depicts the avian attendants of the man-eater who lives at the north end of the world: the long-beaked *huxwhukw*, the shorter-beaked man-eating raven, and Crooked-Beak, with its appendage arching over its nostrils. Far more complicated than nineteenth century prototypes, this twentieth century mask demonstrates the creativity and expressiveness of Mungo Martin, who carved for ceremonies that were illegal.

Martin played a major role in perpetuating Kwakiutl artistic traditions. In 1947, when he was sixty-six, the University of British Columbia Museum of Anthropology invited him to restore totem poles and carve some new poles for Totem Park. Then in 1952, he joined the staff of the Royal British Columbia Museum (then the British Columbia Provincial Museum) as a carver in that institution's Thunderbird Park. There he trained his son-in-law Henry Hunt and Henry's son Tony to carve, thus perpetuating the Kwakiutl artistic legacy. Martin also worked with Doug Cranmer (Macnair et al. 1980:185).

flect in some manner the culture that designs them. As Michael Ames (1986:1) has put it, museums are "artefacts of society . . . exhibits in their own right." Pieces selected for acquisition and then for display, the text describing them, the story that they are made to tell, the setting in which they are displayed, and their audience all constitute an "artifact" of the society producing the exhibition. I have described thus far how my planning for *Chiefly Feasts* was informed in part by the questions currently under discussion in anthropology, such as the meaning of authenticity and the importance of history.[12] Although of considerable concern to this discipline, their emergence as central issues reflects the more general late twentieth century concerns of how so-called traditional cultures function within a context largely determined by a dominant society.

Another issue that became part of this exhibit is of central concern to contemporary society, namely the representation of women. A growing body of anthropological literature (as well as literary and historical works) attempts to correct the predominantly male perspective so pervasive in the discipline.[13] This male orientation has often led, we now realize, to an inadequate picture of the culture, since the female perspective is omitted. Because questions of empowering women are fundamental to the modern world, it seemed appropriate to inquire of the means by which women were represented in the Kwakiutl literature.

During the process of creating *Chiefly Feasts*, new and fascinating facets of Kwakiutl culture continually revealed themselves. During my travels, some of the most impressive people I met were women, dignified, charming, and strong individuals. Speaking with them, I recalled Boas's and Hunt's descriptions of Kwakiutl ritual, which contained many references to the participation of women in the potlatches, where they sang, danced, and were initiated into societies. Although Boas and Hunt had described in their publications the role of women in Kwakiutl ceremonialism, their museum displays at the American Museum of Natural History made no reference to that role. Earlier in this essay I mentioned the Kwakiutl figure group at the American Museum as an example of Boas's desire to depict the traditions and lifeways that had by and large been lost. It depicts two male manikins, one taking hot stones from the fire to be placed in a box in order to boil water, the other painting a box. One woman, making a cedar bark mat, rocks her infant in its cradle, another shreds cedar bark for an apron, and a third dries fish over a fire. The female figures, engaged in the essential yet mundane activities of childrearing and costume manufacture, gave no indication to Boas's contemporary audience that Kwakiutl women also play central roles in ceremonies and brought with them into marriage significant privileges. And few of these early visitors would have had the opportunity or the inclination to read through the voluminous texts by Boas and Hunt to gain an accurate understanding of the role of women in this culture.

The representation of women in Boas's Northwest Coast Indian display is especially interesting considering the fact that Boas trained a good many female anthropologists, including Ruth Benedict and Margaret Mead. Although clearly a progressive man, ahead of his time in his encouraging women into the profession, it would probably have been difficult for Boas to have imagined creating a display that focused on women's contributions in Kwakiutl ceremonialism, as he was primarily interested in displaying diffusion, tribal relations, and the context of the artifact (Jonaitis, in press).

Realizing how skewed was the image of Kwakiutl women in past museum displays, I decided to have a separate section on the role of women in Kwakiutl ritual in *Chiefly Feasts*. Because some of the most impressive pieces in the display—the 511-cm-long *sisiyutł* board (fig. 1.35), the 272-cm-high, three-part *dantsikw* (fig. 1.40), and the 523-cm-high *nułami'sta* (fig. 1.37)—were associated with women's dances, there is little doubt that the museum visitor will clearly recognize the importance of women in this culture from the nineteenth century to the present. (The *sisiyutł* and screen are pieces that Calvin Hunt has recreated.)

Kwakiutl Involvement in the Exhibit

Many of the issues discussed thus far—authenticity, traditionalism, history—emerge from the contemporary questioning of a central premise of classical anthropology, namely that the scholar speaks with an authoritative voice and has the right to make value judgments about what is pristine, what is acculturated, what is culturally pure, and what is tainted by western influence. At this time we are undergoing a thorough reassessment of what anthropology is and should be; as a result, the notion of the authoritative scholar is beginning to be replaced by the idea that we are but one of many voices. Of major importance to scholarship on Native culture is the inclusion of the voices of those peoples whose culture we are studying.[14]

There exists a need to understand the contemporary world from the broad point of view of different cultural and historical traditions. While much homogenization occurs, with shopping malls in Brazil, Martinique, and Vancouver bearing a striking

1.33 **Raven and ermine headdress**. L 65 cm. *UCC, 1979*

ORIGINALLY FROM THE OOWEKEENO AT RIVER Inlet, this headdress refers to the story of the Nanwakawe', who were preparing for a hunting trip. Their father advised them that they should find a rocky, sloping place on which to camp overnight. The sons ignored the advice and stopped at a flat, grassy meadow, where they slept. When they awoke the next morning, they found themselves stranded atop a tall pillar of rock, with no way of getting down. The youngest brother said, "Let us tie our ropes together and I will stay here and hold one end, while each of you climbs down." As the third brother reached the bottom safely, the youngest brother realized that he was stuck at the top. He curled up in his cedar bark tunic and fell asleep, waking when he heard a noise. He poked a hole in his tunic and saw an ermine. The ermine said, "I know what you did to save your brothers and I will help you. Touch my paws with your hands and feet, then move down, exactly as I do, with your hind end held high." The young man did as he was told and soon joined his brothers at the foot of the rock pillar.

The headdress is rigged so that the ermine moves on a track in and out of the mouth of the raven. Underneath the raven is a *sisiyutł*, representing strength. The absence of dyed red cedar bark indicates that the headdress is used in the *tła'sala* rather than in the *tseka* ceremonies.

This headdress is from the Potlatch Collection, returned by the National Museum of Man (now the Canadian Museum of Civilization) in 1979. It was one of the treasures confiscated in 1922, as a result of the arrests under the law prohibiting the potlatch. GCW

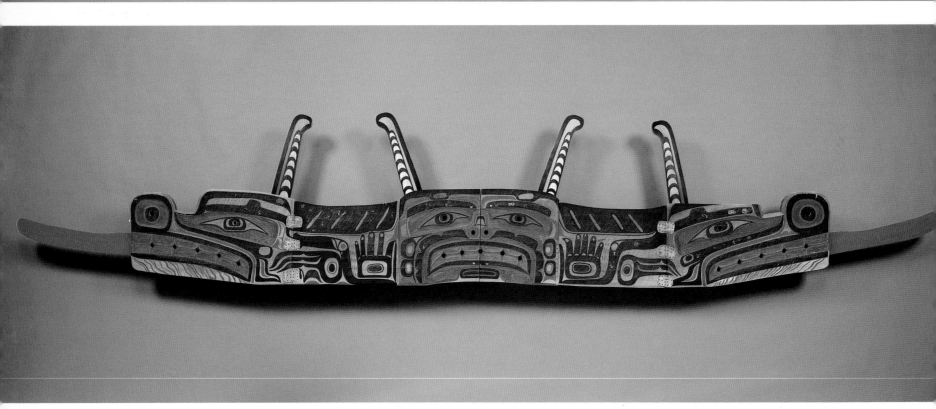

1.34 *Sisiyutł* board. Fort Rupert. Wood, L 511.4 cm, H 47 cm. *Collected by George Hunt, 1904. 16/9583*, AMNH 1904–41

1.35 **Replica of *sisiyutł* board carved by Calvin Hunt**. 1990. *16.1/2631*

THE *sisiyutł* IS A FABULOUS BEING BELIEVED BY THE Kwakiutl to take the form of a double-headed snake, each profile head with its own curled horn and sharp, protruding tongue. In the center of its body is a frontal human face, commonly depicted with bared teeth and two horns. The *sisiyutł* might at times appear in the guise of a fish; this shape-shifting is consistent with its ambiguous nature—sometimes the death-dealing monster the sight of whom brought death, but sometimes the bestower of great power.

A human being who caught sight of this creature might suffer a horrible death; the head would be sharply twisted, dislocated from the rest of the body. Contact with a *sisiyutł*'s blood is also said to petrify human skin (Boas 1897:371–2).

The *sisiyutł* could also be of great service to chosen individuals, especially warriors, able to harness it. Transforming itself into a canoe, the *sisiyutł* could move of its own volition and its eyes might be used as formidable weapons when hurled from a sling (ibid.). Those fortunate enough to acquire its scales, spines, or blood might use them to their own advantage (Holm 1972:57 and Webster, this volume).

Sisiyutł imagery may be displayed either as a crest privilege or as the theatrical prop of a *tuxw'id* dancer, as was the case with this artifact. The *tuxw'id*, usually a woman, would enter the house singing as she moved around the fire. Boas recorded gestures of a *tuxw'id* dancer that gave the distinct impression that she was trying to conjure up this being, compelling it to rise from its underground domain:

She holds her elbows close to her sides, the forearms forward, palms upward. She walks around the fire limping, raising both hands slightly every second step. (1897:487)

These gestures would summon a huge carving of a *sisiyutł* from the ground at the rear of the house. This was accomplished through the impressive sleight-of-hand and puppetry techniques, which effectively established the supernatural abilities of the *tuxw'id* (see also figs. 1.39, 1.40, and 2.29). A smaller *sisiyutł* might be made to fly through the air, a larger one might poke its horns up from a trench dug in the ground, appearing to drag the *tuxw'id* down to the underworld (ibid:488).

This *sisiyutł* carving collected by Hunt in 1904 was constructed of wooden slats. It is divided down the middle of the central face, probably so that the *tuxw'id* might appear to split it in two when she struck it with a stick, lance, or paddle in the course of her riveting performance. The flat boards were carved in shallow relief with small punctured areas between the teeth and on the eyes and nostrils. It was originally painted in green, black, white, and red, the red used to outline the horrific teeth and to emphasize the protruding tongues. Thin flakes of mica still adhere to certain parts of the wooden *sisiyutł*, which must have glittered eerily as they caught the firelight.

Figure 1.35 is a reproduction of the 1904 piece made especially for the *Chiefly Feasts* exhibition by the Kwakiutl artist Calvin Hunt (George Hunt's great-grandson). The older piece was too fragile to be displayed. Calvin Hunt wished to produce a new carving as much like the original as possible, and so its surface was stained with potassium permanganate and abraded with steel wool to simulate age. In the newer *sisiyutł*, the style of a modern artist is combined with the inspiration provided by an anonymous past master, resulting in an unusual document of a continuously evolving art tradition. JO

1.36 *Nułami'sta* **dancer's apparatus**. New Vancouver. Cloth, wood, L 523 cm, W 165 cm. *Collected by George Hunt, 1904. 16/9584AL, AMNH 1904–41*

1.37 Replica of *nułami'sta* dancer's apparatus by Calvin Hunt, 1990

T HIS UNUSUAL APPARATUS WAS A THEATRICAL PROP, probably used by a female dancer of the Da̱'naxda'x̱w tribe who appeared in the course of the Winter Ceremony. It is elaborately constructed of several lengths of painted cloth, supported at intervals by wooden slats, and framed at two of its rectangular sections. One framing device is made of simple wooden strips, but the other is an intricate arrangement of wooden figures or puppets with movable arms and two finlike projections. It is not clear if this configuration represents the original structure of the piece; certain stylistic differences suggest that this work may have been intended for use in separate segments. In addition, the wooden figures appear to have been nailed to the screen at some point after the original construction of this work (Peter Macnair: personal communication, 1990).

The word *nułami'sta* has been identified as the appropriate title of a particular dance claimed by Agnes Cranmer, now from Alert Bay, who acquired it from her aunt, Mary Johnson, George Hunt's daughter. She, in turn, had inherited it from her own mother, a 'Nak'waxda'x̱w woman. Because Agnes Cranmer's dance is identified by this same name, *nułami'sta*, and she describes the use of a similar prop at the culmination of her performance, it is likely that this version bears some relationship to the Da̱'naxda'x̱w dance. A different family within a different village group, however, would probably vary the dance somewhat.

In Agnes Cranmer's version, the performer appears dressed in a blanket, wearing a piece of cedar bark on top of her head. She is endowed with the special ability to "throw supernatural power," which affects the behavior of her audience in an amusing manner. Entering the house and circling left, she would pause at each of the four corners. Each time she would throw this intangible substance from the folds of her blanket, causing people to laugh hysterically, hug each other, or scratch at an intolerable itch. This power would also animate carved wooden puppets, causing them to rise into the air. After each demonstration she "took that power back," allowing the people to return to their normal state. Then, the long strip of this cloth apparatus might be rigged with strings so that the *nułam'ista* would rise up behind the back of this performer (Agnes Cranmer: personal communication, 1990; see Jonaitis, this volume, for an account of this performance).

It would appear that in this case, as well as in the theatrical display of the *tuxw'id*, a dancer's command over a cooperative audience is a sign of power and of the public acceptance of his or her claim to a particular dance prerogative. Both the physical and

emotional responses of the audiences are essential to the success of these performances.

The newer *nułami'sta* was reproduced by contemporary Kwakiutl artist Calvin Hunt for the exhibition because the original's cloth strip was fragile. Hunt selected an off-white length of canvas for the new piece, feeling that it might approximate the color of the original. He decided, however, to make certain minor changes in the new piece for artistic reasons. One of the painted profile faces, for instance, now faces right instead of left, and a blank background has been added as a support for the apparatus. As with the *sisiyuł* board (figs. 1.34-35), the ideas and techniques of this contemporary artist have been effectively incorporated into a work inspired by a past master. This unique and important work of art documents the processes of both continuity and change that affect the production of Northwest Coast Indian art today. JO

1.38 Calvin Hunt replicating the *nułami'sta*. Fort Rupert, 1990

1.39 **Crab puppet**. Blunden Harbour. Wood, L 44.5 cm, W 28 cm. *Collected by George Hunt, 1902. 16/8946AF, AMNH 1902–46*

THE THEATRICAL EXPLOITS OF THE *tuxw'id* DANCER were designed to astonish the audience, to shock even those familiar with the techniques that produced such spectacles. The proper response of the audience to these displays was a form of validation, a recognition of the performer's right to these dance privileges. The *tuxw'id* dancer was usually female.

Some *tuxw'ids* insisted that a member of the audience try to kill them, to cut through their necks, split open their stomachs, or drive a wedge through their heads. The gory special effects required to create these illusions were perfected by these dancers. A concealed bladder filled with blood would be made to burst at the appropriate moment. Seals' eyes, hidden in the hair, would be released, as if they fell out of the dancer's eye sockets when a wedge was pounded into her head (Boas 1897:489).

In addition to conjuring up a *sisiyuł* (see fig. 1.34), the *tuxw'id* and her helpers manipulated puppets such as birds, which were rigged to fly through the air at her command, and frogs or crabs, which were made to scamper across the floor. Hunt found one of these crab puppets in a cave at Tigwaxste', an old 'Nak'waxda'xw village. The mechanism that would have animated this figure is gone now, but its intent face and wobbly legs, attached with flexible hide hinges, still convey a sense of its incredible and humorous progress across the floor. Its cylindrical eyes are still covered with glue, indicating that some material was used to decorate them, perhaps mica. Traces of red paint can still be discerned on the crab's body. There are four pairs of holes on the underside of the crab. It is likely that there were four wood wheels attached to these holes, allowing the crab to be pulled from side to side, thus emulating the actual movement of crabs (Holm: personal communication, 1990). JO

1.40 _Daṉtsikw_ (dancing boards). Gilford Island. Wood, L 272 cm, W 117.5 cm. _Collected by George Hunt, 1899. 16/6900AC, AMNH 1899–50_

AMONG THE MANY UNFORGETTABLE IMAGES FROM the Edward Curtis film, _In the Land of the Head Hunters_ (later changed to _In the Land of the War Canoes_), is the reenactment of a performance in which a line of Kwakiutl dancers, their backs to the camera, cause a series of _daṉtsikw_ boards to rise from the ground. The boards sway slightly as they emerge from among the huddled group, and the dramatic effect is enhanced as the crisp, pale-painted images appear from the darkness.

These boards are made to represent _sisiyutɬs_, executed in a more abstract manner than the carving which represents the double-headed snake in fig. 1.34. In some performances, the boards are made to separate and assume a horizontal orientation approximating the form of a more naturalistic _sisiyutɬ_.

The _daṉtsikw_ were used in the Curtis film as a part of the _nuntam_ dance (Holm and Quimby 1980:85). Boas, however, described them as the treasures of the _tuxw'id_ dancer, which she causes to rise from the ground as testimony to her supernatural affiliations and skills (1897:491). This example, composed of three vertical segments, is a filigreed network of circular, ovoid, and eye-shaped forms that combine in certain areas as facelike configurations. Some traces of paint remain on the boards, and it appears that the open areas were at one time rimmed with white. Pieces of mica are still glued to the wood, and the effects of this reflective material, combined with the play of shadow and light which would have been cast from the openwork structure, must have made a spectacular display.

Hunt's field notes associate these particular boards with the story of T̓sekame' or Head-Winter-Dancer, a legend of the Ḵwiḵwasutinuxw (acc. 1899–50, AMNH). Hunt specifically refers to Tisamgid, one of the major protagonists in the story, whose name may be translated as Stone-Body. This character, his hands washed as a child in the blood of a _sisiyutɬ_, acquired a body of stone along with the appearance and formidable cry of a _dzunuḵwa_. As no ordinary canoe would support his new form, his father, Head-Winter-Dancer, bestowed upon him a self-paddling serpent canoe, originally a gift acquired from a being called Only-One-on-Beach. The canoe is in fact a double-headed serpent, a _sisiyutɬ_. Stone-Body climbed aboard and embarked upon a series of extraordinary adventures (Boas and Hunt 1905:165–247). This particular _daṉtsikw_ is meant to represent this vessel (Gloria Webster: personal communication, 1990).

Head-Winter-Dancer demonstrated his considerable supernatural power by causing the serpent canoe to sink into the ground at one end of the village and to reemerge at the other (Boas and Hunt 1905). The manipulation of the dancing boards by the _tuxw'id_ dancer, as she causes them to rise from the ground, may parallel Head-Winter-Dancer's impressive display. JO

1.41 Visit of Kwakiutl to American Museum of Natural History, May 1990. From left to right: Emma Hunt, Agnes Cranmer, Irene Hunt Hayman, Elsie Williams, Adam Dick, Tom Willie, Peter Macnair, Ethel Alfred, Gloria Cranmer Webster, and Judith Ostrowitz. *Photo by D.Finnin*

1.42 Visit of Kwakiutl to American Museum of Natural History, May 1990. From left to right: Helen Knox, Alice Smith, and William Hunt. *Photo by D. Finnin*

resemblance to those on Long Island, and television bringing a particular vision of reality to groups dispersed literally world-wide, certain elements of Native cultures remain remarkably persistent. Despite its current economic power and aspects of its culture that seem universally attractive, the west has neither displaced nor absorbed indigenous people, who continually redefine themselves as they experience changes. These redefinitions have been selective, with Native peoples doing much of the selecting. The situation is conducive to more respectful and equal relationships than those characterizing the recent past.

From the inception of this project I knew that I needed to include the Native voice in any representation of the Kwakiutl, so I contacted Gloria Cranmer Webster, a great-granddaughter of George Hunt, who had studied anthropology at the University of British Columbia, worked at that institution's Museum of Anthropology, and was then the Director of the U'mista Cultural Centre in Alert Bay. At first we saw her role as a consultant, to help make sure that what we said in the exhibit did not misrepresent her people, so we shared what we wrote and designed with her. She also agreed to write a catalogue entry on the modern Kwakiutl potlatch, a ceremonial in which she plays an active role.

During the course of development of this exhibit, I listened to Native people, at the Ottawa conference on "Preserving Our Heritage," as well as during less formal, casual conversations, expressing their desire to play the determining role in what was said about their history and culture in museum displays. Museum professionals, particularly from Canadian institutions such as the Royal British Columbia Museum in Victoria and the Museum of Anthropology of Vancouver, reiterated this point from a museum perspective, describing how museums need to begin relinquishing control over how they represent Native peoples. Instead of assuming an authoritative voice in these representations, museums must allow Native people to function not only as consultants, but as actual creators of exhibits.

In response to this changing standard about the appropriate level of involvement of Native people in exhibitions, I asked Gloria Cranmer Webster to curate the modern potlatch section of *Chiefly Feasts*. In keeping with the historical theme of the persistence of a people and their practices, the final part of the exhibition was to be a display of contemporary masks like those worn at the potlatch today. The American Museum owns no art of this kind, as it had, for the most part, ceased active collecting on the Northwest Coast after Boas left in 1905. Thus we were delighted when the Royal British Columbia Museum in Victoria agreed to lend some of its exceptional twentieth century Kwakiutl art. In an appropriate reversal of roles, the anthropological staff at the American Museum of Natural History and I then became Webster's consultants.

As the planning for *Chiefly Feasts* progressed, I tried to involve more and more Kwakiutl people, who complemented the key role played by Gloria Webster. Particularly important was Tony Hunt, distinguished artist who gave us excellent advice on the artworks we were going to display, and welcomed me to Fort Rupert. I also discussed the show with other artists including Calvin Hunt, Doug Cranmer, and Bruce Alfred. It was fascinating to listen to their responses to the sometimes elegant, sometimes rough, sometimes ingenious, but always powerful creations of their ancestors.

The old people of the community store in their keen memories a wealth of knowledge about their traditions; I was especially concerned that the senior members of the Kwakiutl community be consulted during the creation of this show.[15] In addition, it seemed advisable to inform the people living in villages on and near Vancouver Island about what we were doing in regard to their cultural heritage, thousands of miles away in New York City. Thus I traveled as often as possible to British Columbia to visit Alert Bay, Fort Rupert, Hopetown, Quatsino, Kingcome, Gilford Island, and Cape Mudge to show photographs of the objects we were planning to exhibit, and to speak with the old people about them.

Pleasurable and personally satisfying to me as these trips were, they proved inadequate as a means of bringing the old people into the creation of *Chiefly Feasts*. Because of work obligations in New York, my trips to British Columbia were neither as frequent nor as lengthy as I would have wished. Moreover, because the old people could see only photographs, not the actual artworks, they could not be as forthcoming with information as they might have otherwise been. To deal with these limitations and to attempt a more productive dialogue, we invited a delegation of Kwakiutl old people to New York City to discuss the exhibition's carvings and paintings, and to review the label copy and catalogue captions.

In May 1990, the largest group of Kwak̓wala speakers ever in New York City at one time visited the American Museum of Natural History (figs. 1.41–43). They were: Ethel Alfred, Margaret Cook, Agnes Cranmer, Adam Dick, Emma Hunt, William Hunt, Helen Knox, Alice Smith, Elsie Williams, and Tom Willie; accompanying them were Gloria Cranmer Webster, Irene Hunt Hayman, Beatrice Smith, and Peter Macnair of the Royal British Columbia Museum.[16] They discussed the pieces, provided information about their meaning and usage, and re-

lated our nineteenth century artworks to the ceremonialism in which they participate today.

One of the most extraordinary moments of this visit occurred when we brought out an array of masks associated with the Dance of the Undersea Kingdom which reenacted the adventures of the hero Siwidi. When Chief Tom Willie, who today owns the story of Siwidi, saw our Siwidi masks, he stood up and, in Kwak̓wala, recited his version of the story (see Ostrowitz and Jonaitis, this volume). A few days later, the discussion of the *nuɬami'sta* inspired Agnes Cranmer and Ethel Alfred to do a very amusing dance associated with one of Mrs. Cranmer's privileges. The two women danced about in a circle, "throwing" invisible objects at the group; the recipients of these thrown powers started laughing hysterically, scratching themselves, and hugging each other. When the two women finished, everyone stood up and danced in this fluorescent-lit, vinyl-floored, climate-controlled space lined with endless gray metal cabinets and shelves.

One evening after spending long hours in the Museum storage area we spent some time touring New York City. I was driving along Fifth Avenue, with William Hunt sitting next to me. Just as we were approaching the Empire State Building, this grandson of George Hunt began singing some of his *hamatsa* songs. Behind us Margaret Cook, Ethel Alfred, and Helen Knox then began a song women sing to "tame" the *hamatsa*. I realized then how much richer *Chiefly Feasts* has become as a result of the involvement of the Kwakiutl people, and how comparatively impoverished this exhibition would have been had I adhered to the old paradigm and insisted on being the sole authority, creating a display and story line in isolation from the people whose culture was being celebrated.

A Potlatch in Alert Bay, November 1988

During my first visit to Alert Bay in summer 1988, Gloria Cranmer Webster said to me that if I was going to do a show on the potlatch, I ought to see a real one. One day, among the interoffice memos and professional correspondence, I received an invitation to a potlatch hosted by Peter Cook that was to memorialize two deceased members of his family. I made plans to travel to Alert Bay in mid-November. I flew first to Victoria where some friends from the Royal British Columbia Museum picked me up for the eight-hour drive up to Alert Bay. Halfway up the island, where the road races past mountains both forested and clear-cut, the weather turned and it began to rain ferociously. We just made the ferry from Port McNeill to Alert

Bay, and, as we sat on that boat, watched the gray and windy sky become black.

Evening comes early in this part of the world in November, and it was dark by the time we reached Alert Bay. I sat in the big house, eyes filled with smoke from the central fire, and clothes still damp (figs. 5.1, 5.2). It was just as my hero Franz Boas had described it in his letters home from the field: he had watched the Kwakiutl dance for hours, listened to their orations, observed their gift-giving, ate their food. But nothing I had ever read prepared me for actually seeing a *hamatsa* initiate rush around in frenzy, a big *dzunuk̓wa* lumbering sleepily, a sea monster dancing gracefully about. Powerfully delivered orations memorializing deceased individuals filled the house. Men and women of all ages danced gracefully throughout the evening, elegantly attired in button blankets and carved frontlets with ermine trains. And the food was extraordinary: venison stew, grilled eulachon, salmon sandwiches, home-made breads and cakes. The tastes, the smell of smoke, the buzz of the crowd, the beating of drums, the swirling movement of the dancers, the bright red yarn headbands that everyone, even I, wore through part of the celebration, all became part of a single sensation of belonging. And that sense of belonging transported my understanding from the knowledge obtained from books to a reality unlike any I had ever experienced.

I could have anticipated the effects that the masks, dancing, and food would have on me. But the gift-giving touched me in a completely unpredictable way. The distribution of the payments to those of us who witnessed this demonstration of family prerogatives came late in the evening. It took nearly an hour just to bring all the boxes containing potlatch goods out and place them on the big house floor. Then people unloaded carton after carton and gave gifts to the guests, according to their social importance and rank—plastic and glass dishes, towels, pillows, home-baked goods, home-canned summer berries, hand-crocheted doilies and shawls, large blankets, quarters for the children and ten-dollar bills—wads of them, apparently without number (figs. 5.18–20). Some of these items may have been purchased at white markets, but in this context they were undeniably Kwakiutl. For a while I watched objectively, mentally noting what was similar to nineteenth century gifts, what was a manifestation of cultural innovation, what had been purchased in local markets, and what had taken weeks and months to create or prepare. Such speculations lasted a very short time, for soon my attempted scholarly detachment fell away, replaced by awe of this generous and noble family whose prestige was firmly embedded in my consciousness. The ceremony did to me what it was supposed to do; in this sense, nothing had changed since Boas's time.

After the potlatch, a group of people had a small party. The young Kwakiutl, who had earlier been dancing in button blankets and carved frontlets, were now in jeans, dancing to top-forty disco music. But when it was finally time to leave, they all stood up in a line and left, singing in Kwak̓wala the going-away song traditionally sung at the end of potlatches. Regardless of how easily these dancers fit into a youth culture now widespread in the world, they were also without doubt inheritors of a culture which, despite all predictions by Franz Boas, despite all the real changes that it has undergone for decades, remains profoundly and uniquely Kwakiutl. Every time I sit in my New York City apartment and look at my easy chair decorated with the delicately crocheted doily that is my most cherished potlatch gift, I relive these magical experiences. Those of us who have had the privilege of sharing in Kwakiutl culture have been transformed by hearing their songs and speeches, enjoying their feasts, watching their ceremonies, and, most important, celebrating with them their never-dying traditions.

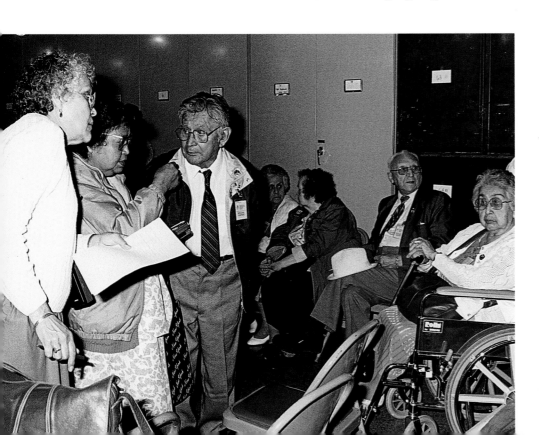

1.43 Visit of Kwakiutl to American Museum of Natural History, May 1990. From left to right: Gloria Cranmer Webster, Elsie Williams, Tom Willie, Ethel Alfred, Alice Smith, William Hunt, and Margaret Cook. *Photo by D. Finnin*

2.1 Knight Inlet, 1881. *Photo by Edward Dossetter.* AMNH 32955

2 / *Streams of Property, Armor of Wealth: The Traditional Kwakiutl Potlatch*

Wayne Suttles

L IKE THE PEOPLE THEMSELVES, THE KWAKIUTL potlatch has continued into the last decade of the twentieth century and will likely endure into the next millennium (see Webster, this volume). Like any social institution, the potlatch has had a history that developed within the changing cultural and social life of the people. My task is to go back in its history to introduce the Kwakiutl potlatch of the nineteenth century as we know about it from oral tradition, eyewitness accounts, and later interpretation, and to tell something about its cultural and social context. I will begin in a time known only from oral tradition in order to discover what that tradition tells us were important events.

This time is the early nineteenth century, half a century after European explorers and fur traders first entered Queen Charlotte Strait, but a few years before 1849, when the Hudson's Bay Company built Fort Rupert on its Vancouver Island shore. The place is Crooked-Beach (Ḵalugwis, the "Karlakwees" of official documents) at the southern tip of Turnour Island, the site of the village of a tribe called the Kwaguł, a name that is the source of "Kwakiutl."

Crooked-Beach is one of a number of villages in the maze of channels and islands around the eastern end of Queen Charlotte Strait (see map). These villages are near the entrance to the great fiord of Knight Inlet, with its early spring harvest of eulachon (candlefish), and they are handy to the Nimpkish and other rivers of Vancouver Island, with their summer and fall runs of salmon (fig. 2.1). Each village is the winter home of one of the twenty or more tribes who speak Kwakwala, the language of the Kwaguł. These tribes, the Kwakwaka'wakw 'speakers of Kwakwala', have come to be called collectively the Kwakiutl. I will use the term 'Kwakiutl' for this larger nation and 'Kwaguł' for the people called by this name in Kwakwala, that is, for the people of the village of Crooked-Beach before the founding of Fort Rupert, and for the four tribes that settled next to the fort shortly afterward.

Crooked-Beach must have been a village of several hundred people living in a row of great cedar-plank houses. Their gable ends all faced the curving shore, the larger ones with painted fronts and with decks extending over the beach, where people could rest and talk, or work, or make speeches (figs. 2.2–3). The beach would have been lined with large and small canoes. In warm weather the men and children would be quite naked, the women dressed only in skirts of shredded cedar bark. In wet, chilly weather, people would be wearing basketry hats and blankets of cedar bark or furs. A few, by now, might wear sailors' pants and shirts.

Entering one of the larger houses, we are struck first by the four great carved posts that hold the two heavy beams supporting the roof (fig. 2.4). The posts stand at the ends of an open central area with an earth floor and a fireplace in each corner. Beside each fire is a pair of settees (fig. 2.5). Above the fires are racks loaded with drying fish and baskets of other foods. A raised platform extends from the walls on all sides. Several compartments resembling small houses are built on the platform and serve as bedrooms. Elsewhere it provides space for wooden boxes for storing preserved foods and oil, carved feast dishes (figs. 2.6, 2.8), and chests filled with fur blankets, coppers, masks, rattles, and other treasures.

The events that occurred at Crooked-Beach, which are narrated below, form only one episode in "Marriage with the Comox," one of a number of long family histories recorded in Kwakwala by George Hunt and translated by Franz Boas (1921:951–1002).[1] The whole history begins a generation earlier, with the marriage of a man of the Comox tribe, the Coast Salish people at the northern end of Georgia Strait, to a woman of the Ligwiłda'xw tribe, the southernmost Kwakiutl group. The history ends four generations later at Fort Rupert, where the Kwaguł and three other tribes had built a new village, with the marriage of George Hunt to his first wife, and the privileges that went to their four sons.

The leading figure in this episode is a Kwaguł man of the Sintłam numaym (a social group we will examine later), whose

2.2 Hope Island, c. 1900. *Photo by C.F. Newcombe,* RBCM PN 238

2.3 Alert Bay house façade, 1873. This was the first painted house façade in Alert Bay. According to Peter Macnair (personal communication, 1990), a northern-style box inspired this whale and thunderbird design. *Photo by R. Maynard.* AMNH 329173

2.4 New Vancouver house interior (late Jack Peter's father's house), c. 1900. Parts of the bird posts are articulated. Behind the central man is an anthropomorphic carving dressed in a button blanket. *Photo by C.F. Newcombe.* RBCM PN244

2.5 **Settee**. Kingcome. Wood, L 236.6 cm, H 73.7 cm. *Collected by George Hunt, 1901. 16/8432, AMNH 1901–32*

THE KWAKIUTL PLACED THE SETTEES AT THE REAR OF the house or on either side of the fire. Although used as backrests for the chief and his family, they were more than simple furniture, for they displayed the crest emblems that were such treasured possessions of the family. Settees had four distinct parts: the backrest itself, the plank resting on the floor, and the two armrests. Hunt did not collect this floor plank, which was made later at AMNH.

Hunt did not connect this settee to a specific history. It appears to depict a *sisiyutł*, the double-headed serpent, as well as a winged figure (Macnair: personal communication, 1989). The *sisiyutł* is represented by the two long scalelike bands emanating from the sides of the central image and running along the bottom of the backrest; the two heads of the serpent appear on the armrests. Flanking either side of the central circle are designs that appear to be wings. The central circle seems to represent the face of both the *sisiyutł* and the winged creature, suggesting a simultaneous representation of two different creatures. SAM

2.6 **Seal dish**. Probably Quatsino. Wood, H 29 cm, W 29.5 cm, L 86.4 cm. *Collected by George Hunt, 1898. 16/4687A, AMNH 1898–41*

Possibly a companion piece to fig. 1.3, this seal-shaped dish is similarly carved, but is actually a bit smaller and more completely covered by a painted design. One eye retains its circle of inlaid material, perhaps a mirror or once-shiny button, which would have made the eye luminous, as if moist.

The rim of the bowl has been delineated by the shallow carving of delicate, parallel grooves, while the rest of the seal's body is completely smooth and shiny. A hole at the bottom of the dish appears to have been deliberately punched through, and Peter Macnair (personal communication, 1989) has suggested that someone may have tried to "neutralize" this object, making it unsuitable for further use. This act might have insured that the dish would not be used by any group lacking the right to display it. (See fig. 1.11, also a Quatsino piece, similarly damaged.) JO

2.7 Interior of Quatsino house, illustrating house post. Although this house seems to be abandoned, it may not be. Instead, the inhabitants might have taken the roof planks from this winter house to use in their summer village. *RBCM PN 335*

2.8 Double-headed wolf dish. Quatsino. Wood, L 166 cm, W 42 cm. *Collected by George Hunt, 1898. 16/4690* AMNH 1898–41

THIS DISH IS IN THE FORM OF A WOLF WITH TWO heads and two tails. Each head bares its teeth of sharpened bone and displays a small wooden copper in its mouth. The vessel is carved and painted in the relatively naturalistic "Old Wakashan" style, which is characteristic of sculpture collected among the G̱usgimaxw.

The Dzawada̱ʼenux̱w have a story about four wolf siblings who survived the great flood by climbing to the top of a high mountain called Having-Phosphorescence. The wolves, all of them possessing some degree of supernatural power, took off their wolf skins and became the ancestors of the Dzawada̱ʼenux̱w. They wondered if they were the only people in the world, and the oldest brother,

Listened-To, put on his wolf mask so that he could call out in a howl to any other survivors. According to the legend, Howling-About-in-the-World answered his call all the way from G̱usgimaxw, indicating that another person was still alive (Boas and Hunt 1906:28–43).

The Kwakiutl also danced as wolves for the ʼwalasax̱aʼaḵw, wearing blankets and wolf headdresses. They imitated the movements of the wolf in the course of their dance, crawling on their hands and feet and resting as if poised on their toes and knuckles (Boas 1897:477). In the ɫugwala, another wolf dance probably related to the ɫuukwaana of the Nuu-chah-nulth, those individuals who have been initiated by wolves wear a frontlet that represents this animal, black and red facial paint, and a blanket. They then dance in a circuit around the fire (ibid.: 478–89). (See fig. 2.30.) JO

name changes from Ye<u>k</u>wa<u>k</u>walagalis (Sound-of-Giving-Property-Around-the-World, hereafter Giving-Property) to A'udzagolas (Place-Where-They-Keep-Thronging-Together [attending his potlatches], hereafter Thronging-Place). He has been married to the daughter of the Comox-Ligwiłda'<u>x</u>w couple, and she has just left him to return to her people, leaving behind with him a son, Kwaxsi'stala (Smoke-All-Round), and a daughter, <u>H</u>amalaka<u>l</u>ame'ga (Head-Food-Giving-Woman).

It was not very long after Gagawu<u>l</u>alaga went home when Giving-Property wished to marry again. His numaym, the Sin<u>t</u>łam, wanted him to marry Ringing-Copper, the princess of Wrong-Round-the-World. Giving-Property at once obeyed their wishes. All the Sin<u>t</u>łam got ready and went to Facing-Inland, the village of the ancestors of Ławitsis. In the morning, when day came, the numerous numaym of the Sin<u>t</u>łam started off; and when they arrived, they paid the marriage price at once; and after they had paid the marriage price, they were still sitting in their wooing-canoes. Then Wrong-Round-the-World, the head chief of the Ławitsis, came out. He belonged to the numaym Sis<u>a</u>n<u>t</u>łi', the first one of the numayms; and he said this: "Welcome, numaym Sin<u>t</u>łam, welcome! Come out of your wooing-canoes and take the wife of your chief Giving-Property aboard your canoe!"

Thus he said. Then the crew went ashore out of the canoe—those who paid the marriage price on behalf of Giving-Property and also Giving-Property himself. And when they had gone in, Wrong-Round-the-World told him to sit down on a mat that had been spread in the house. When all the men of the crew were inside, Giving-Property went in and sat down in the rear of the house. There he was given food by his father-in-law, Wrong-Round-the-World. And after they had eaten, Chief Wrong-Round-the-World spoke. He said:

"Now listen to my speech, son-in-law! She will be your wife, and her mat will be forty dressed [elk or deer] skins and twenty boxes of [eulachon] oil. Now your name will be Thronging-Place, O son-in-law! Now your prince Smoke-All-Round will be called Valuing-Each-Other-Place, and your princess Head-Food-Giving-Woman will be named Giving-Away-Property-Woman in the secular season. You will be named Head-Winter-Dancer, your prince Smoke-All-Round will be named <u>K</u>anga, and your princess Head-Food-Giving-Woman will be named Warming-Place in winter. And you shall have those house-dishes—the grizzly-bear house-dish and the wolf and beaver and killer-whale house-dishes. Now take the four house-dishes aboard your canoe, so that your tribe may eat out of them, son-in-law Giving-Property."

Thus he said. Immediately Giving-Property arose. He called his four speakers and they sang at the same time their sacred songs, and Giving-Property also sang his sacred song. And after he had sung, he thanked Wrong-Round-the-World for what he had said.

Then they carried down to the beach the dressed skins and the boxes with oil and also the four house-dishes. And when they had put them aboard the wooing-canoe, Giving-Property came out of the house of his father-in-law, walking by the side of his wife, Ringing-Copper, and they went aboard his canoe.

2.9 **Eagle headdress**. Kingcome. Wood, parts assembled around a baleen ring, cedar bark, L 45.5 cm, W 10.5 cm. *Collected by George Hunt, 1901. 16/8431, AMNH 1901–32*

HUNT DESCRIBED THIS HEADDRESS AS HAVING been worn by a "chieftainess" and as representing a prerogative derived from a history that involved Kwalili, one of the four wolves that survived the flood (acc. 1901–32, AMNH). The woman would wear this atop her head during the *tseka* ceremonies. According to contemporary accounts, the woman would stand near the center of the floor by the singers. Her movements were slow and steady, following the rhythms of the singers, her hands flat with palms facing up (Webster: personal communication, 1990). SAM

Now they went home to Crooked-Beach. And when they arrived, the four speakers stood up in the canoe, and they reported to the Kwaguł that Giving-Property had married Ringing-Copper, the princess of Wrong-Round-the-World. Then they promised to give away forty dressed skins to the Ma'amtagala and the Gixsam, and to the Kwakwakwam, and also to the La'alaxs'andayu. And they promised twenty boxes of oil to these four numayms. (The forty dressed skins were on account of Smoke-All-Round, for now he changed his name, taking the name Valuing-Each-Other-Place obtained in marriage from Wrong-Round-the-World. And the twenty boxes of oil were on account of Head-Food-Giving-Woman, the name obtained in marriage from Wrong-Round-the-World.) And as soon as the speakers stopped speaking, the crew and their chief Giving-Property, with his wife, went ashore into the house.

Immediately the four speakers went to invite the four numayms to come to a feast to be given with the forty boxes of oil by Giving-Away-Property-Woman, the princess of Thronging-Place (for now Giving-Property had changed his name).

As soon as the four speakers had gone to invite them the young men cleared out the house of Giving-Property. They took ashore the dressed skins and the boxes of oil, and also the four house-dishes. And when the guests were in, they poured the oil into the house-dishes, and they put the grizzly-bear dish before the Ma'amtagala, and the wolf dish before the Gixsam, and the beaver dish before the Kwakwakwam, and the killer-whale dish before the La'alaxs'andayu. As soon as they had finished the speakers spoke, and said,

"This is the weight of the name of Head-Food-Giving-Woman, whose name is now Giving-Away-Property-Woman, obtained in marriage from Wrong-Round-the-World." And when he stopped speaking, another speaker spoke, and said,

"Now let us give away the dressed skins!"

And then he gave them away. When they had all been given out, another speaker spoke, and said,

"This is the weight of the name of Smoke-All-Round. He has changed his name, and now his name is Valuing-Each-Other-Place, for that was received in marriage from Wrong-Round-the-World by my chief Thronging-Place, for Giving-Property has changed his name now, and this is also obtained in marriage from Wrong-Round-the-World by my chief here."

Thus he said. And as soon as he stopped speaking the guests went out.

When winter came, the Ławitsis came paddling with their chief Wrong-Round-the-World. He came to pay the marriage debt to his son-in-law Thronging-Place. After he had taken ashore dressed skins and many cedar-bark blankets and many baskets of clover roots and boxes of oil and boxes of dried clams—when these had been taken out of the ten canoes, he also gave the copper named Search to his son-in-law, and also the ten canoes that had carried the princess of Wrong-Round-the-World.

That was the first great return of marriage price by Wrong-Round-the-World to his son-in-law Thronging-Place on account of his princess Ringing-Copper. Then Wrong-Round-the-World took a carved box and carried it ashore himself out of his canoe into the house of his son-in-law Thronging-Place, and he put it down in the rear of the house. It

was not long before he came out again and went into his canoe. Then he spoke to his tribe, and said,

"O tribe, now our supernatural power has gone into the house of my son-in-law."

And when he said so, he turned towards the Kwaguł, and said,

"Now, take care, son-in-law! This is the box containing the Winter Dance which I have taken into your home. Now purify for its sake!"

Thus he said. Then he was invited by his son-in-law to eat. When they had all gone ashore out of their canoes, they were given food.

It was evening when they finished eating. They all went to eat with the Kwaguł. Then the chief of the Ma'amtagala called Great-Copper spoke, and said, "Go on, Chief Thronging-Place, go on, and see what is in the crest-box, that you may give a Winter Dance!"

Genealogy of Giving Property

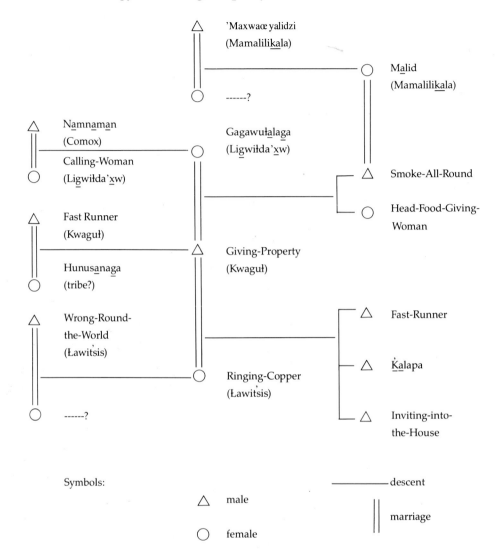

Symbols:

△ male

○ female

——— descent

‖ marriage

2.10 **Grizzly bear dancer's claws**. Fort Rupert. Grizzly bear fur and claws. *Collected by George Hunt, 1897. 16/2339AB, AMNH 1897–43.* Top: L 46 cm, W 23 cm. Bottom: L 4 cm, W 22 cm

GRIZZLY BEAR CLAWS WERE USED BY INITIATES OF the Grizzly Bear Society during the Winter Ceremony. They were attached to the hands of a performer, who might also wear a complete bearskin. The initiate into the Grizzly Bear Society sought to frighten the audience with his potential power, as his role in the ceremony was to act as a policeman enforcing proper behavior. The grizzly bear dancer and the *nuḻamaḻ* (see fig. 2.11) worked together in this capacity. Both the grizzly bear and the *nuḻamaḻ* were powerful helpers of the *hamatsa* and punished all transgressions relating to the *hamatsa* during the Winter Ceremony. Another responsibility was to guard the ceremonial house before the performances (Boas 1897:467).

In addition to wearing a full bearskin, grizzly bear dancers also wore head- and neckrings composed of thick strands of twisted red and yellow cedar bark. If bear's claws were not available, a substitute could be used. The U'mista Cultural Centre, for example, has a claw set used for a similar purpose but made from whale ribs. They are accorded the same status as real bear claws (Webster: personal communication: 1990). SAM

2.11 ***Nuḷamaḷ* mask**. Fort Rupert. Wood, copper, L 37 cm,
W 24 cm. *Collected by George Hunt, 1897. 16/2337,* AMNH 1897–43

T HE *nuḷamaḷ* (FOOL DANCER) PLAYS AN IMPORTANT
role in the Winter Ceremony. This dancer functions in
many capacities, most importantly as a messenger or
helper of the *hamatsa*. His duty is to help enforce the law that gov-
erns proper potlatch behavior. Like the *hamatsa*, these dancers
have been initiated by a powerful spirit. The supernatural beings
from whom the *nuḷamaḷ* derive their power are the *aḥasamk* people, believed to have come from a floating village on an island
lake. They are said to have enormous, continuously runny noses.
The special powers of these beings were brought to humans by a
beaver hunter who accidentally fell upon this community. Later
he returned home exhausted and ill, his nose running constantly.
Soon, his tribe began to think that he was crazy because he would
eat his own mucus or smear it on his body, and he would urinate
and defecate in the house. It took a long time for the people to restore him to normal behavior (Boas 1897:468).

Like the *aḥasamk*, the beings from whom a *nuḷamaḷ* derives his
power, the fool dancer detests anything clean, calm, or attractive.
The mere mention of the word *nose* or anything that will remind
the dancer of smell or mucus will send a *nuḷamaḷ* into a frenzy.
The first indication of the initiates' possession by the winter spirits is the scratching of their heads and bodies. This scratching becomes violent as long as the frenzy lasts. Sometimes an older
nuḷamaḷ gives mucus to a young initiate, thereby throwing "the
winter ceremonial into him" (Boas 1897:469). The theatrical nature
of this dance is emphasized by the use of some sort of slimy substitute contrived to appear like a great amount of mucus being
thrown from the nose.

The *nuḷamaḷ* dance is appropriate to one who detests neatness
and acts deranged. Instead of turning to the left as all other Winter Dancers do, the *nuḷamaḷ* turns to the right. When other dancers
try to correct him, he becomes increasingly more excited, crying
"We! We! We!" while dancing like a madman and looking to destroy everything in sight. At the end of the dancing season, he
pays for any clothes of spectators that he has torn or soiled, or
any possessions that he has broken (Boas 1897:469).

Masks representing the fool dancers have certain distinct characteristics. The mask illustrated here has the typical greatly exaggerated nose. Boas writes that the face of the *nuḷamaḷ* mask is "surrounded by a red ring which represents the red cedar bark"
(1897:469). This mask features a band of red and white twists, perhaps referring to the use of dyed and undyed cedar bark. The eyebrows can be raised to reveal brows of copper. SAM

2.12 *Nuḻamaḻ* axe. Fort Rupert. Wood, metal, H 25.7 cm, 20.7 cm. *Collected by George Hunt, 1901. 16/8548, AMNH 1901–32*

To enforce the laws of the Winter Ceremony, the *nuḻamaḻ* dancer carries a lance, a stick, or a war axe. He uses these implements to "attack" members of the audience whom he believes to be misbehaving. Boas (1897:468) notes that the "method of attack is by throwing stones at people, hitting them with sticks, or in serious cases stabbing and killing them with lances and war axes." The modern day *nuḻamaḻ* does not act nearly so violently as his predecessor did; in contemporary potlatches he inflicts little real damage. In all cases, those the *nuḻamaḻ* injured would receive some compensation, either at the end of the dance or the end of the ceremonial season.

This particular axe would have been held by the *nuḻamaḻ* dancer during his appearance at the *tseka* ceremonies. Like the masks depicting this being (fig. 2.11), this axe depicts the *nuḻamaḻ* with its characteristically large nose. SAM

2.13 New Vancouver, c. 1900. *Photo by C. F. Newcombe.*
RBCM PN 242

2.14 **Attendant figure**. Turnour Island. Wood, H 152 cm.
Collected by George Hunt, 1901. 16/8393, AMNH 1901–32

W HEN A CHIEF HOSTED A POTLATCH, HIS AIDES
supervised the distribution of wealth to guests. According to Hunt's notes about this figure (Acc. file, Dept. of
Anthropology, AMNH), it was called Ḱixtłaxakis. Derived from
'Ḱixtła' (big fire), this name relates to large feasts and potlatches,
and is best translated as "rich or wealth from the beginning, in

front of everyone else and having come from above" (Webster:
personal communication, 1990). Boas (1909:50) refers to this figure
as "representing a Chief's attendant killing Slaves and breaking
coppers."

This figure, like that in fig. 1.15, has a copper design painted on
its chest. Its right arm holds a knife with a triangular blade. That
gesture suggests the aggressive action of breaking a copper, or
perhaps killing a slave. SAM

Thus he said. Immediately the chief of the Ławit's̓is, Wrong-Round-the-World, arose and said,

"Go on, Kwaguł, and begin the Winter Dance this evening! In this box is the *hamatsa* [cannibal dancer], and his name will be Tsax̱wax̱stala; and also the thrower dance, and his name will be Great-Supernatural-One; and also the chief fool-dance, and his name will be Umak̓wuḻala; and also the grizzly-bear dance, and his name will be Fearless-Companion. Now there are four winter dances for my son-in-law, and therefore I wish you to begin a Winter Dance this night."

Thus he said. Immediately they began the Winter Dance. Then Valuing-Each-Other-Place (for now I shall not call him Smoke-All-Round) disappeared, and Giving-Away-Property-Woman (for her name was no more Head-Food-Giving-Woman) disappeared, and also the children of their father's younger brother, the boy Two-Whales-Spouting-on-the-Beach and his younger brother Source-of-Potlatch-Gifts. Now the ancestors of the Kwaguł had a Winter Dance. After they disappeared for a long time, they were caught again. Now Valuing-Each-Other-Place was a cannibal-dancer, and his name was Tsax̱wax̱stala. Two-Whales-Spouting-on-the-Beach, the nephew of Thronging-Place, was a thrower-dancer, and now he was named Great-Supernatural-One. Pot-latching-Woman was chief fool-dancer, and her name was Umak̓wu-ḻala. And Source-of-Potlatch-Gifts was a grizzly-bear dancer, and his name was Fearless-Companion. Now they finished the Winter Dance.

Now Ringing-Copper was with child, and she gave birth to a boy. Then Wrong-Round-the-World came to make another payment to his son-in-law Thronging-Place, bringing forty dressed skins and also a name. And the name given to the child borne by Ringing-Copper was Fast-Runner, and Thronging-Place gave away the forty dressed skins to the four numayms on behalf of his child Fast-Runner. Then she had another boy, and Wrong-Round-the-World gave another name for the child, and his name was K̓alapa. Then she had another boy, and Wrong-Round-the-World gave presents of food to his son-in-law, and he gave a name to the boy. And when Thronging-Place gave a feast, with the cinquefoil roots given by his father-in-law, to the Kwaguł, then he named this new child Inviting-into-the-House. As soon as Wrong-Round-the-World went home, he fainted and died.

Now it happened that Wrong-Round-the-World had no son; his only child was his princess Ringing-Copper. When it was reported to Ring-ing-Copper that her father had died, she immediately went home with her three children, and she gave away property to her tribe. Then Fast-Runner took the seat of Wrong-Round-the-World, and now his name was Wrong-Round-the-World. He had the first seat in the numaym of Sis̱anḻi' of the Ławit's̓is. Then Thronging-Place was sad on account of what his wife Ringing-Copper had done, and he did not want his children, K̓alapa and his younger brother Inviting-into-the-House, to come back. Ringing-Copper then had them give a potlatch and take seats of their relatives who had died before. The two children obtained the seats of those who were dead.

The episode that I have taken from the Hunt narrative is typical of Kwakiutl family traditions. They give great attention to marriages, births, deaths, and the transfer of property, to the exclusion of much else, and they are filled with what to us is a bewildering number of names being passed from person to person. But this really should not surprise us. They embodied the memory of events that were in effect the civil and church registries and the inscribed pages of family Bibles for a nonliterate society that was, like traditional European society, greatly concerned with descent, status, and property.

This particular family history goes on to tell of the marriage of Smoke-All-Round to a princess of the Mamalilika̱la tribe, of his son's move to Fort Rupert and marriages there, and of his grandchildren's marriages there. It was a great-granddaughter of Smoke-All-Round who married George Hunt.

I have begun this essay with this episode in a family history because it illustrates three features of traditional Kwakiutl culture in which the traditional potlatch was embedded. These were the numaym system, the marriage system, and the ceremonial system. I shall explore each of these before going on to the potlatch itself.

The Numaym System

Throughout the family histories, people are identified as belonging to numayms. Giving-Property is the chief of one of five numayms of the Kwagu̱ł tribe. Ringing-Copper is the princess of the chief of the highest-ranking numaym of the Ławitsis tribe.

The Kwak̓wala term 'na̱'mima (one kind), which Boas (1920) anglicized as "numaym,"[2] refers to the basic social group in traditional Kwakiutl society. As Lévi-Strauss (1982) suggests, the numaym was a kind of "house" in the medieval European and Japanese sense (as the houses of York and Lancaster, Taira and Minamoto). It was a social entity that owned one or more plank houses in a winter village, and several seasonal sites where it had the right to harvest certain resources. It had its own tradition of origin, identifying its first ancestor and its rights to its resource sites, hereditary names, and ceremonial privileges. The numaym consisted of a head chief, lesser chiefs, and commoners, together with their families. The numaym chief was identified as the descendant of the founding ancestor and inheritor of his power, but other families within the numaym might have other origins (Boas 1935b:43).

The numaym can also be described (Boas 1966:50) as a set of ranked positions, each associated with a name and certain privileges. These were positions in a literal sense in the seating arrangements at ceremonial events, and they governed the order in which their occupants were served food at feasts and received gifts at potlatches.

2.15 Man carrying staff, c. 1910. He is giving away the pile of blankets behind him, as well as the bracelets carried by man on the right. RBCM 1098

2.16 **Staff**. Turnour Island. Red cedar, H 150 cm. *Collected by George Hunt, 1899. 16/6810, AMNH 1899–50*

HUNT COLLECTED THIS STAFF FROM A SPEAKER OF the Ławitsis tribe in 1899 at their village Crooked-Beach on Turnour Island (acc. 1899–50, AMNH). Ceremonial staffs served an extremely important function among the Kwakiutl. At the turn of the century, as well as today, the "chief's talking stick" (Hawthorn 1967:175) was the piece of regalia most closely associated with the speaker of the chief. This was an extremely important hereditary position to hold within the numaym. The speaker was so closely associated with the essential power of the numaym that he would live with his numaym chief in the same house. Similarly, the chief, when making a point, might use the speaker's staff (Holm 1972:56). When in use, the staff was held by the speaker or chief and then "used for emphasis—pounded against the floor or jabbed into the ground" (ibid.).

While Holm describes talking sticks as usually resembling "miniature totem poles" that display an array of crests (ibid.), the carved portion of this staff is relatively simple. At the top, only one image is represented, fingers clasping a copper.

The construction of this staff is rather unusual. The shaft was split and then hollowed out, pebbles were placed inside, and then it was sealed. When the staff is lifted, it sounds like a rattle. Possibly these sound effects were quite persuasive when the stick was lifted to emphasize a point during a speaker's oration. SAM

The numaym chief is identified in the Kwakwala texts with terms translated as "head chief" or "one in first position" or "one with the office of giving away property." His oldest son is identified by a term translated "prince" and his oldest daughter by a term translated "princess." Giving-Property is chief of the numaym Sintłam (Real Sintłe', this being the name of the founder, said to have come from the sun). This numaym is said to be numerous, and it is clear from an earlier episode in the family history that his house is only one of those belonging to it. It is likely that it held several nuclear families, including that of a brother, the father of his nephews who were initiated into the winter dance along with his prince and princess. Slaves are not mentioned in this episode of the history, but are mentioned later on in connection with the marriage of Smoke-All-Round, and they too must have occupied space in the house.

The chief was responsible for the management of his numaym's resources, and he received a share of fish, game, roots, and berries harvested in his numaym's territory. He was also responsible for maintaining relations with other numayms in his tribe, which he did with property. When Giving-Property marries, he necessarily looks for someone of his own rank in another tribe. In choosing a bride, he follows the wishes of his numaym; they help him with the bride price and when they return with the bride's "mat," a gift of hides and oil, it is distributed to the other four numayms of the Kwaguł.

The numayms in a tribe were ranked. The Sintłam probably ranked third among the five Kwaguł numayms. The narrative identifies the other numayms twice and in the same order—the Ma'amtagala (Descendants of Matagala), the Gixsam (First Ones), the Kwakwakwam (Real Kwaguł), and also (as an afterthought?) the La'alaxs'andayu (Cut-in-Two?). The first three probably outranked the Sintłam, who outranked the last. Later in the nineteenth century, after the Kwaguł had moved to Fort Rupert and changed their name to Gwitala (Northerners), this tribe consisted of seven numayms; two new ones appear in Boas's list (1966:39), but the five in this narrative are ranked in the order in which they are named in it.

The position of chief was transmitted, at least in theory, from oldest child to oldest child, whether son or daughter, though it appears that a male usually occupied the position. Thus when Ringing-Copper's father dies, she, as his only child, must return to her own tribe, but she immediately installs her oldest son, still a child, as her father's successor. We must assume that she made whatever decisions were required until her son grew older. It seems a son-in-law might also succeed as chief, keeping the position for his own son, the grandchild of

ALTHOUGH PORTRAYED IN FAR FEWER HISTORIES than other animals, such as the bear or raven, insects played important roles during the time of the first ancestors. Among these, wasps had special powers. In one tradition told to Hunt in 1894 by Kumgalis of the Nakamgalisala tribe, for example, the wasp manifests sufficient strength to kill the powerful thunderbird (Boas 1910:243). When Hunt collected this wasp mask in 1901, he recorded that it belonged to Kawadilikala, one of the first chiefs of the Dzawada'enuxw people (Acc. file, Dept. of Anthropology, AMNH). He did not, unfortunately, provide any more information about it, such as the history with which it is associated.

According to contemporary traditions, the right to wear the wasp mask came originally from the Kwikwasutinuxw of Gilford Island (Adam Dick: personal communication, 1990). SAM

his predecessor. Later in this family history, Smoke-All-Round plays this role; when his father-in-law dies, his wife gives him her father's position.

The other positions (literally "standing" or seats) in the numaym could be transmitted to collateral relatives or even affines (in-laws). For her other two children, Ringing-Copper finds seats vacated by deceased members of her numaym. Later on we find seats being turned over to brothers-in-law.

The assumption of a seat in a numaym and the associated name required a potlatch. When Ringing-Copper returns to her father's house, she immediately gives away property to establish her position as his heir, and this enables her to put her son in her father's seat with his name. Then when her husband indicates his wish not to have their children back, she gives property again in their behalf. Even the bestowal of an ancestral name to a child required at least a feast, as when Ringing-Copper's father named her youngest.

To aid the numaym chief in dealing with other numayms, there were other hereditary offices. Each numaym had a speaker, whose badge of office was a speaker's staff (fig. 2.16), who spoke for the chief or other members at public events; an assembler (or master of ceremonies), who invited the guest groups; and a tally-keeper or name-keeper, who kept a mental record of the numayms' seats and their occupants so that he could advise potlatchers of other tribes. Most or all had songmakers, who composed songs in praise of chiefs, enumerating their accomplishments.

Privileges were traced back to myth times (Boas 1935b:47–53. Numaym traditions tell of first ancestors, who typically came down from the sky in nonhuman form, took off their masks and became human, had encounters with Ḵaniḵi'lakw (the Transformer), and were aided by animals or fabulous beings. House posts, house dishes, and other utensils were carved to represent numaym ancestors (that is, the ancestors of the chief) and their nonhuman helpers. Beings represented included wolves, grizzlies, sea lions, orcas (killer whales), thunderbirds (of two kinds, Kwaṉkwaṉxwaliga or Tsuna and his young brother Ḵulus), sisiyuł (huge two-headed serpents; fig. 2.18), dzunuḵwa (a race of child-eating ogres with deep-set eyes, open mouths, and pendulous breasts), and Ḵumugwe' (lord of a world under the sea).

Individual Kwakiutl assumed their numaym seats and names and exercised the associated ceremonial privileges as numaym members, and the numaym myths seem to identify these rights as numaym property. And so they may have been in Kwakiutl theory. But as Drucker and Heizer (1967:113) point

2.18 **Sisiyuł belt** (*front and back*). Gilford Island. Wood, leather, L 125 cm, H 2 cm. *Collected by George Hunt, 1899. 16/6902AB, AMNH 1899–50*

BOAS DESCRIBED THE *sisiyuł*, A DOUBLE-HEADED SERpent with a central human face, as one of the most important supernatural beings among the Kwakiutl (1897:371) (see fig. 1.34). Although the *sisiyuł* could harm people who looked at it, it was most benevolent to those with the correct privileges. The Ḵwiḵwasutinuxw, for example, had the right to display the *sisiyuł* on a belt such as this inherited from an ancestor (Boas and Hunt 1905:165–235; acc. 1899–50, AMNH).

When George Hunt collected this *sisiyuł* belt, he recorded that the prerogative came from an ancestor named Tseḵame, 'Head-Winter-Dancer,' whose history he learned from Tsuxtsa'is, a Mamalilikala descendant of the numaym Wiwumasgam of the Ḵwiḵwasutinuxw. According to this version of the tradition, Thunderbird and his wife came down to this world to become Head-Winter-Dancer and Winter-Dance-Woman, and to begin their own tribe (Boas and Hunt 1905:165–247). Just after Winter-Dance-Woman gave birth to her fourth son, Head-Winter-Dancer caught a strange-looking salmon in his trap. He tried in vain to kill the salmon in the usual way, by clubbing it. Each time he hit the fish, it became wilder and wilder. Finally, remembering the advice of his wife, he bit the sides of his tongue and spit his blood onto the fish. As the fish calmed down, Head-Winter-Dancer saw that he had in fact killed a double-headed serpent. He immediately brought the *sisiyuł* back to his wife, who thanked him on behalf of their newborn child. The next morning Winter-Dance-Woman cut the serpent in half, and Head-Winter-Dancer bathed their new son in warm water and rubbed the child's body with clotted blood from the spine of the serpent. The child quickly became a full-grown man whose body appeared to be made from stone. His face began to take the form of a giant *dzunuḵwa*, the wild woman of the woods. He grew twice the size of an ordinary man. His parents were pleased, because he would be a great warrior.

And so this son, Food-Giver-Stone-Body, set out to "make war all over the world." He received a special death-bringing canoe. At each end of the canoe were "large double-headed serpents putting out their tongues, and in the middle there was a head of a man." This canoe was self-propelled and would follow all navigational directions obediently. Its paddles would enter the water on the owner's command "Wo." With this vehicle Food-Giver-Stone-Body made war around the world and brought back wealth, prerogatives, and slaves for his family (Boas and Hunt 1905:200, 202).

As well as establishing a prerogative for this numaym, the tradition also illustrates the more general connection between the *sisiyuł* and warfare. The person who wore this belt was most likely a warrior dancer, or *hawinalał* (Webster: personal communication, 1990). A *sisiyuł* belt signified that the wearer was a great warrior who brought wealth to his family; this particular example also associated the wearer with Tseḵame and his son. SAM

out, in practice the Kwakiutl treated them as individual property, vigorously defending their individual claims to them against rival claimants.

The Marriage System

For the Kwakiutl, marriage was not simply the way to establish a new nuclear family. Marriages were the means by which another large class of names and ceremonial privileges were transmitted, and marriages were often arranged simply for that end.

The name Giving-Property was transmitted in this fashion. The man who bore it when we first met him had received it as a marriage gift from his Ligwiłda'xw father-in-law. Before that his name had been Gayusdes. And as we have seen, he later gets the name Thronging-Place from his Ławitsis father-in-law, while his son and daughter by his first marriage also receive names through this second marriage. Later on, when his son Smoke-All-Round marries the Mamalilikala princess, his son's father-in-law gives him the name Giving-Potlatches-in-the-World ('Maxwalagalis). Three generations later this name will be given to George Hunt.

The image that gave form to noble marriages was that of a suitor making war to force a chief to yield up his princess and his privileges. In reality a marriage was a carefully negotiated alliance. If the two families were not of different tribes, they pretended they were, the suitor's party pushing out in a canoe as if going to another village and then paddling back in front of the prospective bride's house for the formal announcement of their intentions. In the next stage, when the groom came for the bride, on a catamaran made of planks laid across two canoes, the bride's people resisted in a sham battle (Boas 1966:53; Curtis 1915:130).

In the family history, the marriage of Smoke-All-Round is on a grander scale than the marriages of his father. When he goes to sue for the hand of the Mamalilikala princess, he is accompanied not only by his own numaym but also by parties from the other three tribes who later joined the Kwaguł at Fort Rupert, and when they arrive at the Mamalilikala village, they are met by the local people throwing stones.

Customarily, upon arriving in front of the bride's house, the groom gave to her father a bride price, and the bride's father gave a return gift, the bride's mat, usually not amounting to as much in value as the bride's price, and one or more privileges. At this point, Giving-Property receives names and four carved house-dishes from his father-in-law. With this exchange, a

2.19 (*below*) ***Gisaxstala*** **box lid flange**. Fort Rupert. Wood, sea otter teeth, L 85 cm, W 23 cm, H 20.3 cm. *Collected by George Hunt, 1897. 16/2264,* AMNH *1897–43*

THE LIDS OF OLD KWAKIUTL BOXES WERE SLABS OF wood with one raised edge, forming an L-shape (see Holm 1987:96 for a photograph of one of these old-style box lids on a box). The flange often had a painted face emphasized by inlaid sea otter teeth. These special boxes were once used to transfer prestigious paraphernalia from father to son-in-law. The flange portions of the lids, the last remnants of these boxes, became symbolic of the wealth and prestige the boxes once carried, and were valuable family heirlooms (Boas 1897:421–24).

Soon it became de rigeur for a high-ranking woman's family to give her husband a stack of box lids; fig. 2.20 shows such a stack of lids piled up for a wedding payment. SAM

2.20 *Gisaxstala* box lids piled up for wedding payment, Fort Rupert, 1915–16. *Photo by S. Barrett.* MPM *3667*

marriage was accomplished. Usually the groom immediately took the bride home to publicize his victory and divide the spoils.

But custom did not absolutely require that the groom return to his home with the bride. Earlier, Giving-Property had stayed with his first wife's tribe for several years before bringing her back to Crooked-Beach. Later, Smoke-All-Round stays permanently with his wife's people.

The return gift at the wedding day was only the beginning. A marriage was not complete until sometime later when the bride's father repaid the bride price, giving considerably more than he had received from the groom in material goods and giving more names and ceremonial prerogatives. When Ringing-Copper's father comes to Crooked-Beach to return the marriage price, he brings goods and foods, a copper, and a carved box identified as a "crest-box." The term *kis'u*, which Boas translates "crest," refers to almost any kind of right transmitted through a marriage. In this instance the rights were to performance in the Winter Dance. The box may have actually held some of the paraphernalia used in them; symbolically it contained them all.

In the family histories, there are instances of a father-in-law giving his very house with its carved posts and its name to his son-in-law. In later times, the return payment typically included a number of what have been identified as "box lids" (figs. 2.19–20) decorated with sea-otter teeth (Boas 1897:421–24).

Although it is not stated in this family history, from other accounts we know that with a return of the marriage gift, the marriage was formally dissolved (Boas 1966:54). Modern tradition says it took four return payments to finish (*gwał*) the marriage—precisely what Wrong-Round-the-World made. The husband could pay another bride price for his wife and marry her again, or he could let her go, in which case her father could accept the suit of another. For a man, marrying another woman gave him the opportunity to acquire more names and privileges from another father-in-law. For a woman, being married several times added to her honor.

When Ringing-Copper's father repays the marriage debt, he brings the copper named Lita ('Search,' perhaps meaning that it searches for property to pay for it). A copper (fig. 1.16) was appropriate as part of this payment. The repayment of the bride price was perhaps the most important source of wealth for a major potlatch, often financed by the sale of the copper.

In all of this family history, there is little if any indication that the princess sought as a bride has anything to say in the

2.21 **Headring and neckring**. Village Island. Cedar bark. *Collected by George Hunt, 1899.* AMNH 1899–50. Top: 8 cm; *16/4750.* Bottom: 48 cm: *16/4751*

CEDAR BARK DYED RED WITH THE INNER BARK OF the red alder signified the *tseka* season. At the beginning of the *tseka* ceremony, hosts distributed pieces of red cedar bark to everyone; this indicated the commencement of the event. Various participants wore cedar bark neckrings, some of which were made of strips of shredded cedar bark; others were made of more finely twisted or plaited bark (Holm 1987:104).

Hunt collected this headring and neckring as a set from a family from Village Island in 1899. He was told that they were worn together, representing "the first ring of the *hamatsa*" (acc. 1899–50, AMNH). Boas states that they were "the first ring(s) worn after removal of the hemlock during the *hamatsa* initiation" (ibid.). This occurs after the *hamatsa* has passed through the stage of frenzied possession during which he craves human flesh as a result of his cannibal urgings, which are caused by his encounter with Baxwbakwalanuxwsiwe'.

Before the initiate has been tamed and has reentered human society, he wears the hemlock that signifies his association with the other world. Once he has been tamed, assisted by the attendants who continually restrain and guide him, he dons cedar bark ornaments dyed red and worked into rings that rest on his shoulders or forehead; these rings are two examples of the type. SAM

2.22 Two men wearing *hamatsa* regalia; woman wearing button blanket and headband. AMNH 13801

matter. Boas (1966:55) says that marriages were arranged without either bride or groom's knowledge. Curtis (1915:124) was told that the girl usually had the right to refuse, but the prospective groom had no choice. In the family histories it seems that in the marriage of a chief or a prince, his numaym had to approve. It also seems that while the young may have had decisions made for them, with maturity came freedom. A woman whose marriage payment had been properly returned, like Ringing-Copper, could become powerful.

Privileges acquired through marriage were ordinarily transferred to another through the marriage of a daughter or a sister. George Hunt received privileges from his wife's brother. But if a man had no way of transferring the privileges he had acquired from his father-in-law through a real marriage, he might do it through a fictitious marriage. He could declare a half or a part of his body a woman and then marry her off to a fictitious son-in-law (Boas 1966:55). However, some chiefly families prevented the transfer of privileges to others by marrying the princess to a close kinsman such as her father's brother or her own half-brother born of a different mother (Boas 1940:361; Holm 1983:176).

The Ceremonial System

Each year, beginning in late fall and lasting well into winter, Kwakiutl social life was dominated by the *tseka*, the Winter Dance.[3] This was the sacred season, its beginning marked by the distribution of shredded cedar bark dyed red with alder bark, when people set aside their secular names and numaym affiliations and assumed their winter names and identified themselves according to participation in the ceremonies, as dancers (Seals), managers (Sparrows), or uninitiated persons. The managers, who were former dancers, were further divided into groups based on sex and age, and the dancers were grouped according to the kinds of dances they performed and whether these belonged to the major (*laxso*, passed through) or minor (*wixso*, not passed through) series (Boas 1966:172–75). These are the groupings identified by Boas (1897) as "secret societies." One house in the village was set aside for them, secular things were removed, and it was provided with a central fire, a room for the dancers, and a plank for beating time.

Winter names and rights to dances were usually acquired through marriage. In Ringing-Copper's marriage, when her father gave her husband her mat, he gave winter names along with secular names to her husband and his children. Later, when her father returned the marriage gift, he gave her hus-

2.23–26 Four photographs of a *hamatsa* initiation, 1902. In the early stage of the initiation, an initiate wears hemlock boughs. As he is progressively tamed, he puts on cedar bark neckrings. *Photos by George Hunt.* AMNH *22858, 22891, 334020, 104469*

ritual procedures could control this power and restore the initiate to human society. Many performances included actions calculated to horrify the uninitiated, but most of these were illusions achieved with extraordinary inventiveness and skill (Boas 1897:393–418, 437–500).

According to legends, Baxwbakwalanuxwsiwe' and his attendants lived in the mountains, where certain ancestors encountered him and acquired his power and the songs and ritual procedures. The most important initiate he possessed was the *hamatsa*, the cannibal dancer (figs. 2.21–26). The young man selected to be a *hamatsa* initiate was taken away into the woods for three or four months. During this time people occasionally heard a whistle and cry of "Hap, hap, hap!" (Eat, eat, eat!), signifying his craving for human flesh. Then he reappeared to get an attendant who was supposed to procure food for him. Finally he returned, sometimes entering the house through the roof, and in a mad frenzy he ran around biting people, removing bits of flesh from their arms or chest. Other men who had been cannibal initiates might also become frenzied, and other measures were reportedly taken to satisfy their craving. The attendant might break into one of the grave boxes put up in trees near the village and steal a mummified corpse, from which the cannibals were seen to devour strips of dried skin and flesh. Or a slave might be killed, and they were seen to butcher and devour the body.

The biting was certainly real, though the bits of flesh were really cut off with a knife. Probably corpses were actually torn apart and slaves killed. But there was so much sleight-of-hand involved in the Winter Dance that it is uncertain whether human flesh was actually swallowed or simply hidden somehow.

During the first stage of the performance, a screen of cedar boards called the *mawił* was set up to separate a room for the initiate and his attendants from the rest of the house, and a tall pole was erected behind the screen. A face was painted on the screen with an opening for the mouth. Early in the performance the initiate was seen climbing the pole and later emerging from the mouth.

The course of the *hamatsa* performance[5] showed the progressive return of the initiate to a normal state. At first he wore only hemlock branches and danced in a squatting position with his arms extended to the sides and trembling. A certain word uttered by one of the singers made him wild, and he had to be restrained by his attendants. They pushed him down and tamed him with fire, burning his hemlock branches and dressing him in red cedar bark. He danced again, now upright, as several songs were sung. Then a singer sang another word that

band four winter dances with names for the dancers. At that point, her husband's son, daughter, and two nephews "disappeared" and later returned as dancers.

As explained to the uninitiated, the initiates were suddenly seized and taken away by one of the powerful beings that returned in winter to possess those given over to them. The most powerful of these beings were Baxwbakwalanuxwsiwe'[4] and Winalagalis (Warrior-of-the-World), but there were many others. In reality, an initiate was selected by the person who had acquired the right to the performance, and he or she was taken off to some isolated spot (in the major series) or into a special chamber in the house (in the minor series) and taught the songs and dances and how to play the role. After the proper time, the initiate reappeared, naked except for rings of hemlock boughs, crying out or singing, trembling or showing other signs of possession, and danced (always counterclockwise) around the fire. The performance demonstrated two things: first, that the initiate had received great power from the nonhuman being that possessed him, and second, that the

2.27 **Raven** *hamatsa* **mask**. Blunden Harbour. Wood, cedar bark, feathers, L 100 cm, H 29 cm. *Collected by George Hunt, 1901. 16/8944, AMNH 1902–46*

2.28 *Huxwhukw* **mask**. Smith Inlet. Wood, L 107.5 cm, W 20 cm. *Collected by George Hunt, 1905. 16-9975, AMNH 1905–40*

THIS MASK, ALONG WITH THE *huxwhukw* AND THE Crooked-Beak-of-Heaven, depict the avian attendants of the Cannibal-at-the-North-End-of-the-World. These masks appear during the *hamatsa* ceremony after the initiate has completed his first circuits around the fire and has disappeared behind the screen. At this point, cries are emitted from the back room and soon the masked dancer enters, backwards. His cedar bark costume hides hands from view so that he can manipulate strings that snap the bird's beak open and shut. After this dancer makes four circuits around the fire, he disappears behind the screen.

Hunt sent this raven mask in July 1901 to Boas with the information that it was a "gwazwewe Hemsewe found at tegwEXste Nak!waxdax cave" (acc. 1902–46, AMNH). In a letter dated August 12, 1901 (APS), Hunt describes Tigwaxte'as the site of one of five caves he explored in 'Nakwaxda'xw territory. In this cave Hunt discovered "two old dishes and two *hemsewe.*"

One curious characteristic of this particular mask is the unusual yellow color of the eye sockets. This mask is simpler in form than twentieth century raven masks (Macnair: personal communication, 1990), as a comparison between it and Henry Hunt's raven mask (fig. 5.5) makes clear. The *hamatsa* privilege is the most prestigious, and has been continually displayed from the nineteenth century to the present. SAM

THIS MASK REPRESENTS *huxwhukw*, ONE OF THE BIRD attendants of Baxwbakwalanuxwsiwe', the Cannibal-of-the-North-End-of-the-World. The *huxwhukw* lives with Baxwbakwalanuxwsiwe' and continually craves human flesh. When this bird finds a victim, it breaks open the person's skull with its long beak and devours his brains (Boas 1897:394–95). This mask, like the raven and Crooked-Beak masks, appears during a *hamatsa* ceremony after the initiate has made his first appearance.

Hunt wrote to Boas in July 1905 (Acc. file, Dept. of Anthropology, AMNH), to describe this *huxwhukw* mask:

. . . now in this thing you will find it Different from the Hamsewes we get for instade of it made out of two Peses I find it is made in seven(7) Peses all Patched together so it is a new thing for me.

As Hunt points out here, this mask is not carved from a single block of wood, as is usual, but is instead made from several slats of wood, giving it a somewhat boxy look. Compared to later *huxwhukw* masks (see fig. 5.6), this example is simpler in form as well as in painted design. According to Peter Macnair (personal communication, 1990), this kind of austere mask is characteristic of older Kwakiutl pieces, particularly from the Blunden Harbour region.

Hunt catalogued this mask as *aloxsaak* (acc. 1905–40, AMNH). In 1962, Bill Holm showed the Kwakiutl a picture of this mask. They translated *aloxsaak* as "put together"; they also recognized this mask as a type of *huxwhukw* made of different pieces of wood (Holm, personal communication, 1990). SAM was taboo for him, and again he went wild and ran behind the screen.

Next the audience heard a clacking, and out came a dancer moving backwards and wearing a huge raven mask (fig. 2.27) with its great beak opening and shutting. The raven was followed by a dancer wearing a Crooked-Beak mask (see fig. 1.31) and then by a dancer with a long-beaked *huxwhukw* mask (fig. 2.28).

After these great birds retired, the *hamatsa* reappeared and ran around wildly again and out. He was then dressed in a blanket and brought out, led by a female attendant making taming gestures and followed by male attendants shaking their rattles. In his final appearances he danced calmly. The healing power of the ceremony had triumphed, for the time at least, over the madness of the cannibal.

The *hamatsa* was the highest ranked performance and appeared first in the Winter Dance. Several other performances were inspired by Baxwbakwalanuxwsiwe'. The *hamashamtsas* (Eater-of-the-Ground) dancer was like the *hamatsa* but did not dance squatting and cried "Wip!" instead of "Hap!" (fig. 4.13). As in the *hamatsa* performance, masked dancers also appeared. They wore simple animal masks or transformation masks, consisting of an outer form that opened to reveal a different inner form. The *ḵuminoga*, a woman, appeared with (stage) blood in her hair and a skull for the *hamatsa* in each hand. The *nunłtsi'stalał* played with fire, throwing burning wood at the audience. The Grizzly dancer dressed as a grizzly bear and wore sharp claws to attack anyone showing disrespect for the Winter Dance (fig. 2.10). Sharing this function with the grizzly was the *nuḷamał* (fool dancer), who wore a mask with a huge nose (figs. 2.11-12). During the Winter Dance the fool dancers ran around crazily, going the wrong way around the fire, and breaking things. The *madam* dancer jumped down into the house from the roof and danced on the tops of the bedrooms. He wore only a headdress covered with mica made to look like quartz crystals, which were believed to have great power. The *'mitła* (tease) dancer carried a clapper and a club carved to represent a *sisiyutł*.

Warrior-of-the-World was described as a tall, thin, black man with a small head and batlike eyes, who constantly traveled about in his invisible canoe. He was believed responsible for three kinds of performance, the *tuxw'id*, *'ma'maḵa*, and *hawinalał*. The *tuxw'id* was always a woman. She appeared in the dance house in a costume of hemlock boughs. To show her ability to withstand anything, she asked for some terrible death, such as to be cut into pieces, be disemboweled, have a

wedge driven through her skull, or be burned to ashes. The attendants tried to dissuade her, but she insisted, and so they appeared–to the audience–to comply with her wishes, actually faking it with artificial severed heads and limbs, animal blood and guts, and other devices. Later, of course, she is miraculously restored. In one account (Boas 1921:1133–35), after being dismembered, her body rolls to her head and then to each of her limbs, which magically become reattached, and she rises, sings, and with her power brings a flood that extinguishes the fire. During her performance she could also cause a huge *sisiyutł* appear to rise out of the ground (see fig. 1.34). She could also give birth to a frog or cause birds to fly, fish to jump, or puppets and carved animals to move (figs. 1.39, 2.29).

The *'ma'maḵa* (thrower) performed a dance in which he appeared to throw a disease-causing worm through the air and to catch it in his mouth, causing him to bleed from the mouth and vomit the worm.

The *hawinalał* (war dancer) actually did endure torment. He first appeared with small wooden paddles sewed to his arms and chest and carrying a knife shaped like a *sisiyutł*. He then had slits cut in the flesh of his legs and back and ropes passed through the slits, so that his attendants could hold him back as he ran, while cutting his head with his knife. The climax of his performance was to have himself suspended by his ropes from a house beam. All of this was to show that the power of Warrior-of-the-World made him insensitive to pain.

Other performances during the Winter Dance involved a wolf dance, similar to that of the Nuu-chah-nulth (Nootka), in which a line of dancers appeared with wolf masks extending from their foreheads (fig. 2.30); the *xwixwi*, acquired through marriage with the Comox, with masks having protruding eyes and tongues (fig. 3.14); and dances inspired by *dzunuḵwa*, Yagam (badness, an underwater monster), and other beings.

All these performances required property. The sponsors of initiates paid the singers and other participants. The *hamatsa* had to pay those he had bitten. The fool dancers paid for the damage they did. And there always had to be gifts to the audience.

These Winter Dance performances were not only acquired from fathers-in-law as marriage gifts, they could also be acquired by killing their owners. According to one tradition, the Kwaguł acquired the *hamatsa* by killing a group of Heiltsuk chiefs on their way to a ceremony and seizing their paraphernalia. But the family histories give instances of *hamatsa* performances, at an earlier time, being transferred as marriage gifts (Codere 1961:448).

2.29 Frog puppet. Quatsino. Wood, cloth, string, wire, glass beads, H 22.3 cm, W 35.5 cm, L 51.2 cm. *Collected by George Hunt, 1899. 16/6812, AMNH 1899–50*

ANOTHER TREASURE OF THE *tuxw'id* DANCER (see fig. 1.39), this frog figure was originally made so that it could crawl along the floor. Its legs were joined with wires to move in tandem, the oversized frog's progress eased by the wooden roller attached beneath it. This wooden creature was worked like a marionette and functioned as an example of the many wonders that seemed to be animated at the command of the *tuxw'id*.

Whoever constructed the puppet went to great lengths to produce the semblance of a living being. Large, blue glass beads make convincing eyeballs. The throat has been hollowed out and then covered over with cloth, speckled in exactly the same manner as the rest of the underbelly. This area was then rigged to pulse in and out, producing the intermittent bulging throat that would identify it as a living specimen.

Hunt's notes (acc. 1899–50, AMNH), indicate that this object too was linked in some way with the story of Head-Winter-Dancer (see figs. 1.2, 1.40, 2.18, 3.30). Indeed, many of the demonstrations of power performed by this legendary hero are strikingly similar to the performances of the *tuxw'id*. At one point, Head-Winter-Dancer threw his magic power into his own body, whereupon his belly began to croak. Frogs emerged from his stomach, and then he used his power to put them back (Boas and Hunt 1905:231). Perhaps this frog puppet was used to commemorate the powerful displays of Head-Winter-Dancer. Most women who claim this dance privilege, however, simply say that they have "given birth" to the frog. JO

2.30 **Wolf mask**. Quatsino. Wood, bone (synthetic hair added for exhibit), L 37 cm. *Collected by George Hunt, 1900. 16/8200, AMNH 1900–73*

THIS FOREHEAD MASK REPRESENTING A WOLF'S HEAD was probably part of the *długwala* dance, which means "received treasure" (Webster: personal communication, 1990). This mask has its origin in the history of Mink, who slew the four sons of Wolf (see fig. 4.7). The rights to this dance belonged originally to the numaym La'alaxsandayu (Boas 1897:478).

The general term for this type of forehead mask is *xisiwe'*, "bared teeth on forehead" (Webster: personal communication, 1990). This mask's open mouth is outlined in red to emphasize the lips of the wolf and also to accentuate its sharp teeth. The deliberate slant of the teeth and the naturalism with which the tip of the nose is depicted show the carver's virtuosity. The simple and direct carving style suggests that the mask is associated with the Nuu-chah-nulth people from the west coast of Vancouver Island, who perform a wolf ritual (Macnair: personal communication, 1989).

A contemporary interpretation of the use of this mask involves the legend of Kawadilikala and his three wolf-siblings. After the deluge, when the wolves dispersed, one of them landed in Gusgimaxw. With him he brought the right to wear the wolf mask whose name is Huhuxwalagalis (Adam Dick: personal communication, 1990). SAM

2.31 Alert Bay potlatch, c. 1905–5. *Photo by George Hunt. AMNH 104463*

The Potlatch

As the episode from "Marriage with the Comox" illustrates, among the elite of Kwakiutl society the assumption of a name or seat, a marriage, or the initiation as a Winter dancer, in order to be recognized as legitimate, had to be announced before an audience at a feast or a potlatch.[6]

Although similar, feasts and potlatches were clearly distinguished. A feast was a gathering to which people were invited to share food, while a potlatch was one to which they were invited to receive "gifts" (perhaps better defined as payments) of nonperishable goods—property. A potlatch was usually accompanied by one or more feasts, but a feast could be given without a potlatch. When Giving-Property returns to Crooked-Beach with his bride Ringing-Copper and her mat, he gives a feast with the eulachon oil and then potlatches the dressed skins. Later, when Ringing-Copper has her third child, her father brings cinquefoil roots for a feast; the child is named, but there is no mention of any distribution of property.

For feasts, each numaym had its feasting songs. Numaym chiefs had great carved feast dishes and feast names, which were distinct from potlatch names. Without a feast name, a chief could not attend a feast. The most honorable feast foods were eulachon oil, high-bush cranberries (viburnum berries), and seal meat, in that order, but other valued foods were huckleberries, salmonberries, crabapples, and cinquefoil roots. Veg-

2.32 Counting blankets, Fort Rupert potlatch, 1898. *Photo by H.I. Smith.* AMNH 411810

etable foods were usually served with eulachon oil. Guest chiefs were served feast foods in the great feast dishes or even small canoes, while commoners were served in smaller boxes (Boas 1921:750–76).

A potlatcher's usual reason for having a potlatch was to present claims before an audience composed of chiefs and people of the other numayms in his tribe or of other tribes and to have his claims recognized. He was successful if his guests accepted his gifts and in their speeches acknowledged his purpose, if no one objected to his claims, and—especially— if his guests later invited him to their potlatches, addressed him by his potlatch name, and included him in their distributions of property (Barnett 1938; Drucker and Heizer 1967:99). A potlatcher might also be trying to show his superiority to a rival.[7]

Because of its purpose as a validator of status, a potlatch was usually not an isolated event but a complement of other events; it was a distribution of property, accompanied by speeches, that marked the conclusion of any ceremony or combination of ceremonies making a change in the status of one or more members of the host's family. Perhaps the only exceptions were occasions when an embarrassing accident or affront was followed by the immediate distribution of property "to wipe away the shame." But such distributions, too, had the aim of maintaining status.

The family histories, with their focus on marriages and the transfer of privileges with marriage, do not tell us much about some of the other occasions for distributions of wealth. But another text that focuses on an individual complements the family histories in this respect. In this long narrative, called "The Acquisition of Names" (Boas 1925:113–357), Hunt gives the ceremonial life history of Facing-Seaward (Tłasutiwalis), the son of Copper-Obtaining-Place (Tłakwudlas), the head chief of one of the numayms of the Ḵumuyoʼe, one of the four Kwaguł tribes then at Fort Rupert. This history tells how a father prepared his son to be his successor with a series of distributions of ever wider scope and quantity.

When the son is born (probably in the 1850s), he is called simply Tsaxis, 'Fort Rupert,' from his birthplace. When he is ten months old, after proper ritual observances, the father gives him a second name and distributes kerchiefs to the men and children of the four tribes. Four days later the father distributes, in his son's name, kerchiefs to all the young men and announces that the son is taking a third name. Four years later, the father gives his son a fourth name, the young men sing a song honoring him, and the father gives them shirts and other store-bought garments.

Some time later, the father gives a tłapa (spreading out), which gives the son a man's name (his fifth name) and the right to attend feasts. After the father distributes blankets to initiate the event, the head chief of the Gwitala, the highest-ranking Kwaguł tribe, acts as host and has four chiefs formally escort the son into his house, where the father distributes several hundred blankets. Later, when the son's canoe capsizes, the father distributes blankets to "wipe away the shame" of the event.

Next the father, with help from his Ławitsis father-in-law, gives a Winter Dance to his fellow Kwaguł, allowing the son to appear as a Winter dancer. He is an Eater-of-the-Ground, a grizzly, and a fool dancer, and after two winters retires as a sparrow. In the next event, the father gives the son blankets to distribute in a potlatch (pʼasa) to the other Kwaguł tribes, at which songs composed for him are sung, his sister dances, and he takes a sixth name.

Now the father and son give an intertribal potlatch (ʼmaxwa), with the Mamalilikala, Ławitsis, and ʼNamgis tribes as guests, and the son receives the name Facing-Seaward and succeeds to his father's position. For this event, the father and son exercise the privilege, said to have come down from the first ancestor of their numaym, of mounting a scaffold identified as the watchtower of a salmon weir and announcing the arrival of "salmon," which are, first, the blankets they will distribute, and then the arriving guests. Various chiefs promise feasts and potlatches, and the feasts are given over four days, with much speech-making. Then poles are set up in the hosts' house, and blankets are piled up between them. The son breaks a copper and gives two pieces to chiefs to honor them, but throws a third down to dishonor another. Then the new chief, Facing-Seaward, tells the Kwaguł to give away the blankets; they are distributed, and the guests go home. Four days later, Facing-Seaward empties his house, inviting the other Kwaguł tribes to remove all the empty boxes, baskets, dishes, and spoons. After another four days, he gives away all the roof planks, announces he will seek a wife, and goes with his father to stay with relatives. In the remainder of this history, Facing-Seaward marries, celebrates his sister's coming-of-age, and builds a house, all events requiring the distribution of wealth.

In another family history, Hunt describes events (Boas 1925:79–89) during a potlatch following the death of a Mamalilikala chief. Thirteen tribes attended, and their name-keepers reckoned a total of 658 seats. For the seat-holders the dead chief's numaym had two piles of blankets, 2,000 to a pile. On the morning of the distribution, the dead chief's numaym

2.33 **Ghost masks**. Kingcome. Wood, hair. *Collected by George Hunt, 1901.* AMNH 1901–32. Top: *abadikala'ls* ghost mask, H 29.5 cm, W 22 cm, *16/8396*; left: *kamwikala* ghost mask, H 26.5 cm, W 20 cm, *16/8397*; right: *lulabo'yi* ghost mask, H 27 cm, W 14 cm, *16/8398*; bottom: *leluwatame'* ghost mask, H 27.5 cm, W 18 cm, *16/8399*

IN HIS ACCESSION RECORDS, HUNT PROVIDED NO information on how these four masks were used. He only described *lulabo'yi* (right) as representing "the soul of the living," and *leluwatame'* (bottom) as a "ghost dancer." All four masks, with their roughly carved surfaces, white pigmentation, and tufts of hair, demonstrate a skeletal quality suggestive of ghostliness. Their separate names suggest that they might depict four different ghostly characters.

Boas offers no insight into how these masks might have been used, or in what context. He does, however, provide a useful account of the appearance of ghosts during Winter Ceremonies, during which there is a "mimetic representation of a visit to the lower world" (Boas 1897:482–83).

The performer, an initiate and his family, might have worn head- and neckrings set with carved skulls. Before the actual performance, assistants secretly dug a ditch in the house behind the fire and installed tubes of kelp under the house floor. The ghost dancer would enter the house, make four turns about the fire, and then slowly disappear as if falling into the fire; in fact, he fell into the ditch dug earlier. Soon otherworldly voices could be heard from within the fire; these were actually sounds made by people outside the house speaking into the kelp tubes.

It was then announced that the ghosts had taken the dancer, who would return after a certain number of days, at which time a new dance would be performed. At that time, a carving representing a ghost would rise up from the ditch, carrying the dancer.

A Dzawada'enuxw history that Hunt recorded describes the existence of four ghost masks (Boas and Hunt 1906:39–40). At one point, one of the ancestors, Listened-To, looks through a crack into the wolves' house to see ghosts dancing. Four ghosts, each with a separate name, are called out to the dance floor by the speaker of the house. They make four circuits about the house, singing four sacred songs. When they are finished, the four ghost dancers begin to disappear into the ground, each at a corner of the house. Then the speaker addresses Listened-To, describing the ghosts:

O friend, Wealthiest Listened-To! Now listen! The first one has the name Maggot-on-Back and the one who came next to the first has the name Hemlock-Leaves-on-Back. That one often masks the dead come back. These are the ghosts of the dead that do not stay away, but Wrapped-Around and Chief-of-the-Ghosts have no way of coming back, for Wrapped-Around lives in the house at the very edge of the village of the Ghosts . . . . The reason why Chief-of-the-Ghosts carries the war axe while he is dancing is to drive away with it whatever is profane.

The descendants of Listened-To have the right to perform a dance representing this history, perhaps by wearing masks such as the ones illustrated.

Adam Dick of Kingcome recognizes the bottom mask as a type danced by his mother in his youth; that dance no longer uses carved representations of ghosts (personal communication, 1990). Gloria Cranmer Webster and Peter Macnair (personal communication, 1990) saw this dance performed at Alert Bay, also without any masks. At this performance, a large, cone-shaped wicker tube is placed in the center of the house. Four female dancers, led by a fifth woman, circle around the cone, moving their arms above their head as if to catch or scare the ghosts. The facial painting of these dancers—the leader with a black stripe painted across her face, the others with white paint across their eyes—resembles the painting on these four masks. SAM

2.34 Sea monster whistle. Blunden Harbour. Wood, L 85.5 cm, W 8 cm. *Collected by George Hunt, 1902. 16/9006, AMNH 1902–46*

I N 1902 THIS WHISTLE WAS DOCUMENTED AS A "ts!eges nawalakw, Monster fish Dancer of Winter Dances, Nak!waxdox tribe" (acc. 1902–46, AMNH). Unfortunately, Hunt did not associate this whistle more specifically with a dance privilege of this tribe.

Today, this type of reed whistle is used during *Ħa'sa̱la* ceremonies to announce the arrival of a specific mask. Because of the name Hunt associated with this whistle, it is probable that it was blown outside the house, as masks belonging to the sea world were announced from outside. Before it was used, the whistle was soaked in water to swell the wood and close up all the cracks that might affect its tone. SAM

2.35 Blankets piled up in house. *AMNH 22861*

sang their mourning songs and their song-maker sang a song counting the number of times the deceased had invited all the tribes, given away property to his own tribe, given grease feasts, given away canoes, broken coppers, given away the roof of his house, given a Winter Dance to all the tribes, given a Winter Dance to his own tribe, invited each one of the other tribes, and so on, ending with telling how many times he had paid the marriage debt and how he had given a copper when his princess married. After the songs were sung, the speaker introduced the nephew of the deceased as his heir, the blankets were distributed, and the speaker explained that it was the deceased's dying wish that his nephew inherit his various privileges.

At this point the Kwaguł chief Ten-Fathom-Face[8] (Naka-pankam) asked pointedly about some of the privileges being transmitted. His interest, Hunt explains, came from the fact that the late Mamalilikala chief had been his rival in copper-breaking and "their chief's rank was of equal value."

The rivalry of chiefs seems to have been a constant feature of social relations. It is reflected in, and was probably promoted by, the speeches and songs. In Hunt's accounts there are a number of speeches by hosts, speeches addressed to guests in support of a host, and songs composed to honor hosts. All are grandiloquent in style and boastful in content. One song (Boas 1925:187–91) runs:

Now this great one will move; he will move about, this greatest chief of our tribes.
Now this great one will show the face of a great chief, this head chief of our tribes.
It is said they cause people to be ashamed, the ways of our great chief, tribes.
It is said he makes people jealous, the high great one who has the face of which people are jealous, the greatest chief, tribes.
Long ago this, our great chief, gave away in a potlatch the one that has the name Lita, the copper for you, tribes.
Long ago this, our great chief, gave away in a potlatch the one that has the name Bear Face for you, tribes.
Long ago . . .

And so the song goes on, naming the coppers he has given away or broken and then naming his names inherited from his ancestors. In other songs, chiefs are referred to as extravagant, merciless, and causing others to lose rank.

Some of the rivalry was probably mere showmanship, as later accounts suggest (Drucker and Heizer 1967:102–103). But real hostility also existed. In "The Rival Chiefs," Hunt (1906) tells of events said to have occurred when the Kwaguł were still living at Crooked-Beach. Two chiefs who had been close friends became bitter enemies, each trying to outdo the other in the destruction of property—throwing coppers into the fire, burning canoes, and killing slaves. These "rivalry gestures," as Drucker and Heizer (1967:118) call them, were made in the context of feasts and Winter Dances, not in potlatching as such.

Changes in Potlatching

The family histories show clearly that potlatching was important to the Kwakiutl early in the nineteenth century. These histories and later first-hand accounts also show that over the course of time, there were changes that increased the scale and scope of Kwakiutl potlatching.[9] These changes occurred in the context of the European invasion of this part of North America, the most important consequences of which were: epidemics of Old World diseases resulting in great population loss; European commerce with Native labor rewarded with European goods; and European political domination, with suppression of Native warfare and slavery and the attempted suppression of Native ceremonies (see Cole, this volume). These changes can be seen in the social system, the ceremonial system, and in the kinds and quantities of property used in potlatching.

The Social System. The Kwakiutl probably experienced the epidemic of smallpox that swept over much of the Northwest Coast in the 1770s. They certainly experienced epidemics in the 1820s (probably smallpox), in 1848 (measles), and in 1862–63 (smallpox again). From a pre-contact population of perhaps as great as 19,000, the Kwakiutl had dropped in numbers to around 8,500 in 1835 and around 7,650 in 1862. Then in two years they were reduced by nearly 70 per cent, falling to 2,370 persons. The population continued to decline until well into the twentieth century (Boyd 1990; Codere 1950:53).

As Codere (1990) has shown, while their total numbers declined, the Kwakiutl seem to have held on to their organization of about 100 numayms, with the result that the average size of a numaym dropped from about 75 persons in 1835 to about 15 in 1887 and about 10 in 1895. Thus if the reported total of 795 seats (an average of 7–8 per numaym) is correct, the Kwakiutl moved from a situation where there were many adult males without seats to one where there were too few to occupy the seats available. This situation, combined with an increase in wealth available to anybody who could work, seems to have

2.36 Figure of a copper breaker. Quatsino. Wood, L 281.8 cm. *Collected by George Hunt, 1900. 16/8252, AMNH 1900–73*

THIS IMAGE DYNAMICALLY DEPICTS A LARGE FIGURE, his legs bent as if to leap forward, one arm pointed ahead, the other holding a weapon. Hunt collected this large potlatch figure at approximately the same time he acquired another large figure designed to ridicule a rival chief (fig. 3.21); this statue, in contrast, with its energy and force, seems to embody all the great power of its owner.

Hunt described this figure to Boas as "Ts̲am'lela pointer figure" (acc. 1900–73, AMNH). Large pointing figures set out on the beach, facing the water and incoming canoes, appear to have been common at the turn of the century (fig. 2.37). Boas identified this carving as a "copper breaker," probably because the weapon it carries in its right hand could be the knife or dagger symbolically used to cut coppers (see fig. 1.16). SAM

led to an increase in competition of claims for vacant seats, and so more potlatching. The increase in wealth and rise of a few *nouveaux riches* even led to the creation of a new series of positions, the "Eagles," who had the privilege of receiving at potlatches before the highest-ranking traditional chiefs (Drucker and Heizer 1967:88–97).

The Ceremonial System. The family histories show that the Kwaguł had been for generations part of a social network that extended beyond the limits of the Kwakwala language. Marriages were arranged with the non-Kwakiutl Oowekeeno and Heiltsuk to the north, Nuu-chah-nulth to the west, and Coast Salish to the south. Yet intermarriage and the transfer of ceremonies did not preclude conflict even among the Kwakiutl

tribes. In fact, conflict or the threat of conflict was perhaps an important component in the larger social system (Ferguson 1983, 1984). But now, with the threat of British gunboats, intertribal conflict stopped, and social ties that had formerly been interrupted by hostility became permanently peaceful. This allowed for, or promoted, the expansion of potlatching and joint Winter Ceremonies.

As the Kwaguł at Fort Rupert expanded their sphere of social interaction, with more and more of the other Kwakiutl tribes involved in their Winter Ceremonies and potlatches, new complexities entered the ceremonial system. Among the Kwakiutl tribes were differences in the kinds of dances they had, in the ways they were ordered into series, in the details of performance, and of course in the myths accounting for them. The tribes on the outer coast differed especially from those originally at the head of Queen Charlotte Strait in that they—the G̲usgimax̲w, Tّłatّłasik̲w̲ala, and others—had two separate series of dances, a *tsitّseka* series that included the performances associated with Baxwbakwalanuxwsiwe' and Warrior-of-the-World, and a *nuł̲am* series that included performances with different animal masks. With joint Winter Dances, the Fort Rupert people were exposed to a greater variety of performances.

Among the Queen Charlotte Strait people, the total number of dances used in the Winter Dance increased. In the at̲łakam performance, acquired from the Oowekeeno, as many as forty masked dancers represented various forest beings (Holm 1983:126–37).

Moreover, through marriages with the Heiltsuk, Oowekeeno, and Kwakiutl of the outer coast, some chiefs acquired dances of a new series called *tła's̲ala* (or *dł̲aw̲al̲ax̲a*), some derived from the *nuł̲am* series (Boas 1897:621–32; Holm 1983:72). This series differed from the *tseka* (Winter Dance) series in that the performances had to be given in the secular season when the secular organization was in force. A *tła's̲ala* performance began with the host's announcing his intention and promising a distribution of wealth, and this was followed by a period during which the distinctive "horns" of the *tła'sala* were heard. On the appointed morning his guests came and were feasted. Then the initiate, a relative of the host, appeared in a Northern chief's costume—a headdress consisting of a carved frontlet, a crown of sea-lion whiskers, and a train of ermine skins on his head, a dancing robe around his shoulders, an apron around his waist, and a raven rattle in his hand (figs. 2.38–40). After dancing briefly, showering white down out of the crown of his headdress, he ran out. Attendants returned displaying his headdress and telling the audience that he had disappeared. Then a dancer appeared wearing a *tła'sala* mask, supposedly the initiate transformed into whatever the mask represented. He made a circuit of the fire and left, and the initiate reentered and finished his dance, with others singing and dancing in his honor. This performance was repeated in the evening of this day and on the following day, and on the next day the host distributed his property. *Tła'sala* masks represent various animals and birds as well as humanoid creatures like the *dzunukwa*, the *bakwas* (woodsman), and *Kumugwe'* (fig. 2.41).

By the late nineteenth century, if not earlier, the *tseka* and *tła'sala* dances were appearing in mortuary potlatches (Drucker and Heizer 1967:130–32). Some time after the death of a chief, his heir held a potlatch that began, before nightfall, with the singing of mourning songs of the numayms present and then a song for the dead chief listing his feasts, potlatches, and coppers sold or broken. The heir sometimes broke a copper and gave away pieces as mementos, without any ill-feeling implied. The guests sang a dirge that asked, "Which way has he gone?" And a dancer appeared wearing a mask representing the ancestor of the numaym of the late chief's father or mother, indicating that he had gone to assume that form. In the evening dancers performed shortened versions of the *tseka* or *tła'sala* dances that the heir was inheriting from the dead chief. Dances of the two series could not be performed on the same night. The event concluded with a distribution of property to the guests.[10]

Property. In our episode of "Marriage with the Comox," potlatch goods consist of dressed hides (in one context Boas identifies the term as meaning specifically elk hides and in another deer hides), cedar bark blankets, and a copper. In the earlier generations of other family histories, potlatch goods also include blankets made of the skins of sea otters, minks, martens, and other fur-bearers, as well as cedar bark blankets, coppers, and slaves. Then, as Codere (1950) has shown, the family histories show a change occurring right after the move to Fort Rupert. Potlatch goods become largely Hudson's Bay Company woollen blankets (called "fog surfaces"), first in tens, then hundreds, and finally—occasionally—thousands. Slavery was no longer practiced, and so slaves were no longer given at potlatches. But coppers were still very much in use, their values measured in blankets. From other sources we know that the blankets themselves were given a value in Canadian dollars, which ultimately became acceptable potlatch gifts.

This shift that we see in the family histories from purely

2.39 **Dancing headdress**. Alert Bay. Wood, shell, abalone, baleen, down, swan's skin, ermine, rabbit, 54 cm x 26 cm; length of train, 169 cm. *Collected from Agnes Cranmer. 19670724*, RBCM *12847*

DURING THE NINETEENTH CENTURY, THE KWA-kiutl borrowed such headdresses from the northern Northwest Coast peoples. This kind of dancing headdress was worn in *tła'sala* performances. A carved wooden plaque depicting a crest animal was attached to a band lined with swan's down and feathers. A crown of baleen gives the headdress height; a long train of ermine and rabbit gives it sweeping elegance. During performances, swan's down would have floated out as the wearer danced.

According to RBCM collection information, this headdress was collected from Agnes Cranmer who was given the piece by Peter Smith of Turnour Island.

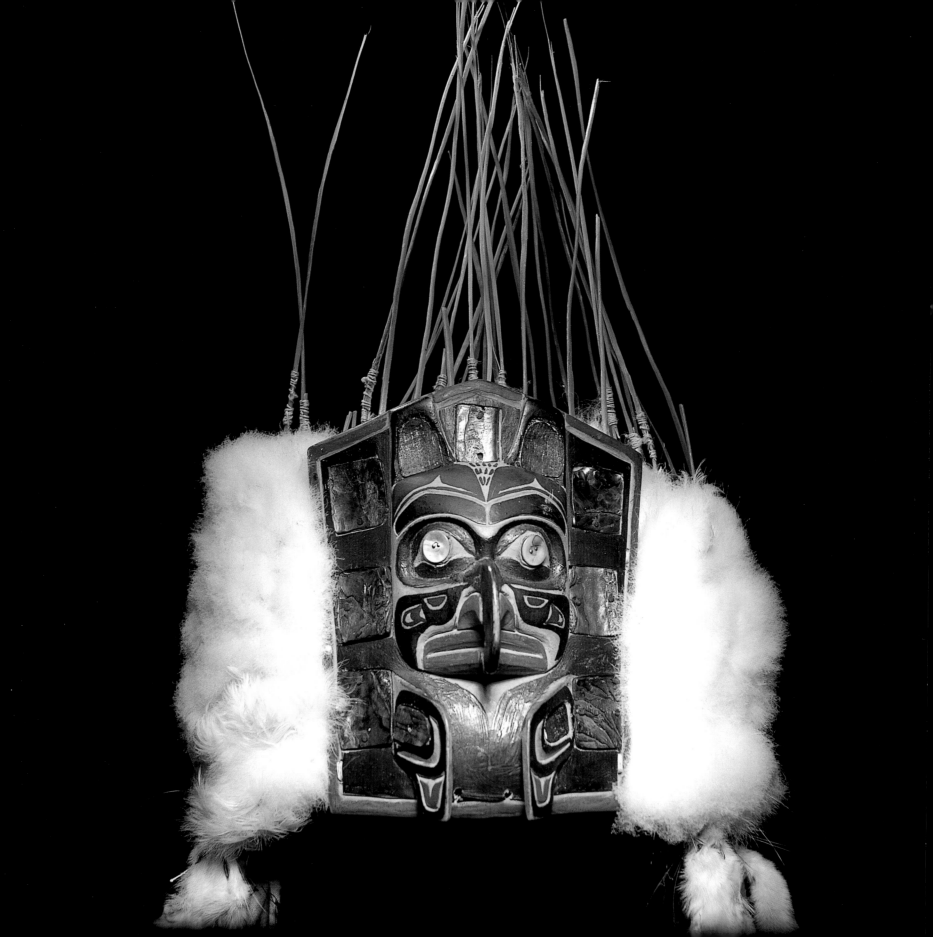

2.40 **Button blanket**. Village Island. Cloth, wool, felt, buttons, beads, 182 cm x 149 cm. *RBCM 13685*

BUTTON BLANKETS WERE USUALLY MADE OF HUDson's Bay Company blankets with borders of flannel. Images were worked out in appliqué flannel and often outlined in mother-of-pearl buttons. This blanket depicts in its center a tree surrounded by broken coppers as well as the T-shaped ridge of the copper. In the border are depictions of complete coppers.

aboriginal goods to blankets is a little too abrupt. As Drucker and Heizer (1967:35–36) point out, by 1849 trade goods would have been available for nearly seventy years, and it is unlikely that they would not have been used in potlatching. The failure of the family histories to mention them may be, like the mislocation of the Comox and Ligwiłda'xw, the result of a reinterpretation of tradition.

But a change, perhaps less abrupt, did occur, and the reasons for it are not hard to find. In the old days, before the fur trade, potlatch goods were entirely of Indian manufacture, and were still so largely after it began. The quantity of goods was limited by this fact. And potlatch goods were largely in the hands of the chiefs. After it became possible to earn blankets—and then money—working for non-Indians, potlatch goods were available to anybody who sold his or her labor for the money.

The use of larger and larger quantities of goods can be seen in marriage exchanges, and marriage may also have been increasingly used as a form of investment. At Fort Rupert, Smoke-All-Round's son 'Maxwakwuḻala seems to have provoked a rivalry between fathers-in-law. He married the princess of one chief and then got her permission to marry the princess of another by telling the former that she would be his chief wife. The second chief agreed to the marriage, but the arrangement goaded him into greatly increasing his daughter's dowry in order to increase her status. Marrying for wealth, however, had its disadvantages. When a father-in-law brought a return payment of double the original bride-price, the son-in-law might have enough for a great potlatch. But then his wife was free to leave him; or, if she did not, the father-in-law could demand an even greater amount as a second bride-price.

The family history we began with tells us nothing about the amassing of property except for the use of marriage as a means of getting it from one's father-in-law. But the personal history summarized above, together with accounts by Dawson (1888:79–81), Curtis (1915:141–55), and Drucker and Heizer (1967) give us a fairly clear picture of the financial transactions used to increase the amount of property available.

One method was to make loans at a high rate of interest. By the second half of the nineteenth century, a man preparing to potlatch would lend blankets to his own people and to his prospective guests with the understanding that they would return the loans with interest up to 100 per cent at the time of the potlatch. In "The Acquisition of Names," when the father and son go to invite the Mamalilikala, Ławit'sis, and 'Namgis to their intertribal potlatch, they take blankets to the other three

villages and hand them out as loans, obligating the prospective guest to bring them to the potlatch with interest.

Another way of increasing one's wealth for a potlatch through a financial transaction was to buy a copper and then sell it at a profit, coppers often doubling in value at each sale. In this transaction, the buyer of the copper often had to call in the loans he had made in order to pay for it. If any of the buyer's debtors could not pay, the seller of the copper (the prospective potlatcher) could advance them the gifts they were entitled to receive at his potlatch. The debtors of the buyer could then pay off their debts and forgo their potlatch gifts. The seller kept track of these advances, not only so he would know to whom he could say, "You've already received your gift," at his potlatch, but because these advances were treated as loans to the buyer and required him to pass them on to the seller with 100 per cent interest.

Boas's description of the Kwakiutl potlatch is wrong on this very matter of interest (Barnett 1938). He identified potlatch gifts as loans at 100 per cent interest and concluded that potlatching itself was a form of investment. But it is clear that a return with interest was expected for loans only. The dressed hides, fur blankets, or woolen blankets distributed at a potlatch were simply gifts. What the potlatcher gained was primarily more secure status and glory. He did not expect that he would get it all back with interest. Some of the chiefs who received his gifts no doubt hoped to equal or even outdo him, but whether they ever did depended on too many variables for the system to work as Boas seemed to think.

Drucker and Heizer (1967: 78–80) question whether a system of loans at fixed rates of interest could have existed before blankets, arguing that no two sea-otter pelts or other items would have been identical in value. However, pelts of fur-bearers (elk and deer hides are excluded) were not used as single whole skins. In 1792 at a village at the mouth of the Nimpkish, members of the Vancouver expedition were entertained and each given a strip or "slip" of sea-otter skin (Vancouver 1984:626; Menzies 1923:87), and in the family histories, people receive blankets made of pelts (or strips of fur?) sewn together. Both strips and blankets might permit a greater degree of standardization than would have been possible using single whole skins.

The Winter Ceremonial of 1894

The time is now the late nineteenth century. The place is Fort Rupert, more than forty years after the post was established

2.41 **Ḵumugwe' mask**. Fort Rupert. Wood, lined rubber boot loops, fabric, H 79 cm, W 50 cm. *Collected by George Hunt, 1897. 16/2370, AMNH 1897–43*

ḰUMUGWE', AN IMPORTANT FIGURE IN KWAKIUTL mythology, is the Chief of the Sea who embodies great wealth. Variously referred to as "Wealthy One" and "Copper Maker," he is conceived of as the strongest power in the sea, as he rules over all beings in his realm—fish, sea mammals, and any land animals that enter his domain, such as the sea bear and the sea raven. His house at the bottom of the sea was made of copper with giant sea lions forming the rafters, house posts, and speaking posts. In mythic times, many heroes sought Ḵumugwe' to obtain wealth and supernatural powers from him (Boas 1935b:128–31).

This elaborate Ḵumugwe' mask was probably used as a *tła'sala* privilege. It incorporates many creatures from Ḵumugwe's realm. On the top of the mask a fish is attached and rigged so that it can spin. Below it is an octopus with its head in the center and tentacles radiating outward. On either side of the central face, fish, possibly bullheads or rockfish, are portrayed. Toward the bottom of the face extend small human hands. A patent date of 1879 and the inscription "RLDS Columbia Exposition" are stenciled on the mask. SAM

and the four tribes now called Kwaguł settled there. Crooked-Beach is now the site of the Ławitsis village (fig. 2.44). The 'Namgis have moved from the mouth of the Nimpkish River to Alert Bay, now the site of a cannery and a sawmill, which offers jobs—and not just to the 'Namgis—an Anglican mission, which offers a new way of life, and governmental authority, which threatens to enforce new laws (see Cole, this volume).

At Fort Rupert (fig. 2.45) the houses of the Kwaguł still have frames of hand-hewn posts and beams, but the front walls are of milled lumber and all the wall planks are nailed on vertically, rather than lashed on horizontally as earlier, and there are a few glass windows. A number of house fronts have painted designs displaying numaym crests, and there are external carvings not seen in earlier times—free-standing totem poles being numaym crests and single figures commemorating potlatches. The interiors of the houses are much the same in arrangement, but there are numerous pieces of furniture, utensils, and personal belongings bought at the local store, at Alert Bay, or in Victoria or some other town to the south. Most of the people are now wearing much the same kinds of clothing as non-Indians.

In November 1894, Fort Rupert is the scene of a Winter Dance to which the Kwaguł (now acting as a single tribe) have invited two other tribes, the G̱usgimaxw (now including the Goṗinuxw, Tłaskinuxw, and Gwatsinuxw), and the 'Nakwaxda'xw. Another guest is Franz Boas. Although no stranger to the Kwakiutl, he had never seen a major Winter Ceremony before.

Boas arrived at Fort Rupert on November 13 and left on December 4. George Hunt provided him a place to stay and, it seems, almost constant guidance. He missed the opening ceremony at which red cedar bark ornaments were distributed, and the reappearance of Yagwis, the new *hamatsa* of the Kwaguł. And the ceremonies continued long after he left. But he had twenty full days to observe.[11]

While at Fort Rupert, Boas gave two feasts. The morning after he arrived, he gave a hardtack (pilot biscuit) and molasses feast, at which he was able to present pictures to the Kwakiutl people who had been in Chicago for the Columbian Exposition of 1893. And on November 28, he gave an apple feast. He attended the Kwakiutl feasts and ceremonies wearing a headband and a blanket (to keep his coat clean), and he tried to eat the food. He passed when offered seal blubber but ate the meat, and he could not down a mixture of dried berries and eulachon grease. He tried to attend every event, getting Hunt to explain what was going on at the time and getting a fuller

2.42 Devilfish dish. Quatsino. Wood, L 188 cm. *Collected by George Hunt, 1900. 16/8161, AMNH 1900–73*

DEVILFISH IS THE COMMON NAME FOR THE OCTOPUS on the Northwest Coast. This dish has been carved so that the curved projections positioned above and below the face probably represent the huge arms of this creature. Because this carved representation includes human features as well, it may be considered a supernatural being, exempt from the requirements of nature to possess an appropriate number of arms or the beak of a true octopus.

The central feature is the vast open mouth surrounded by teeth. The curving lines of the rolled arm at the top of the head are echoed below by the addition of two thicker projections, which terminate in what appear to be serpents' heads. The traces of paint remaining on these heads are some indication of the elaborate design which originally decorated the dish.

Hunt recorded that the Kwakiutl regarded the largest kind of devilfish, the "bear of the rocks," as a sea monster, which may not be eaten because of its ability to kill people (Boas 1921:614–15). JO

2.43 **Grizzly bear figure**. Quatsino. Wood, L 165 cm. Collected by George Hunt, 1900. 16/8250. *AMNH 1900–73*

NANGAMALA IS THE NAME HUNT WAS GIVEN FOR this sculpture when he collected it (acc. 1900–73, AMNH). This literally translates as "Appearance of the Grizzly's Face" (Bill Holm: personal communication, 1990), a common name for a copper with a bear's face at the top. This figure probably was called N̲anga̲mala because of the copper shown on its chest (Webster: personal communication, 1990). Although the face is an animal rather than human, it probably served a function similar to that of other rivalry figures (see, e.g., figs. 1.15, 3.21).

The top of the copper merges with a bear's head, thus depicting the confluence of two concepts. The bear image probably refers to one of the family's important crest privileges acquired through marriage or war, or perhaps through an encounter that a significant ancestor had with a supernatural bear. The copper is an overt sign of wealth. The family's relationship to power and wealth, derived from the past and existing in the present, is greatly reinforced by this display of both copper and crest image.

The smaller figure crouching between the legs of the copper/bear might refer to the work's function in the rivalry context. Holm suggests that this small figure serves a similar purpose as the little figure held in the arms of a larger one (see fig. 1.15), namely, to humiliate a competitor by comparing him unfavorably to the hosting chief (Holm notes, Dept. of Anthropology, AMNH). SAM

2.44 Crooked-Beach, Turnour Island, c. 1900. *Photo by C. F. Newcombe.* RBCM PN 251

2.45 Fort Rupert, 1894. *Photo by O. C. Hastings.* AMNH 336060

2.46 Chief holding copper, Fort Rupert, 1894. *Photo by O.C. Hastings.* AMNH 11577

2.47 Woman holding a broken copper, Fort Rupert, 1894. *Photo by O.C. Hastings.* AMNH 336104

2.48 Piles of blankets for payment during a copper purchase ceremony, Fort Rupert, 1894. *Photo by O.C. Hastings.* AMNH 336066

2.49 Chief in button blanket at the feast Boas gave in Fort Rupert, November 28, 1894. *Photo by O.C. Hastings,* AMNH 335772

2.50 *Hamaṫsa* on the beach, Fort Rupert, 1894. *Photo by O.C. Hastings.* AMNH 336128

2.51 *'Nax'nakagaml mask*. Quatsino. Wood, L 52.5 cm, H 19 cm.
Collected by George Hunt, 1900. 16/8167, AMNH 1900–73

THIS *'nax'nakagaml,* "DAYBREAK" OR "DAWN" MASK, is stylistically similar to Nuu-chah-nulth carvings, with its smooth facial treatment, thin slanted eyes, and openwork around the pupils and between the "lips" of the beak. Inside the wings are serpents painted in a classic Nuu-chah-nulth mode.

Despite the similarity of this carving to artworks from the Nuu-chah-nulth, the G̱usgimax̱w explain that this mask illustrates an episode from their history when Raven stole daylight. The chief of the Gopinux̱w, Counselor-of-the-World, desired to make war on

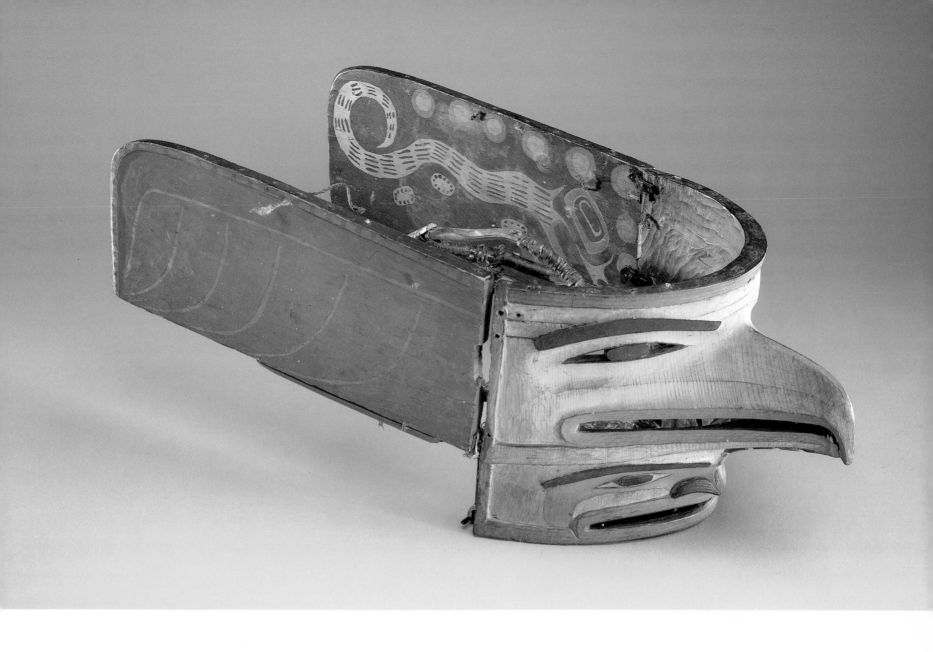

the G̲usgima̲xw to obtain from Daylight-Receptacle-Woman her treasure, the sun, which she kept in a box. One day, Counselor-of-the-World went into the forest to seek supernatural strength, for he knew he would need it to vanquish the G̲usgima̲xw. In his quest he learned how to make himself invisible and enter the womb of Daylight-Receptacle-Woman. After she was impregnated, her belly grew quickly and in four days she gave birth to Counselor-of-the-World who, in four more days, was old enough to walk. Soon he began to cry, and his mother discovered that the only thing that would pacify him was holding the box of daylight. One day, Counselor-of-the-World paddled off with this box. Once safely away from the village, he opened the box, took out the sun,

and removed its *sisiyutł* mask. The world became immediately light. Then the sun offered Counselor-of-the-World his *sisiyutł* mask and his daybreak mask if Counselor-of-the-World would let him go up to heaven and benefit the world by making day (Boas 1897:410–11; Boas and Hunt, 1905:393–97).

While this mask represents an eagle, other types of daybreak masks represent different beings. Many display a central anthropomorphic face with red dash marks on the cheeks. Daybreak masks often have "wings" on either side, which are painted on the outside with a black serpentlike figure. White spots decorate the outside portion of the "wings" and may refer to the night sky (Bill Holm: personal communication, 1990). SAM

account from him later. Then or later Hunt wrote down the speeches they heard. O.C. Hastings, a photographer Boas had hired, took numerous photographs, which Boas supervised (figs. 2.45–50). He also measured people, made casts of faces, collected myths, and corrected songs recorded the previous year in Chicago.

Nearly every day saw events connected with the Winter Dance, with the Kwaguł, the G̱usgimax̱w, and the 'Nakwaxda'x̱w trying to outdo each other in dramatic performance and lavish distribution. The three tribes each had *hamatsa* initiates. Houses were set apart for the ceremonies of each, and they took turns hosting feasts and other events, the seating arrangements reflecting the relations of the three.

There were secret planning sessions early in the morning in the woods, when someone planning an event enlisted the help of his tribe or the participants in a ceremony were taught the new songs. On November 24, one such session was organized for the Kwaguł by Myth-Person (Nuxwnimis), their master of ceremonies, and Listened-To (Hutłalid), their principal speaker. The people sang and beat time, the dancers became excited, and Yagwis, their new *hamatsa*, rushed out of the woods. The organizers enlisted a *tuxw'id* to capture the power of the Winter Dance, and she threw it into the people. She was the center of a procession that marched back to the village—with Boas and Hunt caught up in it. They went from house to house, where the *tuxw'id* threw the power into the people, each time increasing the uproar. The people shook their blankets to show the power had entered them. They laughed and cried and kissed each other's wives, "for during this time there is no jealousy and no quarreling." Myth-Person led them back to the ceremonial house, where Listened-To announced that a boy had been taken by the spirits, who must be pleased with what they had done. He concluded:

Therefore I myself and my friend Myth-Person are pleased with you. We cannot do anything without you, for what is the power of a chief without the help of his tribe? You call me and Myth-Person chiefs of the winter ceremonial, but we have no power without you.

Another morning a *hamatsa* was seen running along the beach trying to bite women who had taken his food, driving them into the water and forcing them to stay there (fig. 2.50). At nearly every event, the fool dancers were teased and threatened people with their lances, while the bear dancers growled menacingly and scratched people with the claws on their mitts.

The feast foods were salmon, berries (probably dried salal,

2.52 **Whale dish**. Quatsino. Wood, L 85 cm, W 43 cm. *Collected by George Hunt, 1899. 16/6895, AMNH 1899–50*

A CROUCHED HUMAN FIGURE SUPPORTS, WITH considerable effort, the weight of an impressively large whale, which functions here as a carved container for food. The rear portion of this animal has been given a face as well. It appears that one eye and one nostril are positioned on either side of the flukes. This configuration corresponds with the G̱usgimax̱w style of representing a grizzly bear (Bill Holm: personal communication, 1990).

There is far less concern here with the conventionalized forms of the north. The expansive oval eye and the carved striations which may be seen across the brow and pupils characterize this piece as a work in the "Old Wakashan" style (Peter Macnair: personal communication, 1990). Moreover, G̱usgimax̱w pieces may incorporate various attributes similar to the art of the Nuu-chah-nulth, the neighbors of this tribe, directly to the south of Quatsino Sound.

The Nuu-chah-nulth were known to remove the dorsal fin or "saddle" from a successfully harpooned whale, decorate it with dyed shredded bark and feathers, cover it with down, and then celebrate this choice part of the whale in song (Drucker 1951:180). The small "lid" or detachable ornament on this whale's back represents an excised dorsal fin. Fin-shaped lids may also be seen on other dishes in this collection (see fig. 6.2).

Hunt recorded in his field ledger that this whale was "speared" by Apotl, a character who appears in a Kwakiutl story about a cannibal woman whose hands were as sharp as knives (acc. 1899–50, AMNH). Apotl's sons have various adventures, which culminate in the marriage of the eldest to the daughter of the cannibal woman. This new daughter-in-law brings several treasures to Apotl's family, including a wonderful box of food that always remains full and the special ability to rejuvenate the elderly.

The imagery of this dish does not correspond with any particular part of this narrative. It is possible that this legendary hero figures in various unrecorded stories, one of which may be more closely associated with this carving. JO

2.53 Fort Rupert potlatch with bracelets and frontlets, 1902–05.
Photo by George Hunt, AMNH 104473

huckleberries, or blackberries) in grease, soapberries whipped into a froth, crabapples, and rice. While eating, the different "societies" among the "Sparrows" gave their characteristic cries. Batons for beating time were issued at the beginning of a feast or other event, and if it was not already daylight when the speech-making was over, they split their batons, lit them in the fire, and used them for torches to find their way home.

Feasts provided the occasion for a man to call in his debts, another to offer a copper for sale, a father-in-law to repay a marriage debt, a man to rub snot on his crying child's face to begin his initiation as a fool dancer, a girl to "disappear," or another to reappear in a state of "holy madness."

There were gatherings primarily for the initiation of new dancers in the *wixso*, the minor Winter Dance, though feasts may have followed them. At one of these gatherings (on November 22) the main event was to be the initiation of a fool dancer, but as a great transformation mask was opened, it broke. Attendants tried to cover it, but the *hamatsa* of the Kwaguł had seen it and became excited, crying "Hap, hap!" The fools and bears caught the excitement. The *hamatsa* rushed to the middle of the house, the fools struck people, and the bears scratched them. This set off the new *hamatsa* of the Gusgimaxw, who jumped up trembling and crying "Hap, hap!" The 'Nak̓waxda'xw *hamatsa* joined in, while a 'Nak̓waxda'xw *paxala* (shaman dancer) started jumping around the fire and throwing burning embers and firebrands into the crowd. Women ran screaming into the bedrooms. The Gusgimaxw left with their *hamatsa*, and most of the 'Nak̓waxda'xw were chased out by theirs. By rights, the "seals" could have broken the walls of the house, and the fools and bears could have driven people through them. But somehow they did not, and as the Kwaguł tried to put the fire back together, the uncle of the man who broke it up ran around it shouting "'Nawalakwai!" invoking the power of the Winter Dance to calm things down.

Feasts were interrupted by comic skits. In one, a man pretended to be a Haida, talking in their funny language. When a woman could not repeat his words, he offered to give her a night class in the subject. In another a girl dressed up like a rich white woman gave away a roll of silver quarters. In a third, a "judge" with a book sent "policemen" to go out and arrest an old woman. When she was brought in in handcuffs, the "interpreter" told her she must pay a fine for her absence. She protested that this is always the way with policemen, arresting anyone who has money. This skit, we are told, was first performed in 1865 and has been kept up ever since.

Every occasion provided an opportunity for bombastic oratory by the official speakers, who (as we can see in films Boas made much later) grasped their staffs and bent their knees so they could bob up and down as they listed the accomplishments of their chiefs. Every occasion provided a reason to distribute property—not only Hudson's Bay Company blankets, but button blankets and silver bracelets on sticks, ten to a stick.

Having missed the first appearance of Yagwis (the new *hamatsa* of the Kwaguł), Boas was delighted to be able to attend a salmon and berry feast given by Yagwis on the evening of November 19. Then, on the evening of November 21, the father of Yagwis gives a feast in his honor. And on November 24, after the *tuxw'id* had thrown the power of the Winter Dance into the people and an initiate had been taken away, people brought blankets into the ceremonial house, and the Gusgimaxw and 'Nak̓waxda'xw tally-keepers came in to give the host a reckoning of those in each tribe who would receive gifts. That evening the blankets were distributed, and Yagwis danced for the last time, wearing a Chilcat blanket—probably a heritage from his Tlingit grandmother.

At the feast for Yagwis given by his father on November 21, the blankets were actually provided by a woman identified as his father's mother, but probably the wife of the powerful Chief Ten-Fathom-Face (Nak̓apankam). She entered the house first, crying out under the weight of her blankets (though not really carrying them). Next the father of Yagwis came in singing, followed by Yagwis himself, his sister, who was his attendant and, carrying the blankets, members of their numaym. The speaker of the numaym rose and addressed the Kwaguł and then the guest tribes, asking them to help tame the *hamatsa*, and while Yagwis and his sister danced, the people sang for them.

During the course of the speeches that preceded the distribution of the blankets, Nułk̓wuła̱la (to identify the father by his sacred name) told how he was taught to conduct himself by his "father" Ten-Fathom-Face and by Owadi (another leading chief), how he had received the names Copper-Maker and Undersea-Lord, and how he had received his *hamatsa* (the privilege being exercised by his son) from his brother-in-law Myth-Person. He asked the people not to call him "little northerner," because his mother was of high station among her people. And he concluded: "I do not give this festival that you may call me a chief. I give it in honor of the two who are dancing here, that the word of their enemies may not harm them. For this purpose I have built an armor of wealth around them."

In response, Listened-To, the speaker of the Kwaguł, said of

2.54 Blankets in canoe, Fort Rupert potlatch, 1898.
Photo by H. I. Smith. AMNH 14206

the father of Yagwis: "His property runs from him in streams, and if one of his rivals should stand in the way he would be drowned by it."

Myth-Person, the Kwaguł master of ceremonies through these events, was a descendant in the fifth generation of the Giving-Property in the family history "Marriage with the Comox." His sister, Made-to-Spout-in-House (Tłaliłilakw), was the wife of Giving-Potlatches-in-the-World (˙Maxwalagalis), at the moment known by his winter name Nułkwułala, and it was their oldest son, Only-One-on-the-Beach (˙Namugwis) who is the *hamatsa* initiate with the name Lying-Dead-on-the-Beach (Yagwis).

As some readers may now suspect, and as readers of Boas who have kept the Kwakiutl names straight will know, these streams of property were running from none other than George Hunt himself. No wonder he was such a good source of information. He had been instructed by the leading chiefs of the Kwakiutl, he was a major potlatcher, his brother-in-law was the master of ceremonies, and his son David was the most important initiate.

In this essay I have tried to present the potlatch in its traditional setting. But as we have seen, that setting has been changing. Practices that might be called traditional in the 1990s were innovations in the 1890s, when George Hunt was recording traditions from the early nineteenth century. I have also tried to present the traditional potlatch as seen through what Hunt recorded. I have been aided by the hindsight provided by the work of Franz Boas, Edward S. Curtis, Philip Drucker, Hèlen Codere, and others, but I have tried to follow Boas's principles of "letting the Indians speak for themselves" and presenting an insider's view. To complement this view, Douglas Cole (this volume) has documented the views and actions of the outsiders, the whites who had great—but, it turns out, limited—power over the Indians. It has been a surprise to me to discover the degree to which George Hunt himself was at the center of the potlatch and the Winter Dance. This glimpse of Hunt is more than complemented by the essay by Ira Jacknis (this volume), which documents Hunt's career as a collector collaborating with outsiders who were determined to preserve material evidence of the extravagant art and ceremony of the Kwakiutl. But Hunt's career as an insider deserves much more attention. Finally, this essay is not an analysis of how the Kwakiutl potlatch may have worked within a psychological, social, economic, or ecological system, nor an analysis of what its symbolic content may have been. A pile made of the books and articles on these subjects would begin to rival one of those piles of blankets at a late nineteenth-century potlatch.

3.1 **War club**. Gilford Island. Wood, bone, L 73.5 cm. *Collected by George Hunt, 1901. 16/8388, AMNH 1901–32*

THIS OBJECT WAS CARVED FROM A HEAVY PIECE OF wood and topped by a crouching grizzly bear, its teeth exposed in a snarl. The head of a sharp-beaked raven is also attached, along the midsection of the stout handle. The ball-like form at the base of this structure has been provided with a human face, its large mouth wide open. The surface is a glossy black, which may result from the addition of graphite to the original paint. Finally, the blade, carved and polished to a uniformly smooth surface, has been fashioned from a rather porous piece of whalebone and mounted so that it penetrates the chest area of the bear at a right angle to the body.

George Hunt called this piece of equipment a war club (*kilagayu*, a tool for killing) (acc. 1901–32, AMNH). It would certainly have been effective for this purpose in battle, but more likely it was used as a theatrical prop, to represent an act of aggression (Peter Macnair: personal communication, 1990).

The carved bear may be a crest of the club's owner. However, grizzly bear imagery was certainly associated with aggression among the Kwakiutl, suggesting an alternate reason for this choice. Initiates of the Grizzly Bear Society were the agents of the *hamatsa*, authorized to punish with death those who behaved inappropriately in the dance house (Boas 1897:467). Boas published a song which accompanied a bear dancer as he made his way around the fire at the time of the Winter Ceremony (ibid., 468). The words are clearly a threat, promising war to the rival tribes:

Haiōō' a haiōō! Let your great name be called, Great Bear!
You will go at once to the chiefs of the tribes, whom you will make your slaves, Great Bear!
Then we shall have war!
Then we shall have trouble! JO

3 / The History of the Kwakiutl Potlatch

Douglas Cole

THE KWAKIUTL HELD TENACIOUSLY TO THEIR potlatch. Only the Gitksan and the Nuu-chah-nulth rival the persistence of the Kwakiutl in retaining the basic features of the potlatch into the twentieth century. The Kwakiutl potlatch declined late, largely as a result of economic, social, and cultural forces that could no longer be resisted. Missionaries, Indian agents, and laws had only limited effects upon it. This essay is partly a history of the institution, and partly an account of the attempt at its legal suppression and of Kwakiutl resistance.[1]

The history of the potlatch is a study in contrasting values. The Canadian government, while sometimes misdirected, had its reasons for the law. The potlatching Kwakiutl, even when subjected to an increasingly authoritarian paternalism, were convinced that nothing was wrong with the potlatch and that the law was mistaken. Exploiting the government's weaknesses, they were able to thwart the law at least as often as it thwarted their potlatches. They remained significant participants in their own destiny. Except for a brief period between 1919 and 1927, the Kwakiutl did with their potlatches pretty much what they wanted to do. Most Northwest Coast groups did too, though the course chosen by the Kwakiutl was to resist, more strongly and for a longer period than most, the external forces that inevitably undermined the potlatch.

The Kwakiutl, like other coastal groups in the pre-contact era, possessed a decent abundance of natural foods and so often gave feasts to those with whom they were in frequent contact and with whom they intermarried. Potlatches, on the other hand, were probably few; while food was abundant, transferable wealth—in the form of animal skins, mats, perhaps some canoes and slaves—was modest. Only the highest chief, perhaps the second highest as well, of a lineage group (numaym) potlatched, with the entire group behind him.

Contact changed this in several ways. The gradual diminution of warfare under British influence increased intergroup relations, especially intermarriage, and thus the exchange of crest privileges—and allowed for an expansion of the guest group invited to feasts and potlatches. At the same time contact also brought an increase of wealth. A further change, perhaps the most telling of all, was the dramatic decline of population from introduced diseases and alcohol.

While the exact process is unclear, it is plain that depopulation, increased wealth, and the end of warfare brought great modifications to the Kwakiutl social system. Kwakiutl society was based on hereditary rank: the over 700 named positions among the Kwakiutl. The loss of population meant that there were more positions than men clearly marked by heredity to fill them. Even more, the potlatch became a means of accession to positions where inheritance was now cloudy. With this, the potlatch became, to a degree, individualized and democratized: lower-ranking people could, by means of wealth, claim positions for which they had only a tenuous hereditary link. The availability of transferable wealth items, almost entirely European trade goods acquired through wage and piece labor, commercial fishing, and prostitution, brought a profound change to the old system (Mauzé 1986:25).[2]

In the years following the 1849 founding of Fort Rupert, potlatches flourished as never before, increasing in frequency, in the number of guests invited, and in the amount of goods distributed. Ranks lost much of their old significance but retained their prestige and acquired a new significance—lower-ranked Indians could emulate chiefs through potlatching. A commoner could acquire wealth items, in the form of blankets and other trade goods, as easily as chiefs. This challenge to the previous chiefly prerogatives "primed the potlatch inflationary cycle" as chiefs struggled to retain their prestige, and commoners sought to imitate it (Kobrinsky 1975:40–42; Ruyle 1973:605, 617). At the same time, external influences threatened to stop it entirely. "By the latter part of the nineteenth century the Kwakiutl were going to extreme lengths to hold together what they regarded as the most important part of their social structure." They might allow the means of claiming and validating rank to be individualized and democratized, but they were unwilling "to permit changes in their system of formal social rank, which it was the basic function of the potlatch to define" (Drucker and Heizer 1967:25–26). In a sense, then, the Kwakiutl turned the altered circumstances to their own ends. Instead of adopting the social values of their European employers and customers, they used their earnings to reinforce the most significant aspects of their social system (Codere 1950:8).

Along the coast this was rather exceptional. By 1900 the potlatch was disappearing or becoming "harmless" almost everywhere else. Christian conversion and the accelerating integration of Indians into the European economy and society were having their effect. Potlatching among the Haida and Tlingit, for example, disappeared almost without resistance. Among the Kwakiutl, however, it intensified and provoked a clash with government agents intent on bringing progress and civilization to their wards.

Canadian lay and mission authorities had long regarded the Kwakiutl as the most "incorrigible" of all British Columbia groups. British Columbia's superintendent of Indian affairs, I.W. Powell, wrote of their "almost intractable character." "The testimony of everyone I have met," wrote Anglican A.J. Hall (fig. 3.2) on his 1878 arrival at Fort Rupert, "is that they are a bad set"; they were, he later told Powell, "a most difficult lot to civilize" (*Sessional Papers* 1883, no. 5:xxiv; 1882:140; Hall 1878; *Sessional Papers* 1880, no. 4:112).

Kwakiutl "incorrigibility" persisted. They were behind few others in exploiting the economic opportunities offered by the European economy. They entered commercial fishing and cannery work, hired on as sealers, did hand logging and wage labor, took to the hop fields of Puget Sound; Kwakiutl women, besides working in the summer canneries, worked as washerwomen and prostitutes in cities and camps. According to Powell, the Kwakiutl were industrious, but scarcely progressive: They lagged behind other Indians in the adoption of Christianity, in sending their children to schools, and in personal and community hygiene. European-style frame houses, even when built, were only slept in, the rest of the day being spent in the traditional multifamily lodges "wanted for the gatherings which they hold on every possible occasion" (*Sessional Papers* 1910, no. 27:245).

"The energy which they display in collecting property is certainly remarkable," Agent George Blenkinsop (fig. 3.3) wrote in 1883, though he regretted that so much was squan-

3.2 The Reverend and Mrs. A. J. Hall. *PABC 89312*

3.3 George Blenkinsop. *PABC 2372*

3.4 (*left*) William Halliday. PABC 95771

3.5 (*above*) R. H. Pidcock. PABC 45456

dered. If only the evil influence of the potlatch could be done away with, Agent William Halliday (fig. 3.4) wrote over twenty years later, the Alert Bay Kwakiutl "would forge right ahead" (*Sessional Papers* 1883, No. 5:48; 1907–1908, No. 27:235).

While grasping economic opportunities, they resisted imported values. To a degree almost unknown elsewhere, the Kwakiutl "completely shut themselves off from the European" (Boas 1889:268). They "appear to desire to resist, inch by inch, so to speak," wrote Powell in 1883, "the inroads of civilization upon old savage custom." Blenkinsop, who had been among Northwest Coast people for decades, wrote the following year that "the Kwakewlths evince no desire for improvement; they see plainly that innovation will destroy their old, much-prized domestic institutions, and hence they cling to them with more pertinacity than ever." So they remained to Department of Indian Affairs officials: "antagonistic toward the white race," and "opposed to anything and everything advanced by the white man" (*Sessional Papers* 1884, No. 4:108; 1885, No. 3:102; 1904, No. 27:256; 1905, No. 27:236).

Agents remarked again and again on the importance in which the potlatch was held by the Kwakiutl, to their "determined opposition" to its end. "I was told by the older men," wrote Agent R.H. Pidcock (fig. 3.5) in 1895, "that they might as well die as give up the Custom" (*Sessional Papers* 1904, No. 27: 256; 1905, No. 27: 236). Missionaries, agents, and the presence of a proscriptive statute could not stamp out the custom.

The exceptional conservatism of the Kwakiutl is not easily explained. They were no more remote from settlement than

3.6 **Mask**. Fort Rupert. Wood, hair, down, feathers, canvas, leather, H 43.2 cm, W 35 cm. *Collected by George Hunt, 1897. 16/2375. AMNH 1897–43*

THIS *dadaḵalamł* OR "LAUGHING" MASK WAS WORN during the *tła'sala* ceremony (G. C. Webster: personal communication, 1990). The eyes glance upwards; the exaggerated flared nostrils almost overwhelm the bridge of the nose. Small upper teeth appear in the slightly opened mouth, which can open and shut. Because the lines surrounding that mouth resemble other depictions of fish gills in Kwakiutl art, Peter Macnair suggests that this mask may depict 'Yagis, the sea monster (personal communication, 1989). SAM

3.7 *Dzunuḵwa* **mask**. Fort Rupert. Wood, L 30 cm, W 24 cm. *Collected by George Hunt, 1897. 16/2376, AMNH 1897–43*

THIS MASK REPRESENTS A *dzunuḵwa*, THE CHILD-eating denizen of the forests. Its silvery gleam has been achieved through the addition of graphite to the black paint that covers the face. The circular hollows in the cheeks, the exaggerated pursed lips, and the heavy fur-covered brow are typical of the *dzunuḵwa* (see fig. 4.16). The hair springs energetically from the head, fanning out in all directions. The *dzunuḵwa* is known to be less than alert and certainly clumsy. She appears to be sleeping most of the time. When she enters the house for the Winter Ceremony, she must hold on to a rope stretched between the door and her seat. She makes a circuit around the fire, sometimes having to be guided to the right by an attendant who prevents her from mistakenly lumbering to the left (Boas 1897:479; 1966:182).

Although this mask may have functioned to portray the *dzunuḵwa* at the Winter Ceremonial, more likely it was intended to be used as a chief's mask, or *gikamł*, worn by a chief when he buys, sells, or gives away coppers. With praise of his great wealth and high stature the chief Yaḵał'anlis was called upon to speak during such a transaction:

Let me see you that I may look up to you, Chief! Now call your name Ts'ō'noqoa, you, Chief, who knows how to buy that great copper. You can not be equaled by anybody. You great mountain from which wealth is rolling down, wa, wa! That is what I say, my tribe!

Then Yā'qaLenlis arose and uttered the cry of Ts'ō'noqoa: "hō, hō, hō, hō!" and he acted as though he was lifting the heavy weight of the copper from the ground. (Boas 1897:350)

The chief's version of the *dzunuḵwa* mask is usually a bit smaller and more finely carved than the one used for the Winter Ceremony (Webster: personal communication, 1990). Although its specific use was not recorded by Hunt, this mask appears to belong to that category of masks used by chiefs when they displayed the wealth and power associated with a copper. JO

most central and north coast groups. What probably made the Kwakiutl potlatch exceptional was a combination of the hazy gradation in ranks, especially among neighboring groups brought into closer relations by post-contact developments, and the ability to obtain rank by marriage, even by multiple marriages. Among the Tsimshian, Tlingit, and Haida, marriages were unimportant as vehicles to alter rank and gain prerogatives; among the Kwakiutl and Bella Coola, marriages were the major vehicle for enhancing prestige. Only among the Kwakiutl were serial marriages not only permitted, but honored. This link between marriage and the potlatch became a vexing point for Indian administrators.

In 1885 the Canadian government of Sir John A. Macdonald had outlawed the potlatch, at the instigation of British Columbia Indian agents, missionaries, and a few Christianized Indians.[3] The reasons behind the ban were varied. First was a concern with health: two months of nightly winter feasting, with families moving from village to village in temporary housing, made sickness and exposure inevitable, especially among children. Second, the potlatch encouraged prostitution of native women as a source of potlatch funds. A third, certainly subordinate, reason was that schools could not flourish when the winter was given over to endless, shifting celebrations. A fourth, economic, reason was doubtless the most important: the system was based on the hoarding of goods, not for savings and investment, but for seemingly senseless waste. "It is not possible," wrote Indian Commissioner G. M. Sproat, "that Indians can acquire property, or become industrious with any good result, while under the influence of this mania." The potlatch was not only a waste of time but a waste of resources and incompatible with the government's goal of Indian economic and social progress (Sproat 1879a; DIA files; *Sessional Papers*; Dawson 1885). Outlawed at the same time was the "tamanawas dance," the *hamatsa* or cannibal ritual of the Kwakiutl Winter Ceremonies.

The government, in passing the legislation, acted on the best advice available to it, not just that of missionaries but men such as Sproat, ethnologist G. M. Dawson, and George Blenkinsop, formerly of the Hudson's Bay Company, whose judgments were based on close observation, long personal experience, and a desire to advance the condition of the Indians.

While their case was convincing to prime minister and Parliament, most British Columbia Indians were unpersuaded. The great majority wanted to continue their customary potlatch and could see no reason not to do so. They saw it as their

3.8 *Dzunukwa* **dagger**. Kingcome. Wood, iron, L 5.5 cm, W 9 cm. *Collected by George Hunt, 1901. 16/8561, AMNH 1901–32*

THIS SHARP-EDGED, POINTED BLADE IS SURMOUNTED by the carved head and torso of a *dzunukwa*, her arms curved around as if to rest her hands upon her stomach. The dark skin shines from graphite added to the black paint, and her features are distinguished by contrasting areas completely devoid of color. The grayish hair extends down the entire length of the knife's handle.

Hunt records that the iron used to make the blade was originally bought by an individual known as Ḵ'wamxalagalis, for the price of one slave. This note may simply have been included to inform Boas that the blade dates back to a time when iron was that valuable (acc. 1901–32, AMNH).

The dagger might have functioned at the outset of the *tseka* ceremonies as an implement used to cut cedar bark, the fiber identified with this portion of the potlatch. A woman stood at the center of a large circular coil of cedar bark held by four male attendants. Another man would then approach, hiding a dagger such as this one beneath his forearm. When revealed, it would be used to cut the huge ring, which was then unraveled into small strips and distributed to everyone in the ceremonial house (Elsie Williams: personal communication, 1990).

Similar daggers carved with the images of ravens, bears, or even loons are known and are used to cut cedar bark as well as for the feigned decapitation and disembowelment of *tuxw'id* dancers (see figs. 1.35, 1.39, 1.40, 2.29). These instruments have also been brandished as weapons in the context of the Warrior dance (Adam Dick: personal communication, 1990). JO "oldest and best" festival, one that sustained their property, rank, and marriage arrangements. It was "an innocent pastime," their winter amusement, that worked for the benefit of the old and the destitute. Above all, they appealed to fairness. The law was simply unjust: "We believe it is our right just as much as it is the right of our white brethren to make presents to one another." Although they wished to live within the law, they were prepared to ignore this one and, if necessary, to defy it (DIA files; *Sessional Papers*).

Everywhere on the coast, reports of Indian opinion was the same: the Vancouver Island Nuu-chah-nulth would have to be educated before they could see its folly; the Cowichan said the government was wrong in preventing it; and the Kwakiutl had doubts about its being done away with. The first showdown between Indian opinion and government enforcement occurred among the Cowichan Salish. Chief Lohah (or Lohar) was intent upon repaying his debts and those of his son who had just died.

Lohah's determination to do his duty threw Agent William H. Lomas into something of a panic. With up to 300 Indians gathered to participate in Lohah's potlatch and with no police force available, Lomas appealed to Superintendent Powell for help. Powell, arriving on the spot, quickly realized that enforcement of the law against several hundred defiant Indians would be futile. He capitulated. So long as Lohah was merely repaying debts, it was not really a potlatch (Lomas 1885; Powell 1885). In its first test, the law collapsed.

It continued to be unenforced. All along the coast Indian resistance and government weakness were evident. The Nuu-chah-nulth agent admitted he could not enforce the law; the Northwest agent felt it was almost useless to abolish the custom by law; the Kwawkewelth agent reported defiance. The Fort Ruperts told Agent Pidcock that they would hear nothing he had to say on the subject, and he reported that potlatches were being openly prepared at Alert Bay and Village Island (Pidcock 1886; 1887). Anthropologist Franz Boas described the situation: the law could not be enforced without causing discontent, but with Indian settlements so numerous and agencies so large, enforcement was beyond the government's ability. "There is nobody to prevent the Indians doing whatsoever they like." Boas illustrated his point with the situation of a Hope Island Kwakiutl to whom Pidcock had given a uniform and flag and whom he appointed constable with a special duty to prevent dances and feasts. "Since that time he dances in his uniform and with the flag" (Boas 1888a:636; 1888b:206).

In 1889, however, Pidcock successfully arrested—at night

and after the event—a potlatcher, He'masak of Village Island. The case went for trial in Victoria before Chief Justice Sir Matthew Begbie. Throwing the case out of court on a technicality, Sir Matthew went on to cast doubt on the law itself. The statute did not define "potlatch"; if Parliament wanted to create a new offence, previously unknown in law, then it should be defined (Moffat 1889; Williams 1977:102–103, 118). Begbie's obiter dicta was shattering: the law was "a dead letter" (Pidcock 1893).

Ottawa decided to leave things alone. This was Powell's advice and it was even more the advice of his successor as superintendent in Victoria, A.W. Vowell. Along with most agents, Vowell judged the law as unnecessary, even unjust, and its enforcement unwise.

In all this, the Indians had strong advantages. They were more numerous in most areas of the coast than European settlers, and most white British Columbians prized the peacefulness of the Indians and wanted no provocations. Neither did the provincial government. They would accept conflict over real issues, such as land and resource use, but not something which they thought of largely as a harmless, even picturesque, diversion. This was demonstrated by an 1897 resolution in the provincial legislature that asked the federal government to drop the potlatch law (*Colonist* 1897; *News Advertiser* 1897).

Ottawa did not repeal, but it did accept Vowell's policy of moral suasion and restraint and his counsel of leaving the problem to time, not the police. Although Parliament later amended the law to fit Begbie's objections, it did so much more to control the Prairie Sun Dance, with its "giving-aways" and corporal self-mutilation, than the coastal potlatch and *hamatsa* initiations. The federal government allowed Vowell to follow his own policy: to leave things alone, in the belief that education, missionaries, and the passing of time would bring an end to the potlatch.[4] By 1900 Vowell's policy of suasion, not coercion, his "sunny ways," seemed to be working. The great exception to this remained the Kwakiutl.

Most British Columbia agents were content with Vowell's policy of discretion, but, amid the blossoming Kwakiutl potlatch system, the men posted to the Kwawkewlth Agency were as exceptional as their wards. Blenkinsop had intended to enforce the law within the measure of his ability; Pidcock had enforced it against He'masak and complained about the "dead letter" produced by Justice Begbie. G.W. DeBeck, Kwawkewlth agent from 1902 to 1906, became so enraged by the flagrant transgressions against the law that he tried stern action to stamp out the evil (fig. 3.11).

A major concern to Kwakiutl agents was the potlatch's con-

3.9 **Ladle**. Quatsino. Wood, L 89.5 cm, W 22.5 cm. *Collected by H.R. Bishop, 1869. 16/706, AMNH 1869–90–94*

THE OPENWORK HANDLE OF THIS LADLE IS CARVED in the form of a composite being with the head of a bird. In its sharp beak it grasps the short stem of the spoon's bowl. A necklike extension is composed of two long, linear elements that recall the "arms" seen in the other ladle in the exhibition (fig. 1.12). At the end of the handle is a round face, its mouth wide open. A checkerboard pattern of carved parallel lines decorates the underside of the bowl. The ladle appears quite clean and may never have been used. JO

3.10 **Mask**. Fort Rupert. Wood, paint, feathers, cordage, H 31 cm, W 22 cm. *Collected by George Hunt, 1897. 16.2363, AMNH 1897–43*

T HIS BLACK MASK WITH FEATHERS COVERING THE top of the head was identified by Hunt as that of a war dancer, *hawinalał*. This performance is said to have begun with the great warrior Winaxwinagam, of the numaym Ma'amtagila, who always desired to make war. His village, however, wanted peace and attempted to restrain their great warrior with ropes. He broke through these bonds easily, ran out of the house, and, with his *sisiyutł* knife killed all those who crossed his path. The villagers finally captured him and this time, rather than simply binding him, cut holes in his thighs and through his back and threaded rope through them. With these ropes they strung him over the rafters of the house and sang songs, hoping to appease his spirit. Still holding his knife, Winaxwinagam cut his own head as he could not reach anybody else. His wounds gave him pleasure and eventually he calmed down. After this, whenever he returned from war he requested that the people of the village treat him in this same manner (Boas 1897:495).

The *hawinalał* performance closely follows the experiences of Winaxwinagam. A man with this privilege would ask his fellow villagers to pull ropes through his back and hang him from the roof. They also tied onto his back a *sisiyutł* image to which they attached ropes. Then they stretched heavy ropes from the beach to the roof of the house and used these to raise and lower the performer (Boas 1897:496). In his detailed description of this ceremony, Boas does not mention the use of any masks. SAM

3.11 George DeBeck and his wife. *PABC 96512*

3.12 Alert Bay potlatch showing frontlets, bracelets, and basins to be distributed. *Photo by William Halliday.* RBCM 10628

3.13 **Grizzly bear dish**. New Vancouver. Wood, L 63.3 cm, H 28.5 cm. *Collected by George Hunt, 1901. 16/8408, AMNH 1901–32*

Hunt identified this animal as a grizzly bear (Boas 1909:519), and its wide snout and pointed teeth support this designation. At the back of the dish is a *dzunukwa* figure with typical hollow cheeks and eyes, large ears, and completely circular mouth, shaped to pronounce the penetrat-ing cry "ū, hū, ū, ū" for which this being is so well known (Boas 1897:372). Boas has illustrated a carved dish from Fort Rupert, now in Berlin, which includes an identical figure similarly positioned (Boas 1897: Plate 20). Its circular mouth is also contiguous with the rim of a bowl. Boas calls the figure on the Berlin dish a *dzunukwa*, reinforcing the identification of this figure (ibid.:390).

This configuration is wonderfully conceived but is carved in a somewhat crude and blocky manner. Peter Macnair has suggested that this rough execution may indicate that the composition was copied in part from an older example (personal communication, 1989). JO

nection to sexual relationships. The potlatch's role in native prostitution had been cited at the time of the law's passage. The exodus of women to cities and camps remained a complaint in the following years. Pidcock went so far as to order a group of Kwakiutl women bound for Victoria off the *Sardonyx* in 1889. Rev. Hall blamed Kwakiutl moral retrogression on "the wholesale migration of their young women to southern towns to procure by illicit [intercourse?] property which enables their male [relatives?] to carry on the 'Potlatch' " (Hall 1889).[5] Vowell minimized the problem. There were, he reported, now few Indian women living an immoral life in the province's towns and cities, and they were "less in number as a rule than that of their white sisters."[6] It was only a matter of time, Vowell thought, before Native women would, through example and teaching, be induced to abandon such practices (Vowell 1891). Pidcock, however, left no doubt that the potlatch had a share in encouraging prostitution, but he introduced another factor, Kwakiutl marriage practices, that would overshadow prostitution as a concern of Kwawkewlth agents.

The Kwakiutl marriage law, "which allows parents or guardians to compel a woman to leave her husband unless he can furnish money or its equivalent, and then forcing the woman to take another husband as a means of raising money to carry on the 'Potlach'," shared a blame in what was seen as the immorality of Kwakiutl women (Pidcock n.d.). Kwakiutl marriage practices became the great concern of Pidcock's successors. The Kwakiutl marriage system was anathema to agents DeBeck and Halliday. If marriages were regularized, they thought, the potlatch would die a natural death.

The marriage issue is complicated (see Suttles, this volume). Boas had already written that "marriage among the Kwakiutl must be considered a purchase," but the object bought was not only the woman but the right of membership in her clan for future children of the couple (Boas 1897:358). Kwakiutl practice was for alliances to be arranged by parents or families, often without the knowledge and usually without the consent of bride or groom. The groom's family made a payment to the bride's, but repayment was required. Indeed, the preponderance of giving was by the bride's side, with the bride price relatively unimportant, only "an opening of negotiation" (Goldman 1975:77).

What bothered both agents was not so much bride price, but that once repayment was made, the marriage was at an end. A couple, wrote Halliday, do not live together long. The man must either buy his wife again, or she is taken and sold to someone else. The agents cited examples. Halliday wrote of a

3.14 *Xwixwi* **mask**. Gilford Island. Wood, feathers, H 25 cm, L 63 cm, W 54 cm. *Collected by George Hunt, 1901. 16/8382, AMNH 1901–15*

BOAS (1897:497) WROTE THAT THE *xwixwi* WAS WORN by a dancer who carried rattles of strung shells and that the dance was believed to "shake the ground and to be a certain means of bringing back the hā'matsa who is being initiated" (Boas 1897:497). A family history recorded by George Hunt gives an account of *xwixwi*, describing how this privilege came to the Kwakiutl through marriage from the Coast Salish Comox (Boas 1921:891–938).

This family history begins with Ḵumugwe', the chief of the numaym Ma'amtagi'la who lived at Crooked-Beach. Ḵumugwe' announced to his tribe that he wished to marry the princess of Chief Down-Dancer of the Comox. His tribe was pleased by this news and soon they traveled to Comox to woo the princess. When they arrived at the beach at Puntlatch, they immediately made the marriage payment. They were told to wait in the canoes while the princess gathered her possessions. When they heard the ancestors of the Comox beating on the front boards of the house of Down-Dancer, all the men of Comox cried "Hum!" and shook their shell rattles to announce the coming of the princess, who was led by four men wearing *xwixwi* masks. As she was entering Ḵumugwe's canoe she sang her sacred songs (Boas 1921:891–92).

Down-Dancer invited Ḵumugwe' and his numaym into his house, and all the while the shell rattles did not stop. When they entered the house the rattles' sounds were coming from behind the screen. Ḵumugwe' and his wife sat at the back of the house in front of the screen while Down-Dancer requested that the men of Comox pacify *xwixwi* so Ḵumugwe' could see and take this treasure home with his new wife.

After he had spoken, the song leader of the ancestors of Comox . . . arose and shouted, "Wooo!" Then the ancestors of Comox shouted "Wooo!" while they were beating time on boxes which were turned upside down. Then four naked dancers came out, their bodies painted with ochre and wearing *xwexwe* masks on their faces. Four songs were sung for them; and when the last song was ended, then the four men dancers walked with quick steps and all of the men of Comox beat time quickly. Then the speaker of Down-Dancer . . . arose and spoke; and he said, "Look at this Chief Down-Dancer! and bring something to drive the supernatural ones into their room." Thus he said. Then they cut goat-skins into strips and put them down and after they all had been put down, . . . [the Speaker] shouted "Wooo!" while they were beating time fast. They shouted "Wooo!" four times and the four *xwexwe* dancers went back behind the curtain (Boas 1921:893–94).

Then Down-Dancer gave his new son-in-law names and treasure. The couple stayed with him for four days before they returned to Crooked-Beach where Ḵumugwe' shared his new wealth with his tribe (Boas 1921:894). SAM

woman who came to Alert Bay for some winter shopping; on her return to her home village, she learned "that she had been disposed of during her absence to another man." He also cited the case of two young men, kept poor by the avarice of their wives' families who, every time they knew that the husband had collected a few dollars, called upon him immediately to pay it over (Halliday 1907b).

In these charges, there was truth. Once the bride price had been repaid to the groom's side, Kwakiutl custom held that the obligations had been fulfilled and the marriage was ended. If a wife remained with her husband, she stayed "for nothing"—a condition considered undignified. A new contract could be made in the same way as the first, though the payments were generally less. As often, the woman was married to another. After four marriages her rank was established, and she should then stay with her husband, though he was under no obligation to keep her (Boas 1966:54–55).

Not only did the treatment of women seem outrageous to whites and even to many Indians, but it undid the advancement of young men. A boy trained at the industrial school had, willingly or not, to enter the system to secure a wife. One lad told Halliday that he "might as well be a eunuch as keep out of the potlatch" (Halliday 1907a). Young men complained that wives left them to get new husbands, usually old men who had gained influence by potlatching (DeBeck 1902; Halliday 1906).

The goods made in repayment to the groom were given away at the Winter Dances where the newly acquired privileges were celebrated by display and validation. This additional linkage of marriage and the potlatch was yet another source of agent concern. One of the worst features of the marriage contract, DeBeck wrote, was that "it acts as a feeder to the Potlatch." Feasts, potlatches, and marriages "seem to be all blended & interwoven together, with their marriage law as the main spring" (DeBeck 1902; Halliday 1906).

Kwakiutl marriage did have most of the characteristics that bothered the agents, though it made its own sense. The important feature was the status of the child. Confident that their family crests and privileges were their most important possessions, the Kwakiutl wished to have their descendants firmly established within that proud lineage. Marriage, as T. F. McIlwraith phrased it for the Bella Coolas, was primarily a matter "of the ancestral eligibility of the contracting parties" (McIlwraith 1948:373–74). Marriage annulment by repurchase or "buying out" of the wife by her family represented an honor to the wife and her children. It "made her heavy." A woman was esteemed among the Kwakiutl by being married several times.

3.15a **Nose ornament**. Turnour Island. Abalone shell, L 6.5 cm. *Collected by George Hunt, 1902. 16/9002a, AMNH 1902–46*

3.15b **Nose ornament**. Fort Rupert. Abalone shell, L 6 cm. *Collected by Franz Boas, 1900. 16/8078b, AMNH 1900–73*

ABALONE ORNAMENTS LIKE THESE WERE USUALLY worn by women. Boas records that they would be worn particularly at the time the father-in-law repays his daughter's husband the bride price. At this time, abalone in general, not just in the form of nose ornaments, functions as one of the emblems of prestige that are transferred:

She wears a blanket set with abalone shells. A large abalone shell is fastened to her nose by strings which pass over her ears, as the shell is too heavy to be worn suspended from the septum. For the same reason her earrings are worn suspended from the hair. She performs a dance, after which her ornaments are given to her husband (Boas 1897:422).

Although Boas and Hunt did not collect specific information, these ornaments would have been worn by women and may have been transferred as part of a bride price. Bill Holm says that fig. 3.15b is not Kwakiutl in style. The killer whale depicted on this ornament relates stylistically to those found further north and was probably "acquired from the North from either marriage or trade" (Holm, object file, Dept. of Anthropology, AMNH). SAM

3.16 *Hamatsa* **headrings**. *Collected by George Hunt*. Left: Fort Rupert; red cedar bark, fabric, H 7 cm; *1897; 16/2352, AMNH 1897–43*. Right: Village Island; cedar bark, cloth, H 6.5 cm; *1899; 16/4754, AMNH 1899–50*

ALL THE KNOTS, BRAIDS, AND FLAPS WORKED INTO these (and other) *hamatsa* headrings refer to events in the acquisition of the prerogative. Hunt collected the headring on the right in the same location he acquired a head- and neckring set (fig. 2.21). Although he was unable to explain the individual features of this piece, he did note that it represented the "third ring of Hamatsa" (acc. 1899–50, AMNH). He provides even less information on the other headring.

Boas does analyze similar headrings (1897:454–60). He explains there that no two headrings ever have the same significance, regardless of how similar they may be. Boas illustrates some headrings (1897: figs. 83 to 91), and describes their meaning. SAM

Thus a woman married four times (four was an honored Kwakiutl number), whether to the same man or different men, and, freed by repayment, bore the title of *u'ma* and was only then permitted to wear a painted hat and abalone earrings (Curtis 1915:131). The rearing of children presented no problem; they were placed either within the new marriage or taken by grandparents, aunts, or uncles.

While the marriage system had coherence, it clashed with European values, and it certainly acted, as DeBeck and Halliday well understood, as a "feeder" to the potlatch. Prompted by these and other concerns, DeBeck, appointed agent in 1902, determined to enforce the law even against Vowell's wishes. He broke up an Alert Bay potlatch and then ordered one in Fort Rupert to cease, arresting several when it did not.[7] Vowell did not support these breaches of his policy of noninterference, and DeBeck, after protesting to Ottawa (where he got little sympathy), resigned. After this aberration, the policy of non-enforcement continued.

Also at issue in the Kwawkewlth Agency was ceremonial cannibalism. It too, as a ban on "tamanawas dances," had been outlawed in the original 1884 legislation, then thrown out as undefined, even "unknown here," by Justice Begbie. The 1895 amendment clarified the wording to make illegal "a celebration of which the wounding or mutilation of the dead or living body of any human being or animal forms a part or is a feature." Vowell's policy of tolerant discretion had never extended to ceremonial dog-eating as practiced among the Tsimshian-speaking peoples of the northern coast or to ritual cannibalism among the central coast Bella Coola, Haisla, Heiltsuk, and Kwakiutl.

Long before 1895, even before the 1884 amendment, missionaries and agents had sought to end the practices. Blenkinsop managed to control biting of witnesses among the Kwakiutl by threatening prosecution for assault, at least where his threats had force in the sprawling Kwawkewlth Agency (*Sessional Papers* 1883, No. 5: 66). Pidcock was able to make the Kwakiutl omit the worst features of the *hamatsa* wherever he was likely to be present, "but often they perform the dance at some distant Village where they feel secure from observation" (Pidcock 1894). In 1900, however, certain that he had evidence and witnesses that could bring a conviction, he prosecuted George Hunt for mutilating a dead human body.

Hunt was the son of a Hudson's Bay Company man and of his Tlingit wife (see Jacknis, this volume). He had been raised virtually as a Kwakiutl and married among the people. He worked for S.A. Spencer, the cannery owner at Alert Bay, who

3.17 **Mask**. Knight Inlet. Wood, cedar bark, copper, H 68.6 cm, W 67.6 cm. *Collected by George Hunt, 1904. 16/9586, AMNH 1904–41*

ON JANUARY 22ND, 1904, HUNT WROTE BOAS FROM Fort Rupert, describing his imminent plans to go up to Knight Inlet to find a particular type of mask Boas had requested: "Now I am trying to get a grizzly Bear mask and a Hoxhokw Hemsewe from here But we Have none here and now I have to go to the ts!awadaenox tribe to get some of the masks that you wanted" (Acc. file, Dept. of Anthropology, AMNH). Later in the year, this mask arrived at the museum with the attribution "Hoxhokw Hemsewe" and nothing more (acc. 1904–41, AMNH).

Literally translated, the term *huxwhukw hamsiwe'* means forehead mask of the *huxwhukw*, the fabulous cannibal bird larger than a man (Webster: personal communication, 1990). The identification of a forehead mask is suspicious, as this mask is not worn tied around the forehead. Rather, it has a structure in the back made from bark and cord that would permit the mask to sit on the head like a helmet and cover the face. Later, Boas amends the attribution by describing the three birds on the mask as representing a *huxwhukw* in the central position, surrounded by ravens on either side (object file, Dept. of Anthropology, AMNH). The Kwakiutl believed the *huxwhukw* could crack open human skulls with his powerful beak in order to eat the brains as well as the eyeballs. Both the ravens and the *huxwhukw* live with Baxwbakwalanuxwsiwe', the Cannibal-of-the-North-End-of-the-World; during *hamatsa* initiations, masks depicting these birds appear (see figs. 2.27, 2.28). We do not know what the central face depicts. Although the birds are all associates of Baxwbakwalanuxwsiwe', he never appears on masks, and thus this image could not represent him.

The mask itself was most likely used in association with a *hamatsa* performance. It would have made a dramatic appearance, for all three bird beaks are rigged to open and close at the same time that the lower jaw of the central image drops down, revealing a large sheet of copper. Gloria Cranmer Webster (personal communication, 1990) suggests that the appearance of several of Baxwbakwalanuxwsiwe's attendants on one mask indicates a rare and valuable prerogative. SAM

3.18 Alert Bay potlatch, c. 1910, with boxes of pilot biscuits and bags of flour to be given away. *RBCM 1889*

3.19 Alert Bay flour potlatch. *Photo by William Halliday.* *RBCM 10068*

3.20 Alert Bay potlatch identified as Bob Harris's, before 1914. *RBCM 1887*

had married his sister, Annie. Fluent in both Kwakwala and English, and literate in the latter, he often served as an interpreter and translator for officials, including Powell and Rev. Hall. In 1888 he met Franz Boas in Victoria, and the young anthropologist began employing him as an assistant, a relationship that became a collaboration of great significance to them both.

In March 1900 Agent Pidcock instituted proceedings against Hunt for assisting in the mutilation of the body of an old woman dead for several years.[8] The offense had occurred in mid-February at Kalugwis. "There is little doubt from the evidence," Pidcock reported, "that a dead human body was taken into a house and there mutilated in a horrible manner." Hunt admitted that he had taken part in the ceremony, but maintained that he was there to obtain information for Pidcock to act upon, a story which Pidcock thought nonsense. Hunt's actions then and later did not sustain the excuse, since he had said nothing about the matter until charged (Pidcock 1900). The jury trial took place in Vancouver County Court on April 17 and 18, with Chief Justice Angus John McColl presiding.

Witnesses for the prosecution claimed that the *hamatsa* had come in with a dead body covered with evergreens, and that Hunt had complied with a request to "do the carving." Hunt had, they claimed, cut up the body and distributed the portions to the participants (*Province* 1900). Hunt's lawyer, W.J. Bowser, a leading Vancouver barrister (and later attorney general and premier), told the jury that the allegations against Hunt were the result of a vindictive trap set by an enemy. Hunt, while acting as a special constable for Agent Pidcock, had come into rivalry with another constable, who had instigated the prosecution, and every Crown witness excepting one was a relative.[9] (Privately Hunt said that he was a victim of "the missionary people"; Hunt 1900). Hunt had attended the dance purely out of curiosity; he was an authority on tribal customs and had furnished information to scientists on questions of this kind. Hunt, in his testimony, said that he had gone as a mere spectator and, even when called upon, had done no more than observe.

After the body had been brought in and placed in the centre of the room, he was called by name to come and see it. He did so, and when he saw what it was and was turning away the Hamatsas, and bear and dog dancers snatched the body and ate, or pretended to eat it.

The jury doubted the Crown's version; after about twenty minutes' deliberation, foreman George Fletcher brought back a verdict of not guilty (*Province* 1900).

3.21 "Caricature" of a speaker. Quatsino. Wood, L 228.5 cm. *Collected by George Hunt, 1900. 16/8272, AMNH 1900–73*

THIS CARVING OF A MAN WITH A DISTORTED FACE was meant to ridicule a nobleman from a visiting tribe by representing a caricature of his speaker (Boas 1909: pl. 46). Usually speakers are depicted standing tall, with an upraised arm gesturing to accentuate a point (see fig. 2.14). Here the speaker almost leans on his speaker's staff (see fig. 2.16), suggesting that he is not particularly articulate. The speaker's face, almost idiotic in appearance, does not communicate the dignity and pride usually associated with this prestigious office. Although its exaggerated nose resembles the equally large nose of the *nuḷamaḷ* dancer (see fig. 2.11), Boas does not connect this figure with that important prerogative. Instead, he identifies it as one of many ways a host chief could express his rivalry with his guests. SAM

3.22 Kingcome, c. 1900. *Photo by C.F. Newcombe.* RBCM PN 2424

Although the mutilation section of the statute proved ineffective in its only court test, it remained, like the potlatch ban, a proscription and a deterrent. Pidcock, though disappointed at having again lost a case, thought that the prosecution had had a good effect (Pidcock 1901). According to Pidcock's successor, Hunt avoided being present "at any more of these heathen feasts" (Halliday 1935: 10).[10]

By this time the actual use of corpses was passing, with artificial ones being constructed of fish, venison, or even stiff dough. The change among the Kwakiutl may have been caused in part by the death of several *hamatsa*, presumed to have been caused by eating the flesh of a person who had died of poisoning or whose corpse had been deliberately poisoned by people opposed to such "old-fashioned" ways (Ford 1941:114; Halliday 1935:10; Curtis, 1915 10:241–42). The substitution may also have been a result of the Hunt prosecution. Chiefs, seeing the case as a threat, reportedly met in council and decided that henceforth only dummies would be used in the *hamatsa* performances (Drucker and Heizer 1967:87).

By 1913 Vowell's policy of tolerant discretion about the potlatch was ending. He had retired in 1910 and was not replaced. In Alert Bay, the agent was William Halliday who disliked the marriage and potlatch systems, but who would take no action unless told to. More significant, in Ottawa a new Superintendent General of Indian Affairs had come to office, Duncan Campbell Scott.

Scott is best known as a poet, described by Rupert Brooke as "the only poet in Canada" (Keynes 1968:487). Professionally, however, he was a career Indian Affairs official who rose on his merits to the top. Scott, like others in the government and in the country, believed that the future of the Indian was civilization and integration into Canadian society. He doubled appropriations for Indian health and education and, most important here, moved with impatience against practices which, in Canada's fifth decade, still hindered the integration and assimilation of Indians into the Canadian mainstream. In British Columbia, this meant the wasteful potlatch still practiced by the "incorrigible" Kwakiutl.

Scott instructed Halliday to enforce the law, and Halliday did, arresting Johnny Bagwany and Ned Harris when they insisted on holding a potlatch against Halliday's warning. Bagwany was frank: he was, he said, willing to make himself a martyr since he did not consider that the law had any business interfering with their customs. The two Kwakiutl pleaded guilty; with the Vancouver jury recommending mercy, they

3.23 Charlie Nowell displaying potlatch bracelets at Alert Bay.
RBCM PN 1071

3.24 Alert Bay potlatch identified as Bob Harris's, before 1914.
Photo by J. Welsh. RBCM 2307–b

received only a suspended sentence (Halliday 1913a; Halliday 1913b; *Colonist* 1914). Another prosecution, against Cessaholis of Kingcome Inlet, ended similarly, and a third, against Kishwagila of Fort Rupert, was dismissed by a grand jury (*Province* 1915; *Vancouver World* 1915; *Nanaimo Free Press* 1915; Halliday 1915).

Scott and Halliday had wanted conviction and penalties. Instead they got three suspended sentences and an outright dismissal. All four offenders remained at liberty, and one of the judges told Halliday that no crime had been committed even if there was a statute and that he doubted if any B.C. judge would give more than a suspended sentence. After these setbacks, Scott and Halliday quit the campaign.

Five years later, they decided to try again, this time after changing the rules of the game. Scott succeeded in having Parliament amend the act, changing the offense from criminal to summary, a simple but not a minor change. Now, the agent, as justice of the peace, could try a case, convict, and sentence. Convictions were now very likely and penalties even more so. This change gave Scott and Halliday a very strong weapon.

So in the winter of 1918–19 Halliday, under instructions from Scott, again enforced the law. This time it was against Likiosa (Johnnie Seaweed) and Kwosteetsas (Japanese Charlie). Tried before Justice of the Peace William Halliday, they were convicted and sentenced to two months at Oakalla Prison Farm, the first Indians sentenced to penal servitude under the 1885 potlatch law. They appealed, but before the case came up another four charges were laid in Alert Bay. This trial, in March 1919, was again heard by Justice of the Peace Halliday. Appearing for the defence was Vancouver lawyer Frank Lyons. The department countered with the distinguished J.H. Senkler, K.C. Quickly realizing he could not win a clear case before the agent acting as judge, Lyons negotiated an agreement signed by the four defendants, the two appellants, and seventy-three others who were in the courtroom. All agreed that they would potlatch no more but would be free to seek repeal of the law. Senkler and Halliday accepted the proposal. The guilty were given suspended sentences. To Halliday it was "a great moral victory" that would stamp out the potlatch evil in his agency (Halliday 1919).

This was not quite how the Kwakiutl saw it. They took the agreement to mean that the government would investigate the law and, finding it unjust, would change it. They had long been asking for "a good straight man to come and see all the Indians so that you may know exactly what the potlatch is" (Kwawkewlth Agency Indians, 1918). This interpretation, that

3.25 Fort Rupert potlatch, 1898. *Photo by H.I. Smith.* AMNH 42992

there would be an inquiry, lawyers Lyons and Senkler agreed, was an unwritten condition behind the agreement. For the Kwakiutl, the 1919 agreement was their victory too. They were confident that the law was a mistake and that any inquiry would see its injustice.

The promised inquiry, stonewalled by Scott, fell by the wayside. So did the Kwakiutl's promise. But Halliday still had his law, his instructions, and now, for the first time, a Royal Canadian Mounted Police detachment posted at Alert Bay.

In January 1920 RCMP Sgt. Donald Angerman laid eight charges. All were sentenced to two months in Oakalla, the first to actually serve sentences under the law. The next winter came another conviction and imprisonment, and in the winter of 1921–22, five more convictions and imprisonments. Then came the biggest case of all, the result of Dan Cranmer's Village Island potlatch, the largest ever recorded on the central coast.

In February 1922, Angerman summoned thirty-four before Halliday's bench. The first witnesses quickly established the strength of his case (built on two informants who had been there). The defense lawyer was prepared. Changing all pleas to guilty, he asked the leniency of the court based on an agreement, signed by all defendants and fifty others, to potlatch no more. Sgt. Angerman refused to accept this virtual duplication of the 1919 Lyons agreement. That, he said, had been ignored. He wanted tangible evidence of good faith: all Kwakiutl should voluntarily surrender all their potlatch property.[11] Halliday adjourned court for a month, pending acceptance of Angerman's terms. Almost all the people from Cape Mudge, Village Island, and Alert Bay accepted in return for suspended sentences. But those from Fort Rupert and some others did not and were given two-month terms in Oakalla.

Angerman then brought cases against seventeen more participants at Cranmer's potlatch. Twelve were convicted and received sentences. In all twenty-two went to Oakalla in April 1922. Halliday thought that the Kwakiutl potlatch was now dead. Occasional small affairs might occur, but there was "absolutely no danger of any great potlatches taking place again" (Halliday 1922).

The first Indian reaction against the application of the law was a flood of petitions. The Natives defended the potlatch in much the same terms as they had justified it in the 1880s and 1890s. It was an old, good, and harmless tradition, helpful to the old and indigent; it was the chief source of pleasure and amusement; and the law was mistaken and unjust. When petitions failed to have an effect, the Kwakiutl retained a lawyer to lobby Scott and Parliament, attempted to turn the Allied Tribes

of British Columbia to their view, and met with their member of Parliament. All attempts failed.

Indian protests made no impact because they no longer carried any threat. With the Native population now reduced to a minuscule proportion of the white, with communications and transportation transformed, with a federal police force established on the coast, the Department of Indian Affairs policy could be enforced without concern. And yet, as the following years were to show, the Kwakiutl were not supine victims of Scott, nor of Parliament, courts, agents, and mounted police. When their supplications secured neither a modification of the law nor even an investigation, the Kwakiutl gave up on the system. They fell back upon their own resourcefulness; they found ways around the law.

The first dodge was secret and underground potlatches. When Jimmy Sewid married Flora Alfred at Alert Bay in 1927, his grandfather "gave a big potlatch," but "he just went around to the houses and gave money and other things to the people to honor me," while Sewid's mother called the ladies together in the Alfred home and gave them dishes, pails, and other utensils (Spradley 1969:71). Potlatches could be disguised as Christmas dinners and the gift-giving as holiday presents. There were variations on the strategy. Second, "real old-time potlatches" continued at inaccessible locations, notably Kingcome Inlet. The Gilford Islanders moved there to winter in the 1920s largely to be free for potlatching. Their village was two miles up a shallow, snag-infested river that froze over in winter. It was so situated that no one could approach, day or night, without being seen. "There in their frosty isolation they potlatched as much as they pleased" (Drucker and Heizer 1967:32). Less secure villages were second bests: Village Island, Fort Rupert, even Cape Mudge.

A third stratagem, the "disjointed potlatch," was invented in 1931. The law was so written that the giving away had to be part of a festival, dance, or ceremony. The Kwakiutl simply split the thing in half, having their dances on one occasion and then giving away later, making it very difficult to prove that the one was part of the other. Halliday saw a dance at Fort Rupert in 1932 but had no evidence that even a five-cent piece had been given away. The year before he observed 1500 sacks of flour delivered at Village Island. The man just said, "Here is some flour to help you over the hard winter." In 1933 Charlie Nowell landed 900 sacks at Fort Rupert, telling the police that it was nothing more than "an act of Christian charity for the benefit of the people who were hard up" (Halliday 1932; 1931; Newnham 1933). Those strategies defeated all efforts at secur-

3.26 A flour potlatch, Alert Bay. *Photograph by Halliday(?)* RBCM
10083

3.27 **Oil dish**. Quatsino. Wood, L 20.1 cm, W 15.4 cm. *Collected by George Hunt, 1900. 16/8170, AMNH 1900–73*

T HIS OIL DISH IS CARVED AS A SMALL ROUND FORM embellished only by a carved border that follows the sweeping line of the rim. Owned by a chief's wife, it was used as a container for eulachon oil in which dried fish such as halibut and salmon were dipped (Boas 1909:422). Some residue of this oil left a glossy patina on the wooden surface of the bowl.

Eulachon are small fish with high fat content that spawn in mainland rivers in early spring. Large numbers are rendered for their valuable oil, which is still prepared among the Kwakiutl today and enjoyed with fish, potatoes, and other foods (Macnair 1971). JO

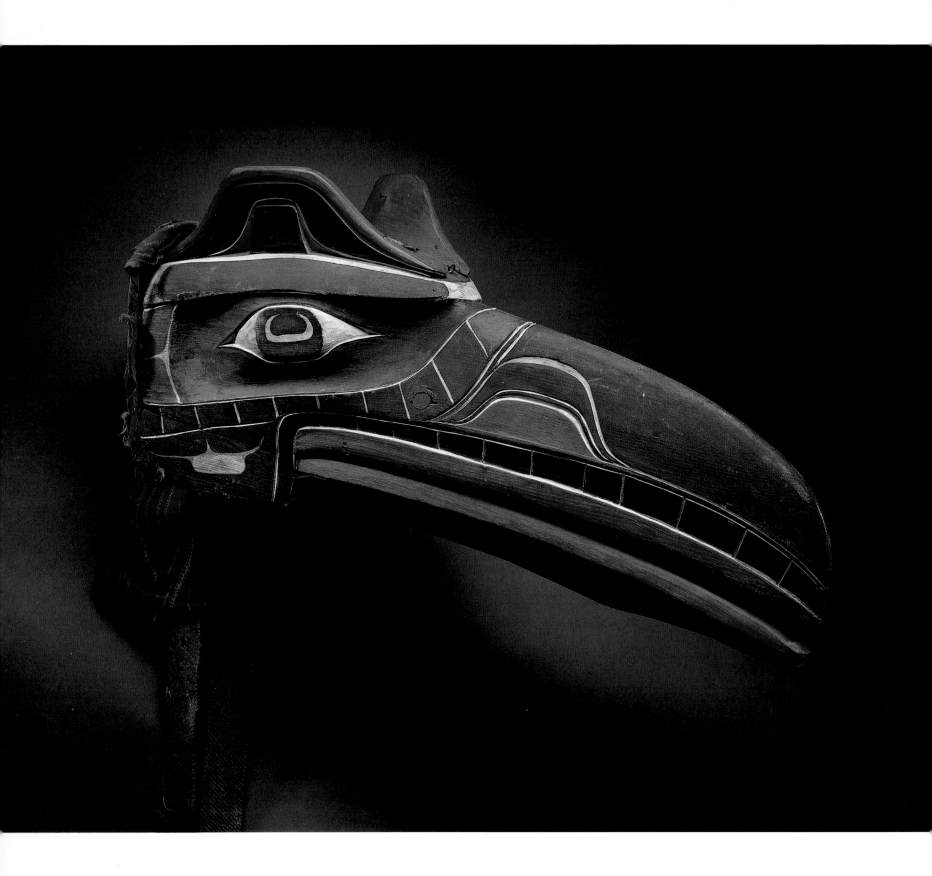

3.28 **Raven mask**. Fort Rupert. Wood, cloth, L 66.5 cm, H 30.5 cm. *Collected by George Hunt, 1901. 16/8533, AMNH 1901–32*

THIS RAVEN MASK MAY HAVE BEEN CARVED BY BOB Harris (X̱aʼniyus), the artist who created the bee mask (fig. 4.10) (Macnair: personal communication, 1990). Both masks share a characteristic of this manʼs art, namely, a chain of squares delineating some feature. On this example, the squares appear above the birdʼs red beak and around its eye socket.

X̱aʼniyus was not only a carver but an accomplished art designer as well. Kwakiutl today recall stories of his elaborate sets for the *tuxwʼid* performances (Agnes Cranmer: personal communication, 1990). Mrs. Cranmer also suggests that the right to wear this kind of raven mask came to Fort Rupert from Blunden Harbour through marriage. SAM

ing evidence. The single Kwakiutl prosecution after 1927 was under the weaker provision against dancing off oneʼs own reserve.

Such evasions rested upon the solidarity of the Kwakiutl. The rivalries and factions of the small Kwakiutl community did not cease, but all ranks closed after the trauma of 1922. Not even the Christian Indians would cooperate. A provincial constable (the RCMP had been withdrawn) found himself "up against a stone wall." To inform meant, as a young Cape Mudge man told Halliday, "I would be an outcast amongst all the Indians" (Clark 1931; Halliday 1931). Enforcement had become impossible. In 1933, Hallidayʼs successor, Agent Murray S. Todd, complained that his position was intolerable: the potlatch, he reported, had reached its greatest height in many years, with the Indians "bolder and quite open in carrying it out." His Victoria superior reported that "we are about as far away from doing anything effective toward the suppression of the potlatch system as when actions against the Indians were started years ago" (Todd 1936; Perry 1934).

Todd and his superiors were not done yet. They attempted still another amendment. In 1936 the government brought to Parliament a bill that would authorize an agent or the RCMP to seize any excess goods that they reasonably could believe to be intended for potlatch purposes. In the House of Commons the independent member for Comox-Alberni, A.W. Neill, himself a former Indian agent who had served under Vowell during the period of deliberate nonenforcement, blasted the proposal as unreasonable, unjust, and un-British. His attacks, seconded by others, forced the minister to withdraw the amendment (House of Commons 1936:1236–1300, 2121–21). After that failure, Indian Affairs left the potlatch alone. It was better, wrote the provincial superintendent, to leave the matter to the good sense of the Indians, hoping that church and school would do more than prohibitive measures to eliminate the practice (Mackay 1938). The department made no more attempts to enforce the law among the Kwakiutl.

Ironically, despite the end of enforcement, the potlatch declined, victim to alterations in the structure of the fishing industry, to the Depression, to Anglican persuasion and Pentecostal evangelization, and to the lack of interest among young people. Dependent upon wealth from the European economy, the system was showing signs of strain in the 1920s with transfers of coppers coming nearly to an end. The change from sail and oar to gasoline fishing boats put the Kwakiutl at a disadvantage against their white and Japanese competitors. Then came the Depression, which, when at its worst, dropped the value of the fish pack by almost two-thirds. The Alert Bay cannery, in production since 1881, closed its doors for some time in 1930. With older equipment and operating at lower efficiency than their competitors, Indians generally lost out in an industry which was already declining. The cash shortage sometimes turned the old competitive rivalry of the potlatch into squabbles and bitterness (Codere 1961:471–83; Drucker and Heizer 1967:50–62). Moreover, attitudes were changing. F. E. Anfield commented that the young men "are not interested," Rev. E. W. Christmas that "the young men will not memorise the ceremonial chants and harangues as their fathers have" (Anfield 1940; Christmas 1945). "I began to feel," wrote Jimmy Sewid about the 1930s, "that it was not right to have these potlatches" (Spradley 1969:110). Altered attitudes affected not just the young.

The Apostolic Mission, a Pentecostal group, had great success in Alert Bay in the interwar period, and it was very strict in imposing among its adherents a renunciation of the potlatch. A Pentecostal revival at Gilford and Village islands stopped dancing between 1942 and 1944. After the death of his first wife, Charlie Nowell, long a campaigner against the ban, married a Christian. "We didn't go through any ceremony; we just went to church." His daughter Agnes married in church too (Ford 1941:232). Customary marriages disappeared in these decades; they no longer acted as a "feeder."

Yet the Kwakiutl were an extraordinarily tenacious people. Potlatches continued and, with wartime prosperity, revived. Mungo Martin was carving potlatch artwork, and the decades of the 1930s and 1940s were the period of Willie Seaweed's greatest *hamatsa* mask production (Holm 1983:109).

By the 1940s the potlatch, though some continued to be held, appeared, even to the Kwakiutl, irrelevant to war and post-war problems. In three years of hearings, 1946 to 1948, before a joint Parliamentary committee to revise the Indian Act, the potlatch and the potlatch law went unmentioned. The brief of the British Columbia Native Brotherhood failed to mention the presence of the law or to argue for its repeal (Native Brotherhood 1947). Comments in *The Native Voice* were infrequent and those negative. The potlatch and the law had ceased to be an issue, either to Indian Affairs or to the Indians. Overshadowed by questions of land, enfranchisement, education, taxation, welfare, fisheries, and trapping, "the whole potlatch issue just disappeared" (La Violette 1961:95). Thus, when the revised Indian Act was passed in 1951, it contained no mention of the potlatch.

For the first time since 1885 the potlatch was again legal, and

3.29 **Mask**. Fort Rupert. Wood, abalone, L 41.6 cm, W 30.5 cm. 20th century. *Collected by George Emmons, 1929. 16.1/1872, AMNH 1929–75*

GEORGE EMMONS' FIRST INCLINATION WAS TO CALL this mask a representation of a *dzunuḵwa* (acc. 1929–75, AMNH). This classification is not correct, but was probably triggered by the observation that the lips of this creature protrude forward in a way that recalls the characteristic expression of a *dzunuḵwa* as she cries "Uuuu, uuuu!". This particular type of pouting mouth, however, is characteristic of sculptures carved in the 1920s by artists in Blunden Harbour and Smith Inlet (Peter Macnair: personal communication, 1990).

The mask has been colored with red, black, and green enamel paints, which began to be routinely used by the Kwakiutl around this time. When newly applied, enamel paint gives the dazzling, hard-edged surface seen on works by such artists as Mungo Martin and Willie Seaweed.

The identity of the being so vividly represented here is difficult to verify, but it is clearly composed of some combination of human and animal attributes. It might be the great and wealthy sea chief Ḵumugwe' (see fig. 2.41), depicted here with slightly protruding, fishy eyes, puckered lips, and two gill-like attachments on either side of his head. The inlays of abalone shell on these attachments help to identify this work as the prerogative of some wealthy and high-ranking member of the community. JO

by the 1960s, as part of the revival of Kwakiutl self-conscious-
ness and a renaissance of native art, dance, and music, the
potlatch made a comeback (see Webster, this volume). It may
have been somewhat different from what was once practiced,
but it was, now as then, a very meaningful ceremony and a
symbol of continuity with customs, traditions, and values important to many Kwakiutl.

3.30 **Mask**. Fort Rupert. Wood, H 55 cm, W 62 cm. *Collected by
George Hunt, 1897. 16/2344, AMNH 1897–43*

HUNT IDENTIFIES THIS MASK AS REPRESENTING
"Ts!egamis," a character he does not describe. Gloria
Cranmer Webster (personal communication, 1990)
suggests that this name is an incorrect spelling of Tsekame',
Head-Winter-Dancer, an important player in a Kwikwasutinuxw
tradition. It is conceivable that this mask arrived in Fort Rupert
as part of a marriage transferral.

With its central anthropomorphic face and five radiating projections, this mask resembles other Kwakiutl masks identified as depicting the sun. In Hunt's recording of Kwikwasutinuxw history,
Head-Winter-Dancer gives a sun mask to his son, Real-Chief:

Then he [Head-Winter-Dancer] called the Sun mask, and the mask of
the Sun came out; and Head-Winter-Dancer . . . said, "O Real-Chief!
now look at this. It will be yours. Whenever you show this, the name
of the dancer shall be Head-Chief. (Boas and Hunt 1905:187–88) SAM

3.31 Kwakiutl celebrating the coronation of George VI, 1936, Alert Bay. *PABC 83576*

3.32, 3.33 Winter Ceremony at Gilford Island, 1946. These photographs are said to have been taken by a provincial policeman. *RBCM 15250–42, 15250–20*

3.34 **Dish**. New Vancouver. Wood, L 51 cm, W 27 cm. *Collected by George Hunt, 1901. 16/8402, AMNH 1901–15*

THIS VESSEL IN THE FORM OF A HUMAN BEING HAS long arms wrapped around its body and grasps the lip of the bowl with curved thumbs. The legs are indicated in very shallow relief, but the head is fully carved in the round.

Wooden containers shaped to give the impression that they are grasped and supported by human figures were also made by Berlin Sea, Koniag, and Chugach Eskimos (Fitzhugh and Crowell 1988:302). In addition, stone bowls enclosed by seated human figures are found in the Salish area in sites dating around 2,000 years ago (Duff 1975:60–80). Possibly related to a very ancient tradition, this dish gives the impression that the trunk of the body forms the cavity used to hold food. JO

3.35 *Nuɫamaɫ mask*. Quatsino. Wood, copper, H 33 cm, W 23 cm. *Collected by George Hunt, 1899. 16/6887, AMNH 1899–50*

HUNT DESCRIBED THIS MASK TO BOAS AS REPRE-senting the character Sapaxalis, Light-Shining-Down (acc. 1899–50, AMNH). The legend that Hunt collected with this mask concerns the activities of Chief-Destroyer, one of the ancestors of the G̲usgimax̲w (Boas and Hunt 1905:382–90; see fig. 4.12 for more complete information on this history). According to that story, this mask would be one of the prerogatives Chief-Destroyer received as a result of his encounters with the Sun and Evening-Sky.

Because this mask resembles a type of *nuɫamaɫ* or fool dancer's mask, Boas questioned Hunt's attribution:

First of all, I find that one of the masks, which is undoubtedly a fool-dancer's mask, is described by you as that of Sepaxalis who came down from heaven, one of the Koskimo ancestors. I mean that one which I described in the book on social organization of the Kwakiutl Indians. Besides this one, there are a few others which make me suspect that the Indians may try to impose upon you to a certain extent in giving explanations of masks and connecting them with the stories that you are writing down. (Boas to Hunt, 1/3/1900, APS)

Both Peter Macnair and Bill Holm (personal communication, 1990) agree with Boas that this mask is a particular type of *nuɫamaɫ* mask, possibly an older type that is distinct from the fool dancer's mask with a greatly elongated nose, such as fig. 2.11. Bill Holm (personal communication, 1989) suggests that the red, black, and white twists surrounding the head, which represent twists of dyed and undyed cedar bark, can be interpreted as looking like a lion's mane, and that the whiskerlike patterns on the being's cheeks resemble lion's whiskers. He describes this as a "lion-type *nuɫamaɫ* which might be derived from an image the Kwakiutl could have seen on sailing vessels." SAM

4.1 George Hunt, Fort Rupert, 1898. *Photo by H. I. Smith.*
AMNH *11854*

4.2 Speaker, Fort Rupert, 1894. *Photo by O. C. Hastings.*
AMNH *336118*

4 / George Hunt, Collector of Indian Specimens

Ira Jacknis

N 1907 GEORGE HUNT, THE KWAKIUTL FIELD AS-
sistant to anthropologist Franz Boas, was having problems
with his mail service. Letters Boas addressed to him were
going up to Prince Rupert before coming down to his home in
Fort Rupert. Moreover there seemed to be another George
Hunt in the area. To ensure delivery Hunt recommended that
all letters be addressed to him as "George Hunt / collector of
Indian Specimens" or "George Hunt / collector for the New
York Museum." Boas did indeed follow this practice for the
next several letters, and if Hunt's postal problems did not entirely vanish, at least they greatly diminished.

This self-appellation is a vital clue into the identity of
George Hunt (fig. 4.1). Hunt could have chosen other labels to
identify himself, such as guide, watchman, trader, hunter and
trapper, interpreter, even anthropologist, yet he chose to see
himself as a collector. This essay examines George Hunt's collecting career, particularly for the New York Museum (American Museum of Natural History), and will show that throughout his life Hunt's activity can best be seen as that of a collector.
The primary emphasis in this essay is biographical (cf. Cannizzo 1983). Setting Hunt's collecting in the context of his life
and world, I will pay particular attention to his gradual growth
and development over his twenty-three most active years of
artifact collecting, 1891–1914.[1]

Hunt's World and Early Life

George Hunt was born on February 14, 1854, in Fort Rupert,
British Columbia, just five years after the Hudson's Bay Company had established a post there. Hunt's lifetime (he died in
1933) coincided with the so-called "potlatch period" of
Kwakiutl history, 1849–1921 (Codere 1950, 1961). During this
turbulent time Kwakiutl population declined, and the number
of white settlers increased, as did the participation of the
Kwakiutl in the cash economy (see Cole, this volume). Though
the Kwakiutl adopted elements of western material culture—

including sawn lumber, metal-edged tools, and enamel
paints—they continued actively to produce ceremonial art.
Hunt's collecting of Kwakiutl artifacts took place in this complex, changing situation, and his stance toward it implied a
conscious and defined image of traditional Kwakiutl culture.

George Hunt lived his whole life in Fort Rupert (fig. 4.4),
with some time spent in Alert Bay. These were the largest
Kwakiutl communities at the time and at successive periods
were the centers of Native life as well as white contact. Neither
community was originally a Kwakiutl village. As Codere points
out (1961:455–56), the Fort Rupert Kwakiutl were renowned as
middlemen and interpreters, and George Hunt's career should
be seen in this light.

Hunt's family was an integral part of these multicultural
communities. His father Robert Hunt (1828–93) was born in
Dorsetshire, England, and emigrated in 1850. He went to work
for the Hudson's Bay Company in the new post in Fort Rupert,
eventually buying out their store. George's mother, Mary
Ebbetts (1823–1919), was a Tlingit noblewoman from Tongass,
Alaska. Many of their eleven children married whites, the
daughters, especially, marrying white traders.[2] George's siblings were all fascinating people in their own right. His sister
Elizabeth, for example, accumulated several collections over
the years, composed of European and Asian antiques, as well
as Haida and Kwakiutl artifacts.[3]

Though he was not of Kwakiutl birth, George Hunt grew up
in a Kwakiutl community and was, in effect, raised as one. His
father was fluent in Kwakwala, often serving as an interpreter,
and George seems to have spoken the language as his native
tongue. But his father also saw to it that he was instructed in
English, supplemented by a little formal schooling in 1878–79
from the missionary Alfred J. Hall. In letters to Boas many
years later, Hunt recalled how he came to be initiated into
Kwakiutl ritual. When he was nine, the old Kwagul chiefs called
him into their feasts. This was in recognition of the peace
brought to the Kwakiutl by his Tlingit grandfather. The warfare

4.3 **Speaker figure**. Fort Rupert. Wood, H 129.5 cm. *Collected by George Hunt, 1897. 16/2397, AMNH 1897–30*

THIS FIGURE OF A CHIEF'S SPEAKER IS AMONG THE earliest acquisitions Hunt made for Boas during the first year of the Jesup North Pacific Expedition. It depicts the speaker of the chief raising his arm in a gesture of oration. The faint red facial markings may have depicted patterns associated with the family to which this figure belonged.

The figure wears a type of store-bought shirt worn by the Kwakiutl at this time. Although he often urged Hunt to acquire the oldest pieces that illustrated what Kwakiutl culture was like before contact with whites, this carving was presumably acceptable to Boas. SAM

4.4 Fort Rupert, June 1881. *Photo by Edward Dossetter.* AMNH 42295

4.5 George Hunt and family with Franz Boas, Fort Rupert, November 1894. *Photo by O.C. Hastings,* APS

4.6 Lucy Hunt and family. AMNH 2A 13872

that formerly existed between the Tongass Tlingit and the Kwaguł stopped in 1854 when Hunt's grandfather came to Fort Rupert to visit his daughter and new-born grandson. "So the old chiefs say that through me that the war stoped. and in there feasts I use to go and listen to them telling Each other there *nEmemot* stories. and that is How I know all there old ways" (Hunt to Boas, 1/6/19, APS).[4]

Because of his foreign ancestry, George Hunt had not inherited any Kwakiutl crests or ceremonial prerogatives. Instead, he gained most of his privileges, and not a little ethnographic data, from his two Kwakiutl wives, along with their expanding web of relatives (fig. 4.6). His first wife, Lucy Homiskanis, was a Kwaguł, whom he probably married in the early 1870s.[5] Between her death in April 1908 and the early teens, he was married again, to a 'Nakwaxda'x̱w woman named Francine or Tsukwani (fig. 1.6). For example, Hunt obtained the *hamatsa* dance from Lucy's brother (Boas 1966:190–91; see also Suttles, this volume). Both women supplied him with culinary recipes, and from Francine he learned much sacred material. As Hunt wrote in 1916, "Some times while we are sleeping my wife would start up and sing her *PExEla* [shaman] songs. then when she stop singing she would talk to the spirit. and she seems to get answer Back. next time the spirit comes to her I will write what she say to it" (Hunt to Boas, 12/22/16, APS).

George Hunt's first appearance in white historical documents was in the 1870s, when he was in his late twenties. Hunt was listed in directories as a laborer and hunter for the Hudson's Bay Company, but his most significant work was as an interpreter. In 1877 he acted as interpreter for the Royal Navy in their expedition to bring to justice the native "pirates and murderers" in the *George S. Wright* affair (Gough 1984: 198–204). When Hall arrived the following year, George Hunt assisted by translating his sermons, prayers, and hymns (Gough 1982: 78–80). In 1879 he offered some information to the Indian Reserve Commission survey and interpreted for Indian Commissioner Israel Wood Powell. On this survey trip, Powell also collected Native artifacts, which went to the Museum of the Geological Survey of Canada.[6] This, one of the first organized collecting trips in the region, is also the first recorded instance of Hunt's involvement with collecting.[7]

Hunt's first real collecting experience came in 1881 when he assisted Johan Adrian Jacobsen, collecting for the Berlin Royal Ethnographic Museum. Hunt performed a number of duties: guide, pilot, interpreter, and collecting assistant. Of his visit to the conservative village of X̱wamdasbe' on Hope Island, Jacobsen wrote: "Only the persuasiveness of George Hunt, our interpreter, who was well regarded in the whole region, finally convinced the chief that in return for a goodly amount he should sell some outstanding ethnological pieces" (Jacobsen 1977:32). Hunt also used the opportunity on some of these visits to do a little trading of his own, selling white man's goods from his father's store. This early trading experience— keeping accounts, handling cash, shipping and storing merchandise—undoubtedly prepared Hunt well for a career in artifact collecting. Early the next year Jacobsen accepted the mission of returning to Germany with a party of "longheads" from the west coast of Vancouver Island. These were Kwakiutl people who artificially deformed the head in childhood. George Hunt was recruited to act as interpreter and leader of the group. However, Native sentiment was against the voyage, and all the Indians soon deserted. Hunt again helped Adrian and his brother Fillip when they made another collection in 1885.

In 1888 George Hunt met Franz Boas, an encounter that was to radically transform his life. Boas was then engaged in ethnological surveys for the British Association for the Advancement of Science (BAAS). When he met him in Victoria, Hunt was again serving as an interpreter, this time for the courts. Boas took down several texts, but worked with Hunt more extensively the following year.

1891–93: World's Columbian Exposition (Field Museum)

The first collection made by George Hunt on his own was intended for the World's Fair held in Chicago over the summer of 1893. For the first time at an international exposition anthropology was being featured as a separate subject with its own building. Boas had secured a job as assistant in ethnology, and naturally he wanted to highlight the people of the Northwest Coast. He selected the Fort Rupert Kwakiutl as a "standard tribe," and other Northwest Coast collections were made to supplement them (Jacknis 1991).

We know little about the circumstances surrounding Hunt's collection. In August, 1891 Boas had come up to Victoria from a Chinook research trip in Washington State to instruct Hunt in person. By October arrangements were well under way for Hunt to "collect all necessary illustrative specimens, and to induce a number of Indians to go to Chicago during the Fair .... Mr. Hunt is also to obtain a large house and the model of a whole village, buy canoes and a complete outfit to show the

4.7 **Mink's *sisiyutł* mask**. Fort Rupert. Wood, string, fiber, metal, L 239.4 cm, W 30 cm, H 56.5 cm. *Collected by George Hunt, 1899. 16/6768, AMNH 1899–50*

ACCORDING TO HUNT, THIS MASK REPRESENTS THE *sisiyutł* used by the Kwaguł to refer to Mink, an ancestor of their tribe, and to recount the story of Mink's victory over the four sons of Wolf (acc. 1899–50, AMNH). The *sisiyutł* mask was worn when Mink triumphed over his rival, Wolf, who was seeking vengeance for the death of his sons (Boas and Hunt 1906:105–10).

The story begins at a time when Head Wolf was giving a Winter Dance during which his four sons were to be initiated. The novices were out in the woods with little to eat, waiting for the moment that they would return to the village. Meanwhile, Mink, or Born-to-Be-the-Sun, was busy making and setting his salmon weir to catch fish for himself and his mother. He repaired and set the trap on three consecutive evenings. Each morning when he came to collect his catch, he found the traps had been raided, leaving only the jaws and the bones of the salmon. On the fourth day Mink slept so he could watch his salmon weir at night. He saw nothing until morning, when the four sons of Wolf came to eat his catch. Angered by their thievery, Mink killed them. He cut off their heads, hid their bodies, and attached the heads to a cedar bark neckring. Mink repaired his salmon weir and left to find another place to fish, to avoid Wolf's anger at the loss of his sons.

Mink traveled north toward Islands-in-Front in a canoe filled with cedar. When he arrived, he set his salmon weir into the water and sat on a rock to wait for his catch. From time to time he would ask the salmon weir what it had caught, and the weir would name

the fish. Unsatisfied, Mink asked the weir to return all of them to the water. After the weir had caught an example of every fish in the sea, it at last snared a strange double-headed serpent. Finally Mink was satisfied. He took the serpent home to his village, along with mussels that he had collected for his mother.

Mink knew that Wolf would discover his four sons were dead when they failed to reappear that evening. He took the *sisiyutł* into the house, cut off its heads, skinned it, and hung it up to dry near the fire. He then connived with his friends to quietly gain access to the ceremonial house in which Wolf was giving the dance, and also expedient ways to leave it.

To prepare himself for the confrontation with Wolf, Mink adorned himself with the cedar bark neckring with the four heads and covered himself completely with his blanket. When he entered the dance house, no one recognized him. Mink danced around the fire four times and then uncovered his face. Immediately Wolf recognized his sons, and the whole tribe became excited and wished to kill Mink. But Mink quickly escaped from the house. Then the secret songs of the four princes were heard in the distance, and, just as Wolf thought this meant that his sons were somehow alive, Mink entered the dance once again. He danced around the house with his friends behind him and then quickly uncovered his face, revealing the head of the *sisiyutł*. Immediately, all who saw it died.

The mask displays the *sisiyutł* with its two powerful serpent heads surrounding the central face. Characteristic of the *sisiyutł* are the long, red, protruding tongues and the four horns, one on each of the serpent heads and two surmounting the central face. SAM

daily life of the Indians, and everything that is necessary to the performance of their religious ceremonies" (F.W. Putnam/G.R. Davis, Monthly Rep. for the World's Colum. Expo., 10/91, HUA). Hunt's compensation was to be ninety dollars a month for eight months, from the middle of March, when he would set out from Fort Rupert, until the middle of November, when he would return, plus expenses.

By February of 1892 Hunt had already purchased the large house, ten masks, a staff, a carved image, two dishes, a spoon, rattle, bracelet, two stone chisels, a stone dagger, and fifty abalone shells, the last undoubtedly to be used in the manufacture of crafts or costumes. By September of that year Hunt had apparently completed his collection, though he was probably still gathering supplies for the visit of the Kwakiutl to Chicago.

Stormy weather over the winter of 1892–93 delayed the shipment of Hunt's collection, which was exhibited in the Anthropology Building. Hunt and seventeen Kwakiutl arrived in mid-April and after a delay moved into their "village," where they spent the summer demonstrating crafts and their dramatic ceremonials (fig. 4.9). Boas spent as much time as he could talking to the Kwakiutl and taking notes. With the aid of musicologist John C. Fillmore, he recorded Hunt and others singing on the new gramophone cylinders. It was here that Boas taught Hunt how to write Kwakwala in phonetic characters, thus enabling Hunt to send him texts in the Native language. At the end of the exposition, Hunt's collection of 360 items, along with the other collections, became part of the new Field Columbian Museum, which opened in June of 1894.

1894–95: U.S. National Museum and American Museum of Natural History

Immediately upon his return to Fort Rupert, George Hunt set out to record Native traditions and send them back to Boas. Documentation does not reveal the sources of the funding for this activity, nor exactly what Boas intended to do with the material. In early 1894, when Boas was still with the Field Museum, Hunt, on his own initiative, offered to collect more artifacts on his trips to gather texts. However, the Field Museum was still sorting out its holdings and was not in the market. By June of 1894 Boas had resigned from the Museum, forced out by scientific politics (Hinsley and Holm 1976).

Boas spent the fall in Fort Rupert witnessing for the first time in situ the Kwakiutl Winter Ceremonies, on a trip funded by the BAAS, the U.S. National Museum, and the American Museum of Natural History (see Suttles, this volume). His primary motive was to collect artifacts and data that would enable him to set up "life groups" or dioramas at the New York and Washington museums (Jacknis 1985:76). For the American Museum he planned a group of figures demonstrating the various uses of the cedar tree (see fig. 1.19), while the Smithsonian would have a scene depicting the return of the *hamatsa* initiate. In addition to relying on Hunt for help with interpretation and texts, Boas paid him forty dollars for three masks, three neck- and headring sets, and two cedar bark aprons. As he did not have time to complete the collection, Boas left with Hunt another fifty dollars as an advance for making collections, mostly of cedar bark paraphernalia. Hunt was also paid a salary with expenses. Hunt's collection—thirty-seven cedar bark rings, two masks, a stone hammer, and a bark blanket—reached the Smithsonian in December of 1895.[8]

Boas set up his Washington exhibits in early 1895 and arrived in New York in the fall to arrange his American Museum group. From then until his resignation in June of 1905, he operated out of the American Museum (and from 1896 on, from Columbia University). Boas was able to send small sums to Hunt during 1896 for what appears to have been rather casual collecting around Fort Rupert and Alert Bay.

1896–1905: American Museum of Natural History

George Hunt was central to Boas's grand plan for the Jesup North Pacific Expedition. He was one of the few participants to be listed as in the field for each year of operation, 1897–1902, and he continued to collect for the museum through 1905. Without a doubt, this is Hunt's largest collection (1,022 Kwakiutl, 283 Bella Coola, and 219 Nuu-chah-nulth items), as well as his most comprehensive. It is also the best documented—the artifacts themselves as well as the collecting process. In April of 1897, as part of his preparations for the expedition, Boas wrote Hunt several letters instructing him in great detail. In them we can see the explicit program Boas set out for his Kwakiutl assistant.

Hunt was to work for four months the first year, from mid-May to mid-June among the Kwakiutl, mid-June to mid-July with Boas among the Bella Coola, and two more months after this with the Kwakiutl again. For this he would receive a salary of seventy-five dollars a month plus board and travel. Boas was able to send some funds almost every year from 1894 until

4.8 *Tsa̱tsa̱lkwa̱ḻal* **mask**. Quatsino. Wood, copper, leather (whale baleen added for exhibit), H 42 cm, W 42 cm. *Collected by George Hunt, 1900. 16/8227, AMNH 1900–73*

4.9 George Hunt (second from left) and the Kwakiutl at the Chicago World's Fair, 1893. CHS

HUNT DID NOT PROVIDE ANY DETAILED INFORMA-tion on this mask, other than calling it a *tsa̱tsa̱lkwa̱ḻal* mask. *Tsa̱lkwa'* means "hot," and the designs on the band surrounding the face could be the rays of the sun (Gloria Cranmer Webster: personal communication, 1990). When a dancer performed with this mask, the firelight would be dramatically re-flected from the copper eyes and mouth of the mask. Originally the top of the mask was surrounded by a halo of what seems to have been split baleen from a whale (Bill Holm: personal communi-cation, 1990; Boas 1909: pl. L#6). SAM

4.10 Bee mask. Knight Inlet. Wood, feathers, cloth, brass (twigs, Chinese goat hair and Chinese wild dog hair added for exhibit), L 43 cm, H 17 cm. *Collected by George Hunt, 1904. 16/9587,* AMNH *1904–41*

Although Boas and Hunt both refer to this mask as a wasp (acc. 1904-41, AMNH), the Kwakiutl who recently saw it identify it as a bee. They recognize this type of mask as one still performed as an important *tseka* privilege.

The long spikey stingers of the bee emanate from the nostrils of this mask. The chain of squares articulating the nose are characteristic of the artist Bob Harris, X̱a'niyus (Peter Macnair: personal communication, 1990). Brass accentuates the insectlike eyes. With this mask, the dancer wears a fur pelt that conceals the back of his head.

The dancer who performed with a bee mask appeared only briefly in front of the audience. During that appearance he would imitate the movements of the bee: he entered the room with outstretched arms, imitating the erratic flight pattern of the insect, ran across the room periodically turning and then appearing to "sting" members of the audience (Macnair 1974:102). Then the dancer would quickly exit. Very shortly he returned without the mask, circling the dance floor while finishing his song with his face fully revealed (Macnair: personal communication, 1990).

Hunt also acquired the costume associated with this mask; his photograph (fig. 4.11) shows both being worn. Hanging from the arms of the costume are small wooden slats with pointed ends, approximately the length and thickness of a tongue depressor. During a performance, these pieces of wood would rise and fall as the dancer dashed about rapidly changing his direction. The clacking noise created by these pieces hitting against each other added to the general effect of the bee dance. SAM

4.11 Bee mask and costume (16/9587, 9624), c. 1904.
Photo by George Hunt. AMNH *13797*

Hunt's death in 1933, drawn from a number of changing sources—museums, government agencies, private patrons, and Boas himself. In early 1895, Hunt was receiving fifteen dollars a month for getting texts and was sent some extra money to make collections. Boas's general practice was to pay Hunt a salary and expenses which covered travel and usually board, as well as all shipping costs and payment for the artifacts. Most often Boas would send a lump sum, such as three hundred dollars, against which Hunt would then draw until his expenses exhausted the fund. Periodically Boas would send statements of the accounts to date, and Hunt would usually send an itemized bill with his collection lists. These arrangements were normally satisfactory, though sometimes Boas would have to prod Hunt by telling him he would get no money if he did not produce. During the American Museum years, however, Hunt worked no more than half a year for Boas, and thus had to supplement his income with outside work, trapping, guiding, or as a night watchman in the Alert Bay cannery of his brother-in-law, Stephen A. Spencer.

Boas began his instructions to Hunt by explaining, "Our museum . . . has no collections whatever from the Kwakiutl, therefore any thing that you may obtain will be welcome" (Boas to Hunt, 4/14/97, acc. 1897–43, AMNH). The American Museum also possessed few items from the neighboring Bella Coola, as the bulk of the Northwest Coast accessions to date had been the Haida-Tsimshian collection made by I.W. Powell for Heber Bishop, and the Emmons Tlingit collection (Jonaitis 1988). Boas had been studying the Kwakiutl since his first field trip to British Columbia in 1886 and welcomed a chance to make a more intensive investigation. Thus, while filling an important gap in the New York collections, he also continued the study of his "favorite" tribe.

Although he asked Hunt to collect anything and everything, Boas offered specific suggestions, for both the Bella Coola and the Kwakiutl. As part of Hunt's ethnological education, Boas sent him a copy of his BAAS report on the Bella Coola, "so that you will know about what you may find. We want to get when you are there just as many masks and [bark dance] rings as you can get, but also the ordinary every-day things,—fish-traps, blankets, hammers, pestles, etc. The Bella Coola have very big totem poles and house-posts, and we must try to get those too" (Boas to Hunt, 4/14/97, acc. 1897–43, AMNH). Boas supplied lists of items to acquire, and although domestic goods are on them, he specifically requested Kwakiutl cedar bark objects and Bella Coola masks.

Boas went on to advise Hunt on collecting procedure,

4.12 **Skull rattle**. Quatsino. Wood, H 21 cm, W 16 cm. *Collected by George Hunt, 1899. 16/6897, AMNH 1899–50*

ATTENDANTS AT *hamatsa* DANCES SHAKE THIS TYPE of wooden rattle at the initiate in order to tame his wild behavior. Hunt recorded a Gusgimaxw family history that explains how the owners acquired the right to this specific rattle through the activities of an ancestor named Chief-Destroyer (Boas and Hunt 1905:382–90).

Chief-Destroyer lived in the upper world. One day the sun gave him some abalone ornaments. Later he encountered a canoe bearing four attendants of the constellation Orion, who invited Chief-Destroyer to their house, offered him a name, and gave him a canoe. They also informed him that he could descend to the lower world by paddling along a body of water; when he wanted to return to the upper world, the water would change its course and bring him back home. The hero there met Evening-Sky, who invited him to his house and gave him his *hamatsa* mask and accompanying paraphernalia. Chief-Destroyer then returned to the house of Orion, took the canoe, and paddled to the underworld. There he built a village, took a wife, and displayed to the community all the regalia he had received from Sun and Evening-Sky. Among this paraphernalia was the skull rattle used to tame the *hamatsa*.

Boas was most enthusiastic about Hunt's acquisition of this piece (Boas to Hunt, 9/13/99 APS). SAM

though this was more a reminder after the earlier instruction he must have given Hunt for Chicago: "You will, of course, have to keep a note-book on all things you will collect in Bella Coola, and I suppose it will be simplest if you put a tag with the name of the specimen on each, and then write in your notebook again the name of the specimen, and the number, and what you have learned about it" (Boas to Hunt, 4/14/97, acc. 1897–43, AMNH). Boas suggested wrapping each piece very carefully and storing the collection in Alert Bay until he had a chance to go over the collection with Hunt later that summer.

Beyond these general instructions, Boas tended to leave the actual method of execution to Hunt's judgment: "You know best, of course, what kind of things we want; and if you collect in the same way as you did for the World's Fair, you will do just what we want" (Boas to Hunt, 4/30/97, APS). As a final note, Boas recommended that Hunt follow a device Boas had used in several Kwakiutl collecting trips—giving a feast and explaining his mission. Accordingly, he enclosed a letter addressed to the Kwakiutl tribe. Hunt was to translate the letter, written in English but in good Kwakwala oratorical style, making changes as he saw fit. Hunt gave the feast and, we assume, read the letter.

The collecting activity of Boas and Hunt was guided by a definite—if often implicit—strategy that determined which artifacts to acquire and which to pass up. In their quest to amass a collection that would be representative of Kwakiutl culture, the most important desiderata for Boas and Hunt were objects that had extensive verbal documentation, domestic as well as ceremonial uses, and were old and well-crafted.

Like many scientific collectors, Boas insisted on full documentation. With each of his specimens Hunt was to send basic provenience data, and, on his object tags and lists, he almost always gave the Native name for the piece and its collecting locale, usually notes on its use, and often the name of the owner or maker. (A few of the artifacts are accompanied by Hunt's field photos, see figs. 4.10–11). In addition to this information, Boas instructed Hunt to get a text recounting the traditions that accompanied certain items, telling of their origin and the right of the owner to possess them: "Only we must remember that we want to have the tales and songs belonging to all of them"; and "It is better for us to get a few pieces less and the story belonging to each. We do not want to grab everything, and then not know what the things mean" (Boas to Hunt, 4/14/97, acc. 1897–43, AMNH).

When justifying his subsequent delays, Hunt often protested that it "takes time to Do it Right"; "Only one thing I see it will be harder for me this year, then it was at the World's fair,

for I got to get the stories and songs" (Hunt to Boas, 4/23/95, acc. 1895–4, AMNH; Hunt to Boas, 5/24/97, APS). Later, he wrote, "It is slow work for me to write the stories and buying at the same time" (Hunt to Boas, 2/18/99, APS). Realizing this, Boas generally expected Hunt to do his active collecting in the warmer months when it was easier to get around, and to save his writing for the evenings and winters. Hunt followed this practice, yet he complained of the hard work and lack of time. (During this period he was still working in the Alert Bay cannery to support his family.) When he was sick in the winter of 1897 he used the enforced bed-rest to write out stories. True to Boas's spirit, he would often decide to buy or not to buy depending on whether he could get the story. At one point he had not spent all his allotted funds because he "wont buy unless they have a storie with it," and in another instance he bought a mask because he already had the story (Hunt to Boas, 4/24/99, 4/12/01, APS).

After a year or so of collecting, Boas reviewed the Kwakiutl collections: "It strikes me that we have not yet a full collection of the simple every day implements. . . ." True to his basic ethnographic method, Boas wanted to have the culture described as a Native would see it: "The best thing you could do would be to sit down and think what the Kwakiutl used for cooking, including every thing from beginning to end, then what they used for wood-working, for painting, for making basket-work, for fishing, for hunting, etc." (Boas to Hunt, 1/13/99, acc. 1899–50, AMNH). Hunt adopted this plan and set to writing out basic Kwakiutl technological tasks, concentrating on subsistence. Most of these texts, in Kwakwala with English translation, were published in 1921, though Boas drew upon and partly published them in his 1909 study of Kwakiutl material culture. Hunt's assemblage of domestic articles was supplemented by Boas's own collections and research in the summer of 1900. Although other collectors, especially Charles F. Newcombe, strove to include domestic items, Hunt's Kwakiutl collection at the American Museum is distinguished for its cultural scope and detail. It contains a wide range of artifact types—utilitarian as well as ceremonial—and includes many varieties within those types.

Of all the factors that figured in whether an artifact would be collected or not, by far the primary one was age. Boas's desire for old pieces was emphatic. Of the large carvings (posts and grave ornaments) Hunt had earlier collected, he wrote, "We cannot get enough of these; and the older they are, the better. I will also remind you of my former request to get a number of good old planks, roof boards, etc. If there is any-

4.13 *Hamshamstsas* **mask**. Wood, cedar bark, baleen, red cloth, L 45 cm. *Collected by George Hunt, 1901. 16/8429, AMNH 1901–32*

THE *hamshamastsas* PERFORMANCE, A HIGHLY VALUED privilege, is danced by both men and women. Part of the *tseka*, it has movements similar to those made by the *hamatsa*. The dancer moves low to the ground and shakes his or her hand palm downward. Despite similarities, however, they are two distinct dances, not only in how they appear but in how they sound. The *hamatsa* fiercely cries "Hap!" but the *hamshamstsas* makes the sound "Wip!"

Masks of the *hamshamstsas* dance consist of a small raven frontlet tied around the forehead. Red cedar bark usually covers the dancer's head. The facial characteristics of this mask are articulated almost entirely through painting rather than detailed carved surfaces. The "lips" of the beak, for instance, and the nostrils are delineated through line rather than carving. SAM

where a nice painted bedroom, particularly if it is made of old planks, I should like to have it" (Boas to Hunt, 4/30/97, APS).

This desire for old artifacts was widely shared among Northwest Coast collectors of the time. The logic was that the old customs were vanishing before the onslaught of Euro-American civilization and thus had to be recorded and collected as soon as possible. As in any society, the sources of Kwakiutl culture were heterogeneous. Some items had been handed down for centuries, others were recent innovations. Boas and Hunt made a decision to "abstract" past all the change that had occurred since contact so that they would be left with what they hoped would be a description of traditional Kwakiutl material culture. This they tried to do by collecting all the old objects they could find and by commissioning pieces for which they had other evidence. The result was a "memory culture," similar to the verbal pictures of old times painted by tribal elders. This method had its direct visual parallel in the archaic recreation of Edward Curtis's photography.

Whatever its virtues, and it had many, there were several problems with this approach. As a scientist, Boas advocated cultural documentation that was both broad and detailed. However, by ignoring white trade goods such as Hudson's Bay Company blankets, metal pails, and iron-tipped tools, Boas and Hunt were not making a representative sample of Kwakiutl material culture as it existed at the time of collection. Boas was interested in historical reconstructions, but he faced losing the sense of culture as a dynamic, ever-changing process. If one ignored change since contact as a corrupting and falling away, there was little evidence of the past except gross distributional studies. Old artifacts were crucial for they were the most direct links to the past. Finally, while Boas advocated a holistic approach, the salvage paradigm's focus on isolated fragments often ignored cultural context and interdependence. All these contradictions grew out of opposing tendencies in Boas's ethnological thought (Stocking 1974:1–20).

Despite these retrogressive tendencies, one should note that in an 1897 list of things to get, Boas asked for button blankets and bracelets, both "arts of acculturation" developed after contact and integrated into Native society (Blackman 1976). Scattered throughout the Hunt collection are objects composed of trade goods; most strikingly, a dance apron incorporating glass beads, flannel fabric, yarn, and a recycled cloth bag (fig. 1.22). Such creative adaptations rearrange fragments of white culture into a new, but still Kwakiutl, whole.

The request for "good, old" pieces is a constant refrain in Boas's instructions. Like many collectors of their time, Boas and Hunt seem to have shared a tacit understanding of the meaning of these conjoined terms, often used almost synonymously. Again like most of his colleagues, Boas seems to have conflated age with aesthetic value, the old with the well-carved and painted: "The few old masks from Koskimo, and the old skull rattles, are also very good. I wish you could get more of these old carvings. They are much finer than the new ones. . . . What we need most are good old carvings" (Boas to Hunt, 9/13/99, acc. 1899–50, AMNH; APS).

In a period of rapid culture change, the sources for old-style pieces were necessarily limited. Although some everyday items were still in use, many, such as cedar-bark clothing, had to be made on commission. Other old artifacts, especially of a ceremonial nature, could be found either stored in old chests as family heirlooms, or deposited in cave burials.

Though Boas and Hunt commissioned less than some other collectors, such as Newcombe and his Kwakiutl assistant Charles Nowell, they resorted to this when necessary. For his early collection of cedar bark for the U.S. National Museum, Hunt found that he had to get them made "in the old fasion way." At the same time he ordered a set of house posts and commissioned a painter to fill a book with designs (Hunt to Boas, 1/15/95, acc. 1895–4, AMNH). One of the discoveries of which Hunt was proudest came in 1899:

Yet I have lots of truly old fations things to send to you this year that you and I not no any thing about of ontill you Read the stories carefully. for in the old times I found out that there was no masks made of wood. for they Had no knives to carve with. so all the masks was made out of Red cedar Bark or LagEkw. (Hunt to Boas, 4/24/99, APS)

Hunt sent to New York several of these newly made archaic pieces (fig. 4.14). Boas intended commissioning to produce more than mere artifacts: "If you do not find any, I wish you could get one of the old men to make a real good arrow and bow for you; and when you do so, please ask them very particularly what kind of arrow-heads they used before they had any iron" (Boas to Hunt, 5/18/99, acc. 1899–50, AMNH; APS). Boas hoped Hunt could get a record of arrow-making traditions to parallel his earlier set of canoe-building customs.

Objects newly made after the form of old pieces can be seen in two ways, as reproductions or fakes. The former were perfectly acceptable to Boas:

In regard to other things, I understand perfectly well that they are reproductions of older implements that have gone out of use, and that your friends are making them in order to show what the Indians used to do in olden times. In cases of this sort, I should even be satisfied if you had made them yourself, as long as they are made correctly. (Boas to Hunt, 1/3/00, APS)

Hunt did indeed make some pieces when he could not find anyone else with greater expertise.

Yet Boas warned Hunt "that the Indians may try to impose upon you to a certain extent in giving explanations of masks and connecting them with the stories that you are writing down" (Boas to Hunt, 1/3/00, APS). A particular stone head worried Boas. At first he liked it, but after further examination, he saw it was new.

It gives me great concern to think that in continuing this work you might get specimens that are not in reality what you and I suppose them to be, and I believe it would be better if you did not try to get any more material for some time. I should advise you to continue to collect wood-carving that may come in you way, if they are sure to be old, such as the old rotten rattles and the few old masks that you sent with the last lot; but I wish you would not get more specimens belonging to the dances until we have a chance to talk things over this spring. (Boas to Hunt, 1/3/00, APS)

When searching through caves several years later, Hunt was especially pleased to find a cache of old masks covered with "fine worm Holes. so you see that they must Be old" (Hunt to Boas, 3/10/08, APS). Their site, if not their worm holes, would have ensured their authenticity (at this point in the "market" no one would go to such lengths to fake).

A good proportion (perhaps as much as 25 per cent) of the Hunt Kwakiutl collection at the American Museum, and especially the oldest pieces, was gathered from caves. Although little is recorded in the literature on this custom, evidently it was the Kwakiutl practice to inter family heirlooms along with the deceased in isolated caves and the more common tree burials. Ceremonial regalia was also stored in caves when not in use. Hunt's first cave collecting appears to have been in late 1900, and was by proxy: "I got most of the people to go and look for old Emeges and dishes and masks out of the graves and caves so you will see them when ever they reach New York. I think it is the best old collection I ever made" (Hunt to Boas, 10/10/00, APS). While some of this collecting was for skeletal material, in general Hunt acquired little of this.

Later that winter, when some of the sites he hoped to visit were snowed in, Hunt occupied himself by digging in local shell heaps and was rewarded with artifacts such as gambling stones, pieces of copper, and stone knives. Two years before,

Hunt had assisted Harlan I. Smith's digging around Fort Rupert for the Jesup Expedition. Though the results of Hunt's explorations in caves were catalogued as "ethnology," and those of Smith's excavations as "archaeology," many of the artifacts are the same—from the early post-contact period, c. 1790–1850. Hunt's finds were about the oldest it would be possible to find preserved above ground, while Smith's digging was in shallow, and thus recent, surface and subsurface strata. Thus, in this case, distinctions between ethnology and archaeology were merely methodological, not substantive. For the ethnography of Boas and Hunt was profoundly retrospective.

As Hunt began to search caves more intensively, he sought out all who could give him information about the locations of such sites, and his collecting seems to have taken on a new enthusiasm as he discovered precious old things in remote regions where he had never been. Hunt did find much old material in these caves, but unfortunately many objects were too rotten to be lifted. Hunt's cave finds were so rich that Boas petitioned American Museum president Morris K. Jesup for a supplemental grant to strengthen the collections with this kind of material. Boas also obtained permission from the British Columbia Indian Affairs Commissioner for this work (see below).

For Boas and Hunt the temporal sampling of Kwakiutl culture was often related to its spatial distribution. During the five years of the Jesup Expedition (1897–1902), Hunt visited at least fourteen different Kwakiutl sites—several more than once—covering most of the major communities.[9] Based in Fort Rupert with extended periods in Alert Bay, he naturally collected from these villages whenever he could. However, older artifacts were apt to be found further away from these centers of acculturation. Advised Boas in 1897, "If you should collect any masks, I think it will be better to wait until we get a chance to go to one of the remote villages, where they still have some of the old masks. If, however, there should happen to be any good ones in Fort Rupert, there is no objection to collecting these" (Boas to Hunt, 4/14/97, acc. 1897–43, AMNH). Remoteness had its negative side, too. It made it harder to transport artifacts to metropolitan museums, and, as Cole notes, "Ceremonial objects remained more meaningful and thus more difficult to buy or even to see" (1985:296). As a local and Native resident, Hunt had the opportunity to overcome these obstacles.

After Fort Rupert and Alert Bay, Hope Island was Hunt's next most often visited locale—in 1897, 1898, 1899. Apart from its intrinsic interest as a conservative village, this reflects his

4.14 **Cedar bark mask**. Rivers Inlet. Cedar bark, cloth, string, wood, L 66 cm. *Collected by George Hunt, 1899. 16/6758, AMNH 1899–50*

IT IS NOT CLEAR FROM THE RECORDS WHETHER HUNT collected this cedar bark mask or commissioned it. On February 18, 1899, Hunt wrote to Boas from Fort Rupert:

. . . there is lots of thing that I am bringing now that we did not know anything about before such as the . . . Bear mask made out of all Red cedar bark or Lagekw! for now I bought a fine one and you have stories of it soon. (APS)

On April 24, Hunt wrote again to Boas concerning a mysterious mask made all from cedar bark:

For in the old times I found out that there was no masks made of wood. For they had no Knives to carve with so all the masks was made out of red cedar bark . . . and afterwards the [?] to the first old people found out how to have to emitete the red cedar bark Masks. Then they taked rough sand stone to rub out the carving on the wooden masks. So I got some of the all cedar bark masks of bear and Hemsiwe and some other. (APS)

On September 18, Boas acknowledged Hunt's find with enthusiasm (APS).

At the end of September, Hunt wrote to Boas, providing him with specific information of the manufacture of red cedar bark masks, and indicating their possible status as commissioned pieces:

There is another collector in Alert Bay that is Mr. Hall has gone home to England and taked 4 large case of new made carving with him. So you see we got enemy all around us speaking [of] you. But I don't think you better to let them see the red cedar bark hamsiwe for I am having lots of different kinds making for me by an old woman that made those two for she told me that in the old times there was no wooden masks only red cedar bark of all kind. (APS)

As long as the replication that Hunt alludes to was truly in the old style, Boas did not seem to object. For him, this archaic form of mask would have been evidence of what "true" Kwakiutl culture was like prior to white contact.

It is not entirely clear what this mask represents. Hunt describes it in two of these letters as a bear's mask. Boas, in contrast, identifies it as representing the Cannibal-of-the-North-End-of-the-World. Baxwbakwalanuxwsiwe' (acc. 1899–50, AMNH). Since this being is never portrayed on a mask, Boas was probably mistaken.

This mask was collected among the Oowekeeno of Rivers Inlet, and could be connected to a story of a hero Tlalamin (Boas and Hunt 1905:403–407). A man and his wife and child go out to hunt mountain goats; the boy tires and stays behind. A bear approaches the boy and offers him some meat from his own leg, then invites him to his house. That night the boy witnesses the Cannibal Dance of the bear during a Winter Ceremony performance and acts as the bear's attendant. The bear gives the boy all his dances and regalia. This mask may have been part of those treasures he received.

In 1962, Bill Holm researched a similar cedar bark mask (UBC 3664). He showed a photograph of it to many Kwakiutl. Those who recognized the mask associated it with the legend of Tlalamin as the "mouth forehead mask" used as a taming mask when a woman sang her taming song to the *hamatsa* (Holm: personal communication, 1990). SAM

trouble with the owner of some house posts. Both Hope Island and Quatsino, visited in 1895 and 1900, were major villages close to Fort Rupert. As he exhausted these nearby sites, he began to go farther afield, but most of the Jesup work was confined to northern Vancouver Island and the adjacent mainland. It was not until later work for George Heye that Hunt visited the extreme northern and southern reaches of Kwakiutl territory. In addition to the grave and cave burials, Hunt also searched through deserted village sites. Finally, these were by no means the only sites of which Hunt was aware. Even in these years he often mentioned proposed trips that for some reason or another did not seem to have come through.

Boas and Hunt worked together in the field only twice during these years—several weeks at Bella Coola in 1897, and for a month or so in Alert Bay in 1900. Though Boas did make a collection of domestic items on this latter trip, when he was together with Hunt they spent almost all their time revising texts. Thus virtually all the American Museum's Kwakiutl collections are Hunt's, not Boas's.

As the Jesup Expedition came to an unofficial close in 1902, Hunt began to wind up his Kwakiutl collecting for the Museum, though he sent out a Kwakiutl shipment in the spring of 1904. Much of the years 1903–05 were devoted to collecting from the nearby Nuu-chah-nulth; in the fall of 1904 Boas received some Nootkan material from the winter of 1903 and the summer of 1904. Although Fillip Jacobsen had made a Nootkan collection for the Museum in 1897, Boas desired more and in November, 1901, asked Hunt if he wished to make one. However, Hunt did not get a chance to do any Nootkan collecting until the winter of 1903. The particular object of attention for Boas and Hunt was the Mowachaht Whaler's House in Yuquot, an ensemble of carved figures set up in an isolated place, to which hunters retired for prayer and purification before setting out on a whaling expedition (Jonaitis 1988:182–84). On June 20, 1904, after lengthy negotiations, Hunt managed to buy the shrine, of which he was quite proud: "It is the Best thing that I Ever Bought from the Indians" (Hunt to Boas, 7/27/04, acc. 1904–38, AMNH). While in Nuu-chah-nulth territory, Hunt collected other artifacts and plants, transcribed myths and traditions, and exposed about fifteen photographs, mostly of the shrine (Jacknis, in press; Jonaitis and Inglis, in press).

In reading over the Boas-Hunt correspondence from this period, one is struck by the relative lack of explicit direction from Boas. Having given Hunt basic guidelines and commissioned him to make a general, systematic collection, he left it

up to his field partner to "fill the bill." There are a few specific requests over the years, but the major motif is simply one of goading and encouraging: "I have not heard from you for a very good long time" (Boas to Hunt, 1/13/99, acc. 1899–50, AMNH).

Do not forget that the continuance of your work for the Museum depends entirely upon your success. Unless I can show results of your labors, I cannot get money for continuing. As long as you are not out collecting, I trust that you are writing down more texts for me. Although letter-writing is tedious, you must take the time to let me know fully what you are doing. (Boas to Hunt, 1/7/01, APS)

Later in 1901, Boas repeated his urgings, but added, "Of course, I know that I can rely upon you, and that you will do your best to get together a good collection" (Boas to Hunt, 5/1/01, APS). These proddings were generally successful. By and large, Boas was happy with Hunt's collections: "I think you have succeeded in getting together a great deal of very interesting material," and "Your last collections certainly contain the best old pieces we have obtained so far" (Boas to Hunt, 9/13/99, acc. 1899–50, AMNH, and APS; 5/27/01, APS).

There is really only one instance when Boas took Hunt to task for a purchase he had made. In the summer of 1902, after waiting a long time, Boas finally received one of Hunt's shipments. While generally pleased with the "very interesting specimens," Boas thought that "the price that you had to pay for the Dzō'noq!wa dish is very high; and, although I presume you were very much interested in this specimen, I do not think the purchase was a very good one" (Boas to Hunt, 6/17/02, acc. 1902–46, AMNH). Hunt had paid the (for the time) steep price of sixty-five dollars for a large feast-dish set carved in the form of the giantess dzunukwa complete with smaller dishes for breasts, navel, and knees (fig. 4.16). Justifying his actions, Hunt pointed out that the collector Captain D.F. Tozier of the U.S. Revenue Service (Cole 1985:186) had just offered a hundred dollars for either the same dish or a similar one. As Hunt explained, ". . . the owner would not sell it for that Price so I thought I got it very cheap for if we write about the ways the Indians Handle it in the large feast I think you would like it" (Hunt to Boas, 7/4/02, acc. 1902–46, AMNH). It was hard for Boas to argue with his own collecting principles.

From the Boas-Hunt correspondence alone, it is difficult to form an accurate picture of how the Kwakiutl regarded Hunt and his work. Unlike some occasions—as when Jacobsen was inundated by specimens, some he did not even want—there is no direct evidence that the Kwakiutl were eager to sell to Hunt.

4.16 *Dzunukwa* **dish**. Fort Rupert. Wood, L 270.8 cm, H 59.8 cm. *Collected by George Hunt, 1902. 16/9013–14, AMNH 1902–46*

THE *dzunukwa*, THE WILD WOMAN OF KWAKIUTL legend, emerged periodically from her domain, the heavily wooded back country. Her forays were motivated by her hunger for fish and human children (Boas 1897:372, 1966:307). Although she was a frightening being who attempted to perform antisocial acts, those who outsmarted her came away from her house carrying riches on their backs—dried meats, skins, dance privileges, and the "water of life," which revives the dead (Boas 1910:121, 1935b:163; Boas and Hunt 1905:92; Curtis 1915:297).

A story from the traditions of the Daʼnaxdaxw suggests that the wealth acquired through the gifts of a *dzunukwa* provided the basis for the very first Winter Ceremony. A hunter, searching for the thief who had made off with his supply of dried salmon, tracked a *dzunukwa*'s son through the forest and shot him. A sympathetic young man helped the *dzunukwa* recover the body of her son in order that she might revive him. As a reward, she led the young man to her house.

"Now," said she, "all these things are yours." She pointed to dressed skins and dried mountain-goat flesh, and a mask which was just like her face. "With this," she said, "you will be tsunukwa dancer. (Curtis 1915:297)

Upon his return to the village, the young man gave the first Winter Dance. The *dzunukwa* dance was performed, the meat provided a feast, and the skins were distributed as gifts. The young man's deceased parents were even brought back to life when sprinkled with the water of life.

Following the festivities, the hunter appeared, claiming to be the one entitled to this new dance privilege. The two men quarreled, and this dispute supposedly survives today among their descendants (Curtis 1915:298).

The intense competition and antagonistic displays prefigured in this legend have traditionally been an important part of the potlatch. According to Samuel Barrett, who acquired a *dzunukwa* feast dish set for the Milwaukee Public Museum in 1915, the use of the dish is a prime opportunity to demonstrate rivalry among Kwakiutl numayms.

Such a feast was approached with apprehension; each associated act expressed relative social position. The *dzunukwa* dish was set down before each tribe at this feast in order of rank. If each tribe present was capable of promising to give a feast, then the dish was placed so that its "stern" faced the door. But if a tribe could not make such a promise, then the dish was set down with the stern pointing in their direction. Barrett reports that a fight quickly followed this insult, and the offended group may have tried to throw a part of the dish into the fire. In the course of this disturbance, members of the host tribe and the poorer group attempted to throw each other bodily into the huge dish, a humiliating experience that would be recalled forever as the time that "so and so was washed in my feasting dish" (Mochon 1966:88–89).

When the feasting finally began, the various removable sections of the *dzunukwa* dish, which correspond to parts of her anatomy, were distributed according to the rank of the guests, starting with the head for the chief of the highest-ranking guest tribe, the right breast for the chief of the second-ranking tribe, the left breast for the third, the navel for the fourth, the right kneecap for the fifth, and the left kneecap for the sixth. Other men ate from ordinary dishes filled with food ladled from the large cavity of the *dzunukwa*'s torso (ibid.:90).

The *dzunukwa* feasting dish set in this exhibition was purchased by Hunt for $65.50, an exorbitant sum in Boas's opinion (Boas to Hunt, 6/17/02, Hunt to Boas, 7/04/02, AMNH).

In this dish, the two bowls representing the breasts are heavily coated with grease, attesting to their frequent use. The face is configured around three large openings, the two eyes and mouth, through which Barrett reported that food might be taken (Mochon 1966:88). The bushy eyebrows and pursed lips are typical features of the *dzunukwa* (see fig. 3.7). JO

199   *George Hunt, Collector of Indian Specimens*

This may indicate a change in attitudes over the two-decade period. Though Hunt did encounter some resistance, mainly from owners who were still actively using their pieces, one gets the impression that most Kwakiutl were either neutral towards Hunt or approved. After all, according to Kwakiutl custom, if one sold a mask or rattle, one could go out and commission a new one to take its place. The inherited family prerogative remained.

Around the turn of the century, however, Hunt did encounter some fairly active opposition. Interestingly enough, it came not from conservative, traditional Kwakiutl who might have objected to prized heirlooms leaving the area, but from newly converted Christians, whom Hunt called "Mr. Hall's people." Although he and his father had originally helped Hall set up his mission, George Hunt seems to have thrown in his lot with the conservatives (still, he maintained an ambivalent skepticism towards shamanism). In 1898 Hunt was harassed by children at Hall's school in Alert Bay for sending stories to Boas, and in March of 1900 he was arrested for taking part in an illegal "cannibal" ceremony (see Cole, this volume). He was acquitted with the assistance of Boas, but from then on Hunt was very careful of even the appearance of his actions.

As he had "been learning how to go and look into this greaves and caves," in mid-1901 Hunt asked Boas if he would secure from Mr. A.W. Vowell (I.W. Powell's successor as Indian Affairs Commissioner for British Columbia) permission to remove material from old graves (Hunt to Boas, 8/12/01, APS). Particularly excited about a cache in a cave at Nimpkish Lake, he explained his reasoning to Boas:

there is no man old enough in Fort Rupert to tell when there where Put there, now it will Pay you to ask Mr. Vowel, for I Dont want to tuch anything less than (80) years old. The Indians I know will let me go and get it, But the mission People telling them to lay complaint against me. so you see I got to look out what I am Doing. (Hunt to Boas, 9/6/01, APS)

Boas sent Vowell some publications of the Jesup Expedition with Hunt's name on them, "to show you that Mr. Hunt is doing scientific work of considerable value, and to show that he is assisting me in my undertaking" (Boas to Vowell, 10/7/01, APS). While Hunt at this point was primarily interested in old artifacts, not bones,[10] Boas specifically requested permission to collect bones if they were no longer cared for or claimed by any living Indian. The motives of Boas and Hunt in this appeal were undoubtedly a mixture of pragmatic and scientific impulses. They were trying to describe Kwakiutl culture before

4.17 **Model of a *dzunukwa* feast dish**. Kingcome. Wood, L 43.5 cm, W 14 cm. *Collected by George Hunt, 1902. 16/8951, AMNH 1902–46*

THE IDENTIFICATION TAG THAT GEORGE HUNT affixed to this object explains that it is "just to show the way it is the true Dish is about 16 feet long with all the small ones Belong to it" (acc. 1902–46, AMNH). This tiny dish includes all the characteristics of the full-sized carvings (see fig. 4.16).

The blackened face includes the circular facial depressions and pursed, reddened lips of *dzunukwa* masks. The body cavity had been provided with two breast dishes carved as bears, and a little dish for the navel. The flexed knees support miniature kneecap dishes.

The form of the model is similar to at least two larger *dzunukwa* dishes, both, like the model, of Dzawada'enuxw origin. One example is now in the collection of the Portland Art Museum. The other is a large and unusual set from Kingcome Inlet, which had three face masks, each used for serving a different type of food. Either one may have served as a model for this small carving (Elsie Williams: personal communication, 1990). JO

white contact, so wished for material as old as possible. Yet these would be the very things most likely to be unclaimed, and if so their removal would cause little disturbance. Also, as Hunt noted, digging in caves was cheaper than buying from the Indians. Vowell gave his official permission, though he wanted to be notified of what went on.

Still, the missionized Indians continued to stir up trouble. While traditional Natives may have had no objection to "looting" caves, the new Christians were probably upset by what they saw as the defilement of a sacrament, even if not in consecrated ground. In 1902 Hunt had to store some of his cave collections with his sister in Alert Bay, having his son David bring them over to Fort Rupert in order to avoid talk from "Mr. Hall's people." From then on, though, there are no mentions in Hunt's letters of opposition to his work.

Competition from other collectors, however, was another matter. The years of Hunt's collecting coincided with the "museum age" of anthropology, and curators and dealers often clashed over favored items and sites. One of the biggest feuds involved Boas and George A. Dorsey, curator of anthropology at the new Field Columbian Museum, a post that had once been Boas's. Boas and Dorsey had encountered one another on the coast in 1897. Dorsey had been sent by his director to gather supplemental information they charged Boas had removed from the Museum at his departure. Boas, in turn, was outraged at what he regarded as an encroachment on his scientific territory (Cole 1985:167–76).

As Boas's deputy in the field, Hunt was a constant character in the competitive scene, as the following scenario effectively shows:

Now my Dear friend in the first Plase I want to let you know that one man came here in alert Bay collecting all kind of specimens and afterwards I was told that he wanted to see me. so I went out and I happened to find him Buying a Hat and as soon as he saw me he asked me who I was and Befor I answered he asked me if I new Dr. Boas. then I said what about him. Wel, he said your name is Geo Hunt are you not said he. Wel said I to him I am he you named. then he said I hope that you Dont Expect to see him come out here again. for the museum people would not send him out here again for they say his to Expensive man to them. and now he said I am send in his Plase. so I tryed to find out what his name is He would not let me know. and yesterday I found out that Mr. Dorsey and Dr. Newcomb is coming up to alert Bay and newitty to collect all kind of specimens . . . and still there is another collector in alert Bay that is Mr. Hall his gone Home to England and taken 4 large case of new made carving with him. so you see we got Enimey all Round all speaking you. (Hunt to Boas, 9/26/99, APS)

4.18 **Sea otter feasting dish**. Blunden Harbour. Wood, L 47 cm. *Collected by George Hunt, 1902. 16/8964, AMNH 1902–46*

FOUND IN A CAVE AT OLD 'Nakwaxda'xw VILLAGE, this red cedar bowl is carved in the rounded form of a rotund, well-fed sea otter. This animal is identified by its characteristic posture—lying on its back with its stubby tail turned up between its hind feet. It uses its dextrous forelimbs to lift a small head to its mouth, perhaps an anthropomorphic sea urchin. (Sea otters have the ability to use forepaws to hold rocks in a tool-like manner to crack shells in order to get at their food.)

A broken human figure, only its lower body, back, and one shoulder remaining, clings to the back of the bowl, while the sea otter clasps this small being between its back feet. This configuration may illustrate some scene taken from a local legend. JO

Hunt's interlocutor may have been Dorsey himself; in any case, Charles F. Newcombe and his Kwakiutl assistant Charles Nowell were soon pulled into these feuds.

As the most active Kwakiutl collector after Boas and Hunt, C.F. Newcombe naturally bumped into the New York team in his travels. Though at times their relationship was cool and perhaps a little strained, Boas and Newcombe always managed to be cordial and maintain contact. Yet a constant spur to Hunt's collecting was an ever-recurring fear that Newcombe would get there first. For his part, Newcombe was quite respectful of the superior knowledge of both Hunt and Boas, and twice tried to get Hunt to work for him. When in 1903 Newcombe was collecting for Dorsey and arranging the Field Museum collections, he asked Hunt to come to Chicago. Miffed, Boas shot off a letter to Newcombe saying that Hunt was still very much engaged with him and that he regarded such action "on the part of Dorsey as an interference with my work" (Boas to Newcombe, 12/28/03; see Newcombe to Boas, 1/5/04/ AMNH). Newcombe replied that he merely desired more information on the collections, some of which Hunt himself had collected, but that if Boas had such an ongoing relationship with Hunt, he would certainly withdraw.

However, Charles Nowell was less bound by professional politeness. In 1905 he told the Kwakiutl that Boas would have nothing more to do with Hunt, and, heeding his words, they refused to cooperate with him. At about the same time Newcombe wrote to Hunt asking if he would collect another Nootkan whaler's shrine. With Boas's recent resignation from the American Museum, Newcombe thought that Hunt's contract for collecting was over. Hunt sent off a very worried letter to Boas, who reassured his Kwakiutl friend that their work together would continue (Hunt to Boas, 10/23/05; see Boas to Hunt, 10/31/05, AMNH). Though Newcombe and Hunt maintained fairly friendly relations, Nowell and Hunt found themselves on opposite sides several times in the coming years.

Boas's resignation from the American Museum was stimulated mainly by a dispute over exhibits and popularization; he insisted that he retain full control over the scientific work of the department of anthropology (Jacknis 1985:105–08). Boas was able to fall back upon his professorship at Columbia University, but his departure from the Museum marked a turning point in his collaboration with Hunt and in Hunt's artifact collecting. The days of massive, systematic collecting were over for the team. Although Boas spent several more years preparing his monograph on Kwakiutl material culture (1909), he began to turn to other aspects of Kwakiutl life, especially social organi-

zation and religion. George Hunt continued to collect for a few more years, but his later collecting was more repetitive and not tied into an organized plan of publication.

1906–10: Museum of the American Indian

Although Boas had left the museum setting, he tried to maintain continuity in his research. This is evident in his overture to the wealthy New York collector George Gustav Heye, whose collection became, in 1916, the Museum of the American Indian. In February, 1906, Boas wrote to Heye, asking if he wanted Hunt to collect a Nuu-chah-nulth whaler's shrine. The previous October, Boas had asked his successor, Clark Wissler, if the Museum was interested in acquiring other praying houses, but without a response. Although Hunt was trying as late as 1910 to get another one for Heye, he was unsuccessful. However, he was able to continue his collecting activity among the Kwakiutl.

To some extent his collection can be viewed as a duplication of the comprehensive AMNH collection, as it contained many of the same kinds of items as these earlier ones. "It does not matter whether we have the specimens in the Museum," Boas wrote to Hunt. "You can begin all over again with the ordinary household and hunting things" (Boas to Hunt, 4/13/06, APS). Yet in another sense Hunt and Boas regarded it as a continuation of their efforts, obtaining more "good, old" material, each specimen unique, never to be made again in quite the same way. Finally, this work for Heye was pragmatic, a source of livelihood for Hunt. Steady funding of Hunt's work was always a problem for Boas. "Provided that his first attempt is successful," Boas advised Hunt, "you may get a good deal of work for him. I am glad this new opportunity presents itself, which I anticipate will open up work for you for years to come" (Boas to Hunt, 2/28/06, APS).

Expressing his goals to Boas, Heye wrote: "Of course you will let Mr. Hunt know that I only wish good old material and none of the commercial specimens the Indians are now making" (Heye to Boas, 6/7/06, APS). Accordingly Boas instructed Hunt, "It is our desire to obtain only good old specimens, . . . we want a good and carefully selected collection of masks and dancing-implements, but you must not take any new and shabby mask. We only want good old carvings with good painting" (Boas to Hunt, 6/8/06, APS). These are basically the same instructions Boas had given Hunt in the Jesup Expedition, but one senses in Heye, taken with what we know of his tastes as a collector, a more "acquisitive" desire for fine pieces, almost objets d'art. Although Kwakiutl were making commercial carvings for sale to tourists, many carvers were also producing in modern, contemporary styles for Native ceremonial use. Much of this work was quite good, but not what Heye and Boas wanted.

Boas talked the matter over with Heye and was able to convince him to allow Hunt to continue with his usual methods of collecting: "For every single mask we must have the history written down carefully in Kwakiutl; and if the mask has a song, you must record the song with it, as you have been in the custom of doing" (Boas to Hunt, 6/8/06, APS). The artifacts, with their basic provenience data, were to be sent to Heye and the texts to Boas. Boas instructed Hunt to collect domestic as well as ceremonial items, but beyond these general guidelines, felt he did not have to give Hunt detailed instructions. As was his usual practice, Boas recommended Hunt be given a lump sum—five hundred dollars in this case, in two installments—for which he had to keep accounts, for his wages, expenses, and purchases.

Setting out in July, Hunt should not have been surprised to find most Kwakiutl away from their homes working in the canneries. He went without success to Seymour Inlet, Kingcome Inlet, and Knight Inlet, before he encountered some old people on Hope Island. Hunt found the largest concentration of people at the Rivers Inlet cannery where he made another small collection. The Hope Island collection, fourteen pieces, was all domestic, and the forty-three-piece Rivers Inlet collection was mostly so. Based on a list of Hunt's purchases, Boas reported to Heye that "It seems to me that he had done very well," and Heye agreed (Boas to Heye, 8/31/06; Heye to Boas, 9/4/06, APS). It took Hunt a while to pack up this collection and in the meanwhile he continued his work. Hunt especially wanted to go to Smith Inlet, for in spite of all his collecting, he had not yet acquired anything from the people there. In February and March of 1907 Hunt gathered a second group of 106 items for Heye, this time from Rivers Inlet, Smith Inlet, Hope Island, and Knight Inlet. When Heye finally received all this in the summer of 1907 he was even more pleased.

During 1908, 1909, and 1910 Hunt collected some more, notably seventy-eight pieces from Fort Rupert, but he was sick much of the time and greatly depressed by the death of his first wife in April 1908. In addition to his personal loss, she was a great ethnological resource for him: "I am trying to Do the work for you and I find that it is Hard without the Help I used to get from my Dead wife. for some times I would forget some thing in my writing then she would tell me" (Hunt to Boas,

9/18/08, APS). In fact, he was so worried that when he went up to the Rivers Inlet hospital in 1909 (meeting Harlan Smith on a trip for the American Museum), he instructed his sons to send the collection on to Heye in the event of his death (fig. 4.21).

However, over these many months Boas and Heye worried about Hunt's silence. There are numerous discussions in their correspondence on Hunt's reliability. Boas placed a great deal of trust in Hunt: "I have always found him faithful in carrying out his work." Of a particular specimen he wrote, "Of course I do not know whether it is as old as he puts it, but I have no reason to doubt his statement" (Boas to Heye, 6/5/06, 3/20/07, APS). Yet both men were troubled by a lost check, which Hunt claimed he never received. As Heye exclaimed, "It certainly is not easy to do business with an Indian at a distance of over 3000 miles" (Heye to Boas, 12/18/07, APS).[11] By April of 1910 Boas was beginning to suspect that Hunt was using Heye's money "for purposes other than collecting," perhaps potlatching, and suggested that Hunt might try to cover his "creative bookkeeping" by selling texts to Boas or through return potlatching (Boas to Heye, 4/25/10, APS). For his part, Hunt claimed that at first he misunderstood that Heye and Boas were working together. Another problem he relates at great length concerned a canoe that Boas had instructed him to get. Hunt had commissioned a Hope Island man and paid him twenty-five dollars in advance. Unfortunately, the man drowned and left the canoe in pledge for a debt he owned. In the end Hunt came away empty-handed, but the incident must have tried the patience of Boas and especially Heye. Hunt sent off his final shipment to Heye in December of 1910.

1911–14: Edward S. Curtis (Washington State Museum)

By the time photographer Edward Curtis arrived on the Northwest Coast to gather material for his *The North American Indian*, George Hunt was widely regarded as the local expert on the Kwakiutl, his fame spread largely through Boas's publications. Hunt and Curtis most likely met in the summer of 1910 when Curtis was arranging for future work in the area.

The Curtis film *In the Land of the Head-Hunters* (later re-released as *In the Land of the War Canoes*) was the first of four in which Hunt would play a major facilitating role. In each, material culture formed a dominant subject, and all four were attempts to document the traditional ways of the Kwakiutl.[12] The artifact collecting Hunt did for the Curtis film was not systematic, as he had done in the past, but was more in the nature of gathering props, to be used for their visual effect in front of the camera. Neither Curtis nor Hunt appears to have been concerned about their ultimate disposition.

Hunt spent most of the early seasons—1911 and 1912—working with Curtis's assistant, William Myers, recording traditional customs and history. The collecting and construction of artifacts came mostly in 1913, with final preparations and filming in the summer of 1914. Still photos were made from 1912 to 1914, and some costumes and props had to be gathered for these as well.

Curtis's film required the construction of several false house-fronts and the erection of at least five totem poles and two inside house posts. Apparently all these poles were carved especially for the film, including one said to have been executed by George Hunt himself (fig. 4.22, cf. Holm and Quimby 1980:45). If this attribution is correct, it is the largest and most ambitious carving known to have been done by Hunt. The total film record clearly documents that Hunt had the everyday woodworking skills possessed by other Kwakiutl men of his time. While the "Curtis pole" has relatively shallow carving, the workmanship and design are quite credible.

Several of the twenty-one masks Hunt collected for Curtis in 1913 were made for the film. Other masks and ceremonial artifacts, such as feast dishes and ladles, were old family heirlooms. Surviving documentation indicates that many of these were simply "borrowed" for the film and not collected by Hunt or Curtis. Almost all the cedar bark clothing was newly made, much of it by Hunt's wife. Also bought for Curtis was a large canoe with paddles (Holm and Quimby 1980:44–57, 127–28). Many of the purchased items, particularly some older masks, were donated by Curtis to the Washington State Museum. While one can talk of "collecting" here, as the pieces had to be gathered together, they were not collected for scientific purposes and were not initially intended for a museum.

Some of these masks photographed by Curtis were collected the next year by Samuel Barrett, curator of anthropology at the Milwaukee Public Museum. Barrett spent from February to April 1915 in British Columbia, centered in Fort Rupert, but traveling widely in Kwakiutl territory. His prime goal was to make a representative collection and gather material for a life-group diorama. Barrett had contacted Boas, Sapir, Newcombe, and Curtis before arriving, and all must have recommended Hunt highly, for Barrett wrote that Hunt was "probably one of the best, if not the best, informed men available on the West Coast" (Barrett to Newcombe, 8/10/14, BCARS). Documentation

4.19 *Dzunukwa* **dishes.** Kingcome. *Collected by George Hunt, 1901.* AMNH 1901–32. Left: Wood, L 86 cm, W 34 cm; *16/8556*. Right: Wood, L 94 cm, W 37 cm; *16/8557*

BOTH THESE VESSELS ARE DESIGNATED IN HUNT'S ledger as the "babies" of a larger *dzunukwa* dish set (AMNH 16/8555) of which only the mask cover remains in the American Museum collection (acc. 1901–32, AMNH).

A reference to the offspring of the *dzunukwa* may not have been intended literally, but a great many stories include some information about her children. It is thought that anyone who can make these babies cry will obtain treasures—her magic canoe, water of life, or death-bringer (Lévi-Strauss 1982:82).

The A̲'wa'etḻala of Knight Inlet have a story in which a boy and his father discovered the house of a *dzunukwa*. After they had dispatched her by throwing a stone at her head, they took away her children along with the other treasures of the house. A dance was then called and the two children were displayed to the guests (Curtis 1915:296). In yet another tale of encounter with this being, the *dzunukwa* rewarded those who helped her by bestowing a wife upon them, her own female child, along with other items of wealth (Boas 1935b:163).

The dish on the right must have been used to serve grease because its surface is darkened with an oily residue. An intriguing blocky device protrudes from the bottom of the ladle, perhaps a handle or even an extension that allowed it to rest along the rim of the larger mother vessel. Although the body of the other dish is also roughly carved, the face is slightly rounder, and its bright red mouth protrudes in high relief like a small round cup. The bowl is darkened with use and was probably used to ladle out grease from a larger vessel. The furry eyebrows and hair were probably made from bearskin, a part of the costume of the *dzunukwa* when she appeared as a participant in the Winter Ceremony (Boas 1966:239). JO

4.20 **Dish**. Fort Rupert. Wood, L 33 cm, W 21 cm. *Collected by George Hunt, 1897. 16/2263, AMNH 1897–43*

which served as a condiment in which to dip dried or barbecued fish. Boas's ledgers indicate that it was the property of a chief's daughter. JO

DESIGNATED BY BOAS AS A WOODEN DISH FOR ordinary dining (1909:421), this vessel is heavily coated with grease. It was probably used to hold eulachon oil,

4.21 George Hunt traveling on boat to Rivers Inlet, 1909.
Photo by H.I. Smith, AMNH 26054

4.22 House frontal pole carved by George Hunt, c. 1914, for
Edward Curtis. Museum of Anthropology, UBC. *A50041*

for Barrett's time in the field is sketchy, but it is clear that he made the collection himself, with Hunt as a guide, interpreter, and general resource person. Hunt's role was thus more like his earlier experience with Jacobsen, although this time, of course, he knew so much more. External factors also facilitated Barrett's collecting; religious conversion and constabulary pressure combined to allow Barrett to make a good collection, strong in old ceremonial pieces as well as the few remaining utilitarian items (Ritzenthaler and Parsons 1966). There is no doubt that Barrett would not have been able to amass such a comprehensive collection, even with these external factors, if he had not had the expert advice of George Hunt.

1922–24: American Museum of Natural History

Hunt's last collecting activity came as he was finishing his sixth decade. His work for Boas had fallen off during the years he had worked for Curtis and Barrett, but by 1916 he was busier than ever. From then until his stroke in 1931, he worked steadily, mostly on the textual documentation of religious practices and social organization. Very rarely does material culture come up in the Boas-Hunt correspondence for these later years.

In the summer of 1922 Hunt was visited by Pliny Earle Goddard, a curator for the American Museum (see fig. 4.23). The old Northwest Coast Hall that Boas and Hunt had worked on was undergoing one of its periodic renovations. Goddard wanted to collect more totem poles to place around the pillars in order to suggest the forest atmosphere of the Coast. He also wanted to get a feel for the area at first hand for a museum handbook he was writing.

Hunt's major efforts on Goddard's behalf were the packing and shipping of a wooden sail and the commissioning of four house posts. Goddard asked for "good . . . typical" carvings, leaving their selection to Hunt's judgment, adding, though, that he much preferred the old ones. Hunt entered into negotiations for various sets of poles, but withdrew when the price rose too high. Finally he made a deal with the carver of one set, Arthur Shaughnessy, who would carve the four posts for eighty dollars if Hunt supplied the cedar logs.

Unfortunately, Shaughnessy was one of those arrested in the 1922 crackdown. "I Dont [know] what he will say after he comes out of jail for I see that all these Poor Indians are now frightened to Do any thing. for I tryed to get another man to do this for the Police will have him arrested. yet the government

4.23 George Hunt, Fort Rupert, 1922. *Photo by Pliny Goddard.*
AMNH 118994

Buying there totem Poles" (Hunt to Goddard, 6/23/23, acc. 1924–78, AMNH). Ever resourceful, Hunt revealed that over the years he had collected some pieces, evidently on his own, that he had not sent to museums:

But we will not let them Beat us. for I got a carved cannibal totem Pole under my house. that none of the museums got. and if cant get the carvers to Do the work for us I will send the Pole to you. . . . and I got seven old masks in the House that you Did not see while you was here and all there whistles. (Hunt to Goddard, 6/23/23, acc. 1924–78, AMNH)

As Boas had done before, Goddard wrote to the authorities, in this case local Indian Agent William Halliday, asking special permission for Hunt to collect, or, in this case, for the poles to be carved (Goddard to Hunt, 9/25/23, acc. 1924–78, AMNH).

Shaughnessy finally came to Fort Rupert in early April 1924. By late June he was finished, though Hunt was dissatisfied. He claimed that there were two right hands on the posts and that they were not put on properly. Shaughnessy also omitted the fine adzing. Hunt removed the offending members and carved two of his own (fig. 4.27), indicating that by this point he was more than a mere collector, but a Native authority in his own right who felt responsible for the correct interpretation of Kwakiutl culture in the white world.[13] For instance, Hunt insisted that the artist use Native paints on the posts, "for I Dont like white mans Paint on the Indian poles" (Hunt to Goddard, 3/29/23, acc. 1924–78, AMNH). Hunt's position was conservative, as the Kwakiutl had been using white man's paint for almost half a century, and many leading artists—such as Willie Seaweed and Mungo Martin—preferred the bright enamels.

Although Hunt recovered from his stroke in 1931, he was ill for much of his last few years. Nevertheless, he continued to send Boas texts, and on the evening before his death on September 5, 1933 (at the age of seventy-nine), he was writing for Boas until he had to go to bed.

George Hunt as a Native Anthropologist

I will conclude by discussing George Hunt's status as a Native anthropologist as a way of drawing some of these strands together and of looking at the development of Hunt's collecting work in the context of his total career.[14] Usually "Native" and "anthropologist" are two different people, the latter studying the former. When Natives assist anthropologists they are generally referred to as "informants." It can be argued, however, that Hunt's activities went beyond this to full-fledged research,

at least in the Boasian mode.[15]

Although it may be a cliché, it is true that George Hunt was a marginal man—a man of two worlds, two cultures, and two ages. First, concerning his insider status, Hunt was able to draw on personal knowledge and experience. Of the old sandstones used to smooth down wood, he told Boas, "I use to see them when I was a little boy," and he searched around especially for the old-time things he remembered (Hunt to Boas, 7/4/99, APS). Along with the list of desired items, Boas had suggested that Hunt sit down and write out everything used in fishing, hunting, cooking, basket-making, etc. These verbal descriptions, "from the native's point of view," from Hunt's point of view, in Kwakwala and English, were eventually published, while the artifacts they were associated with were collected for the American Museum. Hunt was also able to draw upon his knowledge of Kwakiutl woodworking to carve a pole for Curtis or fix some arms for Goddard. Yet there is little evidence that Hunt did much of this, preferring instead to go to experts whenever he could.

Hunt's insider status gave him ready access to local sources through family and friends. However, they seem to have been of less help with artifacts. As he was interested especially in old artifacts, he had to go wherever they were, often in caves and in Kwakiutl villages far from Fort Rupert and Alert Bay. Not born to a Kwakiutl family but married into one, Hunt relied greatly on his two wives, especially in his later work with Boas on ceremonialism and social organization. Hunt's command of the language and the local geography and his familiarity with the leading citizens certainly facilitated his work in a manner that Boas could achieve only with great difficulty. There are two occasions that we know of when Hunt made active use of Native privileges, which an outsider would have found impossible to duplicate. As a member of the potlatching system he was able to ask creditors to call in their loans so a certain man would be forced to sell his chief's seat (fig. 4.25), and he was able to purchase the Mowachaht whaler's shrine by trading some Kwakiutl Winter Ceremony songs (Cole 1985:161–62).

Yet Hunt's insider status can easily be exaggerated. Hunt himself was the first to admit that he was learning new things: "Now I have some fine old things that I Did not know any thing about Before" (Hunt to Boas, 8/12/01, APS). His greatest surprise seems to have been the discovery from reading over the texts that in the old days, before white contact, the Kwakiutl used cedar bark masks. He also enjoyed his work in the "exotic" cultures of the neighboring Bella Coola and Nuu-chah-nulth, groups that spoke mutually unintelligible lan-

4.24 Raven transformation mask. Fort Rupert. Wood, feathers, rope, copper, L 44 cm. *Collected by George Hunt, 1897. 16/2381.* AMNH 1897–43

THIS TRANSFORMATION MASK DEPICTING TWO images of the raven came to the Museum with little documentation save the attribution "Raven of the Sea," an image used as part of the *tła'sala* performance (acc. 1897–43, AMNH).

When completely closed, this raven mask appears quite simple. Its distinguishing features include the green band in which the red eyes circumscribed with black are located. The beak is black with a thin red line designating the nostril. At the top of the head a triangular element juts upward. This finlike element may have been one of the characteristics that associated this mask with the sea. A small dab of down is centered between the raven's eyes.

The mask is rigged so that the beak could open. The inside of the beak is painted with various designs accentuated with dabs of down. Bill Holm has suggested that the painting on the inside of the beak may refer to a killer whale (personal communication, 1990). The interior face is anthropomorphic, although the nose has a distinct beaklike hook. The nostrils are constructed of patches of copper.

Typically, a dancer entered the house with the mask sitting high on his head in a closed position. The dancer then manipulated the mask's rigging underneath a blanket to hide the mechanics from the audience. He did this while lowering his head, so that when he lifted his head the audience would briefly see the transformed image. The dancer again brought his face down to change back to the outside form. While there are many variations of this movement depending upon the type of animal depicted, the mechanics of the transformation are usually hidden. SAM

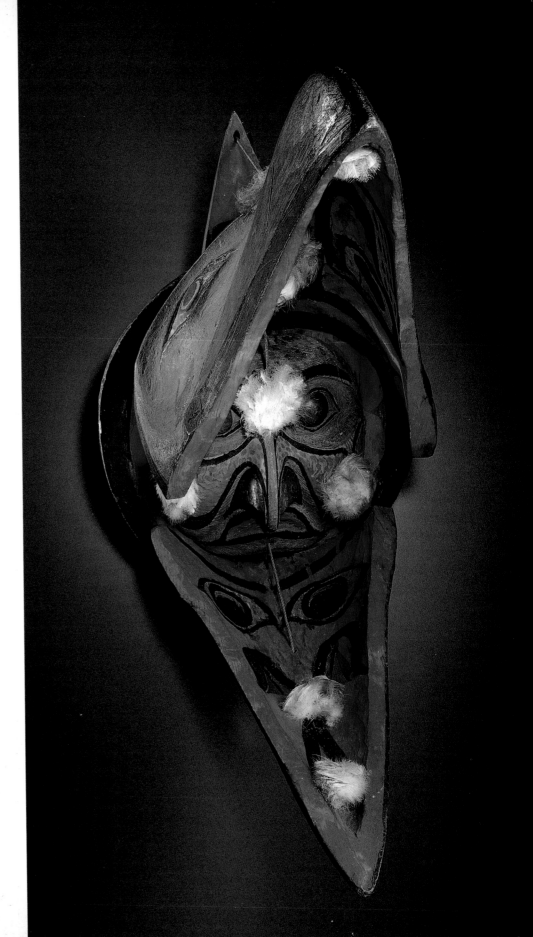

4.25 Settee. Hope Island. Wood, L 297.5 cm, H 99.6 cm. *Collected by George Hunt, 1900. 16/7964, AMNH 1900–14*

Hunt spent several years negotiating the price and transferral of this settee that Boas had already published twice (1888:200, 1897:371). This large settee back depicts the *sisiyuⱡ* or double-headed serpent; its face is carved in shallow relief, and its displayed body is painted on the flat surface. Although the illustrations Boas published included the sides of the settee which showed the two serpent heads, Hunt did not send these side planks to New York along with the back.

Early in their correspondence (Boas to Hunt, 1/4/98, APS), an enthusiastic Boas encourages Hunt to find the Hope Island ("Newitty") house in which can be found the settee as well as house posts and a speaker's post (fig. 4.26). On that same day, Hunt writes to Boas:

I have been to Newitty and I bought the three totem post of Galitis House. But I cant take them yet for Hemtset is using the house now till the winter is over. and about the chief seat they want $50.00 Dollars for it so I want to know if you would be willing to give that price for it. (Acc. 1900–14, AMNH)

It seems that the owner of the settee and posts wanted to display these objects again before he sold them.

On March 14, Hunt writes to Boas describing his clever scheme to get the settee's price lowered. He tells how he persuaded a man to whom the settee's owner was in debt to ask for his money:

. . . so I got a man to ask him to go and get this man to pay his debt to another man so there pressed him so much that he had to come and beg me to buy the seat for 40.00 dollars but I told him that I cant pay him more than 8.00 dollars for it, then he told me to give him another dollar then he will take the price, so I gave him 8.75 dollars for it, so you see the way I have to work it? (APS)

Despite what seems to have been a very clever ploy, Hunt did not take possession of the pieces for quite some time; indeed, he writes to Boas on February 7, 1899, that he still had not been able to actually remove these objects for which he had already paid. He remained hopeful, however:

[I went to] see about the House Posts and asked the man I bought it from to take the House to Peses [pieces] and to let me take them away and he said that he will Do it so I think tht I will send them to you some time in April and the seat. (APS)

But by July 4, Hunt still did not have the carvings. He describes how he went back to the seller:

[I] asked him why he Did not take down the his House and he said that he was going to take it Down as soon as he go home for the Lalasekwata tribe is not working for the cannery this year and I told him that if he tells me another lie that I will have him Rested [arrested] so I think he will do it this time. (APS)

At the end of 1899, Hunt finally managed to send the settee and post to Alert Bay; by January they arrived safely at the Museum. Boas expressed concern that Hunt had sent only the back of the settee, and not the sides (Boas to Hunt, 1/27/00, APS). Hunt had thought (correctly it turns out) that Boas would not want the sides since they had been made from commercially milled lumber and not adzed in the traditional way (Hunt to Boas, 2/24/00, APS). SAM

215   *George Hunt, Collector of Indian Specimens*

4.26 **Speaker's post**. Hope Island. Wood, L 289.2 cm. *Collected by George Hunt, 1900. 16/7960, AMNH 1900–14*

THIS SPEAKER'S POST CAME FROM THE SAME HOUSE as the settee back illustrated in fig. 4.25. Boas first described this post in his publication on Kwakiutl architecture (1888b:212). He described it again in 1897 (p. 376):

[It] represents a statue in a house at Xumta'spē that has a curious explanation. It belongs to the subdivision of the Me'ᴇmaqaae . . . of the Naqo'mg·ilisala. These are the descendants of Lelaxa (= coming often from above) the son of Q'e'q'aqaualis. . . . Their original home is the island of G·ig·e'lem, one of the small islands southeast of Hope Island. Lᴇla'k·en was a later chief of the clan. His daughter was Lao'noqemeqa. They moved to the island of Q'oa;sqᴇmlis and built a village. The chief made a statue like the one represented here. It is hollow behind and its mouth is open. In the potlatch the chief stands behind the mouth of the statue and speaks through it, thus indicating that it is the ancestor who is speaking.

Although the post was published once more in 1909 (pl. 45), Boas provided no further information on it until 1926, when he described this statue as a

figure representing a chief's mind (giges = Chieftaincy inside). The human figure represents a chief's mind and the chief does what the figure tells him; that is to say the chief's speaker stands behind the figure and tells him what to do. The grizzly bear underneath represents the chief in a passion when breaking coppers and canoes. The figure belonged to Q!omkimis, chief of the Nae'nsxa of the Nagᴇ'ngilisala. (Boas 1926:4–5)

Such posts were sometimes erected in the house when a potlatch was taking place; the speaker, positioned behind the open mouth, called out the names of the chiefs as they entered the house. SAM

4.27 House post carved by Arthur Shaughnessy (16.1/1815) in the Northwest Coast Indian Hall, AMNH. *120698*

4.28a *Huxwhukw* **mask**. Wakeman Sound. Wood, feathers, paint, mirrors, cloth, L 100 cm, H 23 cm. *Collected by George Hunt, 1901.* *16/8553, AMNH 1901–32*

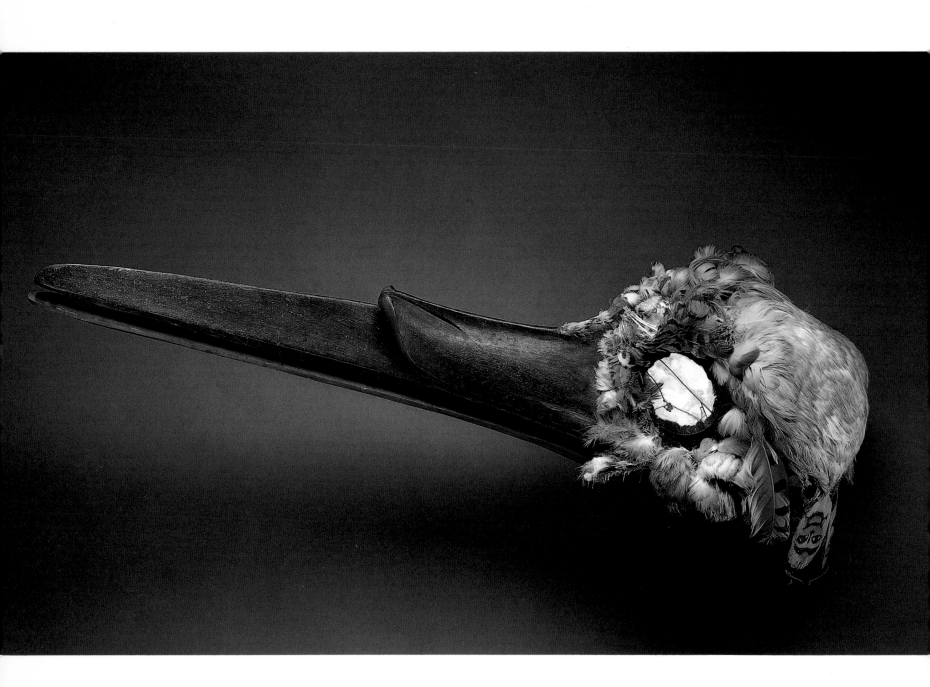

4.28b **Huxwhukw mask**. Kingcome. Wood, feathers, paint, mirrors, cloth, L 96 cm, H 34 cm. *Collected by George Hunt. 16/8425, AMNH 1901–32*

T HESE TWO BIRD MASKS ARE RARE VERSIONS OF *huxwhukw*, a bird attendant to Baxwbakwalanuxwsiwe', the Cannibal-of-the-North-End-of-the-World. They are not the same being as the *huxwhukw* that appears in the *hamatsa* performance (see fig. 2.28). Instead, they represent a bird that reappears in the *tseḵa* as part of a tradition different from the *hamatsa* (acc.

1901–32, AMNH; Adam Dick: personal communication, 1990). The behavior of these birds is similar to that of the *hamatsa huxwhukw*; they all split their victim's heads open with their beaks and eat the exposed brains.

These bird masks have feathered heads and long beaks with large, flaring nostrils. Their large round glass eyes would have reflected the firelight, adding to the drama of their appearance. On fig. 4.28a, the small, paddle-like attachments painted with faces might represent the skulls of the victims of *huxwhukw*. SAM

guages and possessed different, though related, customs. Despite his Kwakiutl status, in his visits to remote villages he probably explored places to which he would not have otherwise gone.

Over Hunt's long relationship with Boas, one can see a progressive education and training in anthropology. We know little of the instruction Boas gave him before the Chicago Exposition, but in the summer of 1893 Hunt learned how to write Kwakwala in phonetic transcription, what a text was, and how to take one. The following year Hunt worked very closely with Boas in the latter's most intense Kwakiutl fieldwork, observing and photographing potlatches and Winter Ceremonies, plus a little collecting. During the Jesup Expedition, especially at the beginning, Boas had offered guidance in letters, but by then he felt Hunt knew his business. Over the years, though, Boas sent him copies of his work and related books, so that Hunt could get a broader background in the discipline. One can see a growth in Hunt's professional roles as he moved from being an interpreter for a collector, to an assistant, to making a rather casual collection from around home, to making, finally, a systematic collection with extensive documentation. Yet it was in his text-based and social research that Hunt showed the greatest growth in sophistication.

George Hunt combined the positions of insider and outsider in his work as a Native anthropologist. As Boas hoped he would, on numerous occasions Hunt initiated projects. As soon as he returned to Fort Rupert in January of 1894, he was out looking for masks, even though Boas was not collecting at the moment. It was Hunt who suggested collecting in late winter, searching in caves for old things, and asking permission from Vowell. In 1900, not satisfied with pen and paper, Hunt asked Boas for a camera and Gramophone, and with his camera took a significant body of photographs (Jacknis, in press). Once Hunt went ahead on his own, bought up all the carved stone heads he could find, and then asked Boas if he wanted any. In December of 1899 Hunt managed to combine personal experience and professional rationale in a typically perfect combination. Hunt's wife had been sick, and "one of this Indian medicine I am using on my wife this last five weeks and it is the only thing that is doing lot of good—so I think it is good to have all this in you museum" (Hunt to Boas, 12/6/99, APS). Upon Boas's reply that it was a splendid idea and that his museum did not have such material, Hunt proceeded to make a rather extensive and unique collection of Native medicines.

As he grew older, Hunt was sought out by many as an expert on Kwakiutl culture. To some extent this was simply

4.29 **Mask**. Quatsino. Yellow cedar, fiber, L 33 cm. *Collected by George Hunt, 1900. 16/8184, AMNH 1900–73*

IN THE COLLECTION DATA SUPPLIED BY HUNT, THIS mask was listed as a "bitten off ear of knee cap of the Nan" (Acc. file, Dept. of Anthropology, AMNH). This attribution is ambiguous. While *nan* is the Kwakwala name for grizzly bear, it is unlikely that this mask was associated with either of the two Grizzly Bear societies that existed when Hunt collected this piece. One of these societies consisted of grizzly bears that had been initiated by Baxwbakwalanuxwsiwe', while the other represented the ordinary grizzly bear. The former was the more prestigious of the two, and its duties were related to those of the *nuḻamaḻ*; members functioned as enforcers during a ceremony, assuring that the proper behavioral codes were upheld (Boas 1897:465–67; see also fig. 2.10).

The formal characteristics of this mask do not correspond to Boas's description of the grizzly's costume. The image of the grizzly bear performer that Boas presented was a dancer clad in a bearskin, wearing bear claws, with a ferocious bear's mouth painted on his face. Boas also illustrated an image that showed the costume of a 'walas nan, the great grizzly, in which the face of the dancer was covered by a mask realistically depicting the snout of the bear down to the details of the sharp teeth (Boas 1897:467, pl. 32).

This mask has no obvious bearlike features. The face is anthropomorphic, the mouth is small, and the lips are closed. Rather than a sharp bear snout, this face has large, round cheeks and an exaggerated human nose. Without further information linking this mask to a particular tribe's history, its significance remains uncertain. Although there is no documentation that such a mask representing a bear's kneecap existed, Adam Dick has suggested a possible connection between this carving and the portrayal sometimes found on totem poles, in which faces appear on the knee joints of bears (personal communication, 1990). SAM

because Hunt was an elder and remembered past customs, but as we have shown, it was more because Hunt was a scholar and had especially investigated these matters. This was particularly true of material culture. Most of the collectors with whom Hunt worked were known to one another, and, if not Boas's students, were in his circle (Edward Curtis was the major exception). A sign of this growing expertise was the demand for Hunt as a "consultant" to review and correct museum exhibits. In early 1903 Boas brought Hunt to New York for several months, and Newcombe tried to get him to come to Chicago later that year. In 1922, when Hunt was working with Boas in Victoria, Newcombe did secure his services to review the Kwakiutl collection at the British Columbia Provincial Museum. Hunt's annotations are quite instructive. Recognizing many pieces, he explained to whom they belonged and with what other pieces they were associated. In many cases he recited the story that went with them, at times giving references to the published works of Boas and Hunt. Hunt made evaluative comments: of a *dzunuk̓wa* ceremonial sword: "This is no good. It is not Indian at all," and of a *sisiyuɬ* mask: "The paint is all right but too much white man."[17] Hunt's expert advice was also sought for the first four films on the Kwakiutl.

When one considers the collections that Hunt himself made, in the Field Museum (1891–92), U.S. National Museum (1894–95), American Museum of Natural History (1896–1905, 1922–24), and Museum of the American Indian (1906–10), one must conclude that George Hunt was not only the largest single Kwakiutl collector, but that he may have collected the majority of the extant Kwakiutl specimens from this period in the world's museums. The total goes even higher if one considers the collections with which he assisted: a little of the 1879 Powell collection (Ottawa), much of the 1881 Jacobsen collection (Berlin), the 1894–95 American Museum and National Museum collections of Boas, the Harlan Smith collection of 1898 at the American Museum, the 1912–14 Curtis collection (Burke Museum), the 1915 Barrett collection (Milwaukee), and a few pieces that Goddard collected in 1922 (American Museum). Hunt monopolizes the sources even more when one considers verbal documentation.

Hunt's anthropological career may be seen as a combination of two distinct roles—interpreter and recorder or archivist. George Hunt had expanded his youthful role of language translator until he found himself spending four decades writing out Kwakiutl culture in Kwakwala and English. He was able to do this by the addition of Boas's phonetic training to his existing English literacy. This, combined with his photo-

4.30 **Headband** (*back and front*). Fort Rupert. Bark, cloth, L 19 cm, W 12 cm, H 7.5 cm. *Collected by Harlan Smith and George Hunt, 1901. 16/8746, AMNH 1901–52*

UNLIKE OTHER HEAD ORNAMENTS IN THIS CATA-logue, this headband was made not from dyed cedar bark but from red cloth, with only small amounts of bark. It was "presented to Harlan Smith, October 31, 1893 by George Hunt of Fort Rupert" (acc. 1901–52, AMNH). Smith, an archaeologist who worked for Boas during the Jesup North Pacific Expedition, subsequently gave it to the American Museum. The shape of the headpiece is like that of other rings worn during the Winter Ceremony. SAM

graphic, film, and sound recording work, allowed him to record Kwakiutl culture for posterity, for both Kwakiutl and whites. By the difficult 1920s, when Hunt was a frail old man, his knowledge was appreciated and treasured by his people. Welcoming Boas to Fort Rupert for what was to be their last time together, Hunt wrote:

I dont know weather you will find any one of these People to talk the old fashean language. for the most of them, one word for every thing instead of using the different word for the different way of answer. one thing I know that lost about two third of their language for there lots of the Indians comes and ask me the meaning of the words. (Hunt to Boas, 3/15/30, APS)

Although Boas and Hunt may been saddened at the loss of tradition, they could at least take comfort from the vast amounts they managed to document and preserve. In the letter that Boas had written for Hunt to read to the Kwakiutl in 1897, explaining why they were there, he said:

My friend, George Hunt, will read this to you. . . . It is good that you should have a box in which your laws and your stories are kept. My friend, George Hunt, will show you a box in which some of your stories will be kept. It is a book that I have written on what I saw and heard when I was with you two years ago. It is a good book, for in it are your laws and stories. Now they will not be forgotten. Friends, it would be good if my friend, George Hunt, would become the storage box of your laws and of your stories. (With Boas to Hunt, 4/14/97, acc. 1897–43, AMNH)

George Hunt, collector of so many Kwakiutl boxes, was, by the end of his life, that storage box for Kwakiutl culture.

4.31 **Drum painted by Willie Seaweed**. Fort Rupert. Wood, deerskin, metal tacks, paint, 45.5 cm by 6 cm. *RBCM 12909*

THIS DRUM IS ELEGANTLY PAINTED WITH A *sisiyutł* design by the twentieth century Kwakiutl master Willie Seaweed. In order to fit the double-headed serpent onto the round surface of this drum, the artist has omitted the creature's snakelike body, including only its central horned anthropomorphic head, which is flanked by profile depictions of horned serpents.

The oldest type of Kwakiutl drum is the wooden box drum. The Kwakiutl originally used this type of round hand-held drum during a game involving gambling; later it was used during potlatches (Holm 1983:68).

In the film *Totem Land* (1930), which Boas made with J. R. Scott for Associated Screen Gems, George Hunt appears playing this drum, which he may have owned. In 1967, the Royal British Columbia Museum purchased it from Mrs. W. Cadwallader, one of Hunt's descendants. SAM

5 / The Contemporary Potlatch

Gloria Cranmer Webster

IN 1951, THE INDIAN ACT WAS REVISED AND THE section prohibiting the potlatch was simply deleted, not repealed as the Kwakwaka'wakw had continued to hope. During the dark years of potlatch prohibition, the people had persisted in carrying on their ceremonies in secret, accepting the changes in form and content that such secrecy demanded. It was a time of fear and confusion for people who believed that "It is a strict law that bids us dance. It is a strict law that bids us give away our property. It is a good law." These words were part of a speech made to Franz Boas when he first visited Fort Rupert in 1886. Almost one hundred years later, one of the two survivors of the 1922 potlatch trials expressed similar feelings when she said, "When one's heart is glad, he gives away gifts. It was given to us by our Creator, to be our way of doing things, we who are Indians. The potlatch was given to us to be our way of expressing joy. Every people on earth is given something. This was given to us."

The causes for the drastic changes in our way of doing things include a period of rapid population decline due to introduced diseases and alcohol. As well, the zealous efforts of the missionaries to "Christianize the heathen" were partially successful. The white teachers of several generations of Indian children devoted most of their energies to "civilizing" their students, rather than providing any useful education. "They were trying to make white people out of us," one woman said in reflecting on a time of her life when she knew little and cared less about who she really is. She, along with others who shared similar experiences, is now trying to make up for those lost years.

Although clandestine potlatches were held before the revision of the Indian Act, it was not until 1953 that the first public "legal" potlatch was held. It was held in Coast Salish territory, a long way from the homes of the Kwakwaka'wakw. From 1952 until his death in 1962, Chief Mungo Martin worked at the

5.1 Alert Bay big house, 1990

British Columbia Provincial Museum, carving totem poles and teaching young carvers. One of his projects was the construction of a big house. When the house was completed, he hosted a potlatch, inviting many people from our area. In a speech to his people, he expressed his feelings about what he was doing, following a rehearsal:

Now, we are finished. That is the way I wanted you to come. Thank you. Thank you, chiefs. You have put strength inside me, for I was very weak all by myself away from home. I almost cry sometimes, when there is no one here to help me. And you have come to help me, you with your famous names, you chiefs. You have strengthened me. Your fame will spread because you are here. You have strength, for you know everything. You, too, have been left to take up the duties which have been passed on to you. So you will help me to finish what I want to do.

The triumph of Mungo Martin's potlatch is evident from the speeches made by the chiefs who were his guests, as recorded during the event. That there were no repercussions from the authorities was a relief and added to the satisfaction felt by those who had participated.

In all probability, the success of Mungo Martin's potlatch encouraged people in Alert Bay to think about building their own big house. Various tribes contributed to the design and construction. The big house was completed in 1963 and was opened with a potlatch hosted by Chief James Knox of Fort Rupert (figs. 5.1–2). He was one of twenty people who had been imprisoned for two months in 1922, for potlatching. Many people attended, some out of curiosity about something they had only heard about, but had never seen.

Since then, there have been potlatches every year, with most of them taking place in Alert Bay, although a few are held in big houses in Kingcome Inlet, Gilford Island, and Comox. For villages which do not have big houses, potlatches are held in community halls and people often comment that "it's just not the same without a fire and dirt floor."

The reasons for giving potlatches are the same as they were in the past—naming children, mourning the dead, transferring rights and privileges, and, less frequently, marriages or the raising of memorial totem poles. Times for potlatching that would not have been known in earlier days were the opening of the Kwagulth Museum in Cape Mudge in 1979 and of the U'mista Cultural Centre in 1980. Our hearts were certainly glad on both those occasions.

A modern potlatch takes much less time to plan than those of earlier days. Our old people say that preparing for a traditional potlatch would take years. It is said that the 1921 potlatch took seventeen years of preparation. Today, there are no longer loans made or to call in. "Nowadays, you just put your hand in your own pocket," one of our old people said, in comparing past and present potlatches. Today, from the time it is decided to hold a potlatch until it happens takes about a year.

During the months of preparation, family members are busy accumulating the goods to be given away. The big house in Alert Bay holds almost 700 people, which gives some idea of how much is needed to ensure that no guest leaves empty-handed. The women produce huge quantities of crocheted articles, including cushion covers, afghans, doilies, and potholders. Glassware, plastic goods, blankets, pillows, towels, and articles of clothing are bought and stored away. Sacks of flour, rice, and sugar may be added. An artist may contribute a design to be silkscreened on posters or shirts.

Tłi'nagila is a special kind of potlatch. *Tłina* is the oil rendered from eulachons and is as highly valued today as it was in the past. As many as 250 gallons may be given away. Today, a gallon sells for about a hundred dollars, so that the distribution of such a valuable commodity greatly enhances the stature of the potlatch-giver. The *tłina* is given away separately from the more common goods, an indication of its importance.

Buying for a potlatch is unlike any other kind of shopping. Christmas shopping doesn't even come close. Some years ago, I walked into a small fabric store and asked for a hundred yards of material that was on sale. The owner exclaimed, "A hundred yards! What are you going to do with a hundred yards?" Earlier that day, I had been asked questions such as, "Are you setting up a boys' camp?" when I bought six dozen pairs of men's socks, and "Are you opening a restaurant?" when I bought 200 coffee mugs. It is difficult to explain what a potlatch is to people in stores, so I told the man that we were going to have a big

5.2 Interior of Alert Bay big house, 1990

party and give it all away. He thought that was such grand idea that he added ten yards as his contribution, saying, "Have a wonderful party." We did.

Sometimes, printed invitations are sent out for a potlatch, but more often, guests are invited in a traditional manner, that is, at a potlatch being given by someone else earlier in the year. Several days before the actual date of the potlatch, the host and members of his family travel from village to village, inviting the tribes. At each stop, the host and his group are fed and given money in appreciation for the invitation. These days, travel is by car, ferry, and boat, rather than by canoe, as in earlier times.

A typical modern potlatch is much shorter than in the past, when one potlatch might last over several days or a week. Today, many of us work at regular jobs, which leaves only weekends free. Some of our family members live away from home, so their travel time must be taken into account. We also have to consider the people involved in the increasingly competitive and uncertain fishing industry for whom limited openings are a major concern. As a result, a potlatch must be compressed into less than twenty-four hours, beginning in the afternoon, so that mourning songs can be sung before sunset, and ending in the late evening or early hours of the next morning.

Several days before the potlatch, relatives and friends begin arriving, staying with local families and visiting other homes, while there is time. Everyone knows that on the day of the potlatch, there will be too many things to do for any more socializing. The big house must be cleaned, wood cut for the fire, hemlock branches gathered to decorate the doorway and screen, borrowed masks picked up, and other chores. Women prepare huge quantities of food, including fish and venison stews, clam chowder, salmon cooked in a variety of ways, smoked and salted eulachons, seaweed, salads, and baked goods. Some of the food is contributed by relatives who live in other villages where certain kinds of food are more readily available. Herring roe on kelp or hemlock boughs is a special treat, as it is difficult to obtain these days.

Early in the morning, as many as twenty women gather to make about twelve hundred sandwiches. One of the periodic functions of the U'mista Cultural Centre, which is probably unique among similar cultural institutions, is to serve as a place for making sandwiches. The work goes quickly, with a lot of joking and gossiping.

Everyone works together with incredible energy and enthusiasm to ensure that everything will be ready on time. While the food and big house crews are finishing their jobs, others are

5.3 End of mourning songs; potlatch given by Tłakwagila
(W. T. Cranmer), 1983. *Photo by Vickie Jensen*

5.4 Red cedar bark ceremony; potlatch given by Tłakwagila
(W. T. Cranmer), 1983. *Photo by Vickie Jensen*

5.5 **Raven mask by Henry Hunt**. Wood, rubber, metal, nails,
string, wool, blanket strips, H 100 cm, W 60 cm. 1973. *1973–1120,
RBCM 14123*

IF ONLY ONE MASK IS TO APPEAR DURING THE
hamatsa dance, it will be the Raven-of-the-North-End-of-the-
World, one of the servants of Baxwbakwalanuxwsiwe`, the
Man-Eater-of-the-North-End-of-the-World. During the dance, the
masked dancer will sit down in front of the singers and again at
the front door, snapping the beak of the mask while making the
sound of a raven. This and other masks of the *hamatsa* appear just
before the last appearance of the tamed *hamatsa*, who is accompanied by a female attendant wearing a smaller version of a raven
or Crooked-Beak mask. The dancer wears a skirt and leggings of
dyed red cedar bark. GCW

loading trucks with potlatch goods and ceremonial gear to deliver to the big house. Such cooperative effort seems to surface only during potlatch time and is probably indicative of another change in our lives; that is, we are no longer able to help each other in any kind of ongoing way. However, it is of some consolation that such cooperation has not completely disappeared and that it does emerge for the right reasons.

While all the other activity is going on, the old people meet to decide on the dances to be performed, the order in which they will appear, and the names to be given. At this time, representatives of various branches of the host family may announce that certain dances and their names will be transferred to the host, explaining the kinship connection and the history of the dance. Relatives and friends may contribute money, varying in amounts from one hundred to one thousand dollars, to show "how I feel in my heart for you." The chiefs present all express their appreciation for the host's determination to follow the path of his ancestors. Food is served, while the host or an older member of his family thanks everyone for attending and expresses the hope that everything will go well. There is an appeal for all to work together, because we are now so few, so poor, and so weak in our world that what we are able to do is only a shadow of what used to be. These statements in Kwak̓wala reinforce our painful awareness of how much we have lost over the years. At the same time, the strong words of our old people inspire us to hold on to what we have left.

At last, it is time to go to the big house. As soon as you enter, another difference between past and present is clear. There is no longer any strict seating arrangement, with people sitting according to their tribal and individual rank. People now sit anywhere, except for the host family, which is always seated on the left toward the back of the house. Chiefs and singers sit on either side of the long drum, with the overflow occupying a row of chairs in front. In earlier times, only those who had received proper names were permitted to enter a big house for a potlatch. Today, anyone may attend. There may be quite a number of white people, some of whom have been invited, others who have not. A few of the white people are anthropologists, who are friends of the host family. There is an old joke about families not having their own anthropologist, who must order one from the "rent-an-anthro" agency, because every potlatch should have one. Sometimes, there have been so many uninvited white people that there has been overt hostility shown by properly invited guests who have trouble finding a place to sit. In more recent years, the message seems to be reaching the outside world that for white people, invitations

5.6 *Huxwhukw* **mask by Doug Cranmer**. Wood, H 178 cm, W 26 cm. 1971. *RBCM 13948*

LIKE THE CROOKED-BEAK-OF-HEAVEN, THE *huxwhukw* is a mythical bird and also a servant of Baxwbakwalanuxwsiwe', the Man-Eater-of-the-North-End-of-the-World. The *huxwhukw* has a long pointed beak, with which it broke the skulls of human beings and ate their brains. Like Crooked-Beak, it cries "Hap! hap!" as it snags its beak. The dancer wears a skirt and leggings of dyed red cedar bark.

This mask lacks the required trim of dyed red cedar bark, which is ordinarily attached to the top of the head and down the back of the mask, to hide its rigging. Eagle feathers may also be tied to cedar bark. GCW

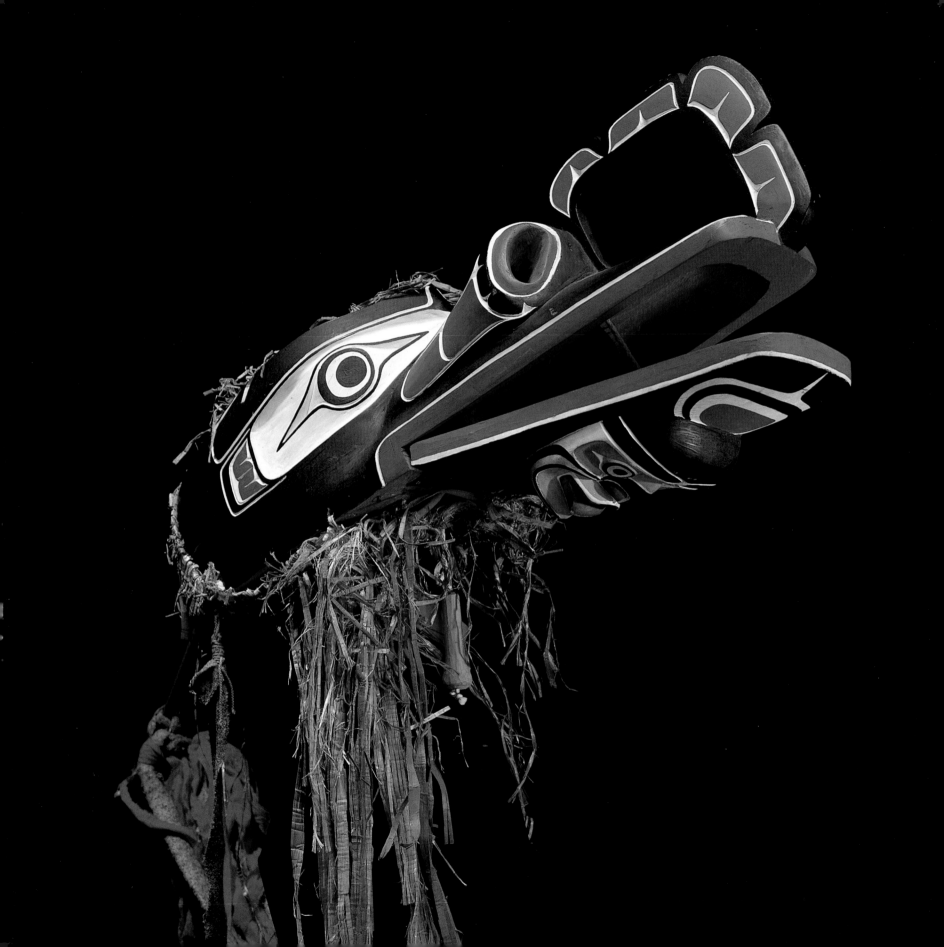

5.7 **Crooked-Beak mask by Henry Hunt**. Wood, cedar bark, H 73 cm, W 24 cm. 1971. *RBCM 13850*

THE MASK REPRESENTS THE CROOKED-BEAK-OF-Heaven, another of the servants of Baxwbakwalannuxwsiwe', the Man-Eater-of-the-North-End-of-the-World. When the dancer sits, snapping the beak of the mask, he cries, "Hap! hap!" His costume includes skirt and leggings of dyed red cedar bark. GCW

5.8 *Hamatsa* masks—Crooked-Beak and raven; potlatch given by Tłakwagila (W.T. Cranmer), 1983. *Photo by Vickie Jensen*

are required, because what we do is not for the entertainment of strangers.

After a welcoming address by the host's speaker, women from bereaved families are called to put on button blankets and to sit in front of the singers, while mourning songs of different tribes are sung. At the end of each song, its origin is explained and words of condolence are offered to the mourners. When all of the songs are finished, the women stand and dance in place (fig. 5.3). This signifies that the sadness is shaken off and the tears are wiped away. Infrequently, if the potlatch is in memory of a high-ranking deceased person, a dancer wearing an *imas* mask appears, accompanied by four chiefs. The mask may take the form of a killer whale, the chief of the undersea world, or whatever is appropriate for the deceased. The dancer and his attendants move slowly around the fire and leave through the front door. The attendants return, without the dancer but carrying his neckring, apron, and blanket, indicating that, although he is gone, he has left his rights and privileges for the use of his surviving relatives.

At the completion of the mourning ceremonies, there may be a transfer or sale of a copper. One of the rules laid down by the old people who were involved in the building of the Alert Bay big house is that the breaking of copper is forbidden there. They say that breaking a copper for a rival was such a serious matter that it was the same as wishing he would die.

If a marriage is on the agenda, it will take place following the copper business. The bride sits with her family near the door, facing the groom and his family, who are standing in front of the singers. Each tribe in order of its rank attempts to capture the bride, circling the fire, while singing a song that refers to one of its ancestors. We, the 'Namgis, are led by a man carrying a bow and arrow, recalling the story of Muksa-ga'wakw, whose magic weapon made him invincible. He had found the scales of a *sisiyutł*, which he rubbed on his arrows. An enemy, when struck by one of the arrows, turned to stone.

Eventually the right tribe wins the bride, who moves to stand with the groom's family. Her family's speaker then announces the names, songs, and dances which are being transferred to the husband, to be held in trust for their children. The total value of money and goods to be distributed is also announced. Older women who have led exemplary lives as wives and mothers are called to feed the bride small bits of food, as they instruct her in the proper behavior expected of her as a wife. All of those who have participated in trying to capture the bride are given money for their efforts. The husband's family sings a song in appreciation for everything being given.

5.9 *Tuxw'id* **head by Beau Dick**. Wood, hair, cord, L 32 cm, H 18 cm. 1980. *1980–27:0, RBCM 16616*

THE *tuxw'id* DANCER HAS THE POWER TO MAKE MAGIC things happen, depending on the particular treasure of her dance. She may cause thunder and lightning, give birth to a frog, or make *dantsikw* boards appear and disappear. This treasure represents the decapitated head of the dancer and is carved as realistically as possible. Concealing the carved head under her blanket, the dancer asks the attendants to cut off her head. They do so, substituting the carved head, which appears to bleed profusely. The sources of the bleeding are containers of animal blood, which have been hidden under the dancer's costume. The attendants circle the floor, holding the decapitated head by its hair. At the end of her dance, the *tuxw'id* once again conceals the carved head and completes her performance as if she has come back to life through her own power. GCW

Now the food is brought out and served by the young women of the host family. Chiefs, singers, and old people are fed before the other guests. At the end of the meal, feast songs may be sung.

The cedar bark ceremony may now take place (fig. 5.4). A high-ranking woman of the host's family, standing in the middle of a large circle of dyed red cedar bark, enters with four chiefs who hold the circle in place around her, as they move slowly around the fire, to stand in front of the singers. One of the chiefs, who has inherited the position of cutter, makes three feints with his knife before actually cutting the bark circle. The bark is then cut into lengths, torn into strips, and distributed, first to the chiefs and singers, then to the rest of the guests. Everyone fashions a headband from the bark and wears it during the *tseka* or "red cedar bark [Winter Ceremony]" dances. Because logging companies now own most of the trees and forests, cedar bark is difficult to obtain, and red yarn or cotton may be substituted.

It is now time for the appearance of the *hamatsa*, the first and most important of all the dances. The sound of whistles is heard behind the screen, heralding the approach of the dancer. If he is a new dancer, he appears first wearing a skirt, neckrings, wristband, and anklets made of hemlock branches. He dances wildly around the fire, crying "Hap!" indicating that he is hungry, while his four attendants try to control him. They escort him behind the screen and reappear with him, now wearing red cedar bark ornaments, instead of the hemlock. Once again, they circle the floor and go behind the screen. The *hamatsa* masks appear, one at a time, representing the servants of Baxwbakwalanuxwsiwe', the cannibal spirit. These are Raven, *huxwhukw*, and Crooked-Beak (figs. 5.5–8). The number of masks appearing vary from one to eight, depending on how many the family owns. During this performance, a few women stand and sing chants while shaking rattles. In his fourth and final appearance, the *hamatsa* is completely tame and dances dressed in an apron, button blanket, or bearskin decorated with carved wooden skulls. He wears either an eagle or thunderbird headdress and is preceded by a female relative, who also wears a bird headdress. An older woman may dance with them, carrying a copper, which she feeds symbolically to the *hamatsa*, as part of the process of taming him. Women in the audience stand and dance in place, honoring the *hamatsa*. For many of us, this is the proudest moment of the whole potlatch. The floor is filled with dancers, the singing is powerful, and there is such an intense feeling of pride and belonging that it is

5.10 *Nuḻamaḻ* **mask by Beau Dick**. Wood, cotton, cedar bark, L 30 cm, H 23 cm. 1980. *1980–270. RBCM 16615*

CHARACTERIZED BY ITS LARGE NOSE, THE MASK IS worn by a dancer who moves very quickly around the floor, crying, "Yi hi!" as he pretends to throw mucus from his nose at people in the audience. In earlier times, the *nuḻamaḻ* dancers were responsible for ensuring that everyone behaved properly in the big house during ceremonies. Armed with sticks, they hit people who did not observe the rules of correct behavior. A *nuḻamaḻ* does not allow his nose to be touched and is easily enraged by any reference to it. A well-known *nuḻamaḻ* was named Kwaxatola, "Smoke-from-the-Top (of his head)." In reality. the name means that he was so fierce that smoke came out of his nose.

On this mask, the red and white fabric coiled around the face represents dyed and undyed red cedar bark. GCW

5.11 Wolf dancers, one with headdress, one without; potlatch given by Pal'nakwala Wa'kas (Douglas Cranmer), 1978. *RBCM*

hard to describe to those who have not been part of something so vibrantly alive.

If this is the first time the *hamatsa* has danced, he and his female attendant receive new names. These reflect the importance of the dance. For example, his new name may be Kwanwatalagalis—Thundering-Around-the-World. Hers may be Gamuti'lelagalis—Howling [like a wolf]-Back-and-Forth-Across-the-World. The speaker expresses his gratitude that everything has gone well and distributes money to the singers, "to soften your throats." He will do so several times throughout the evening, to encourage the singers. Money is also given to the women who chanted during the appearance of the *hamatsa* masks.

The dances following the *hamatsa* are in the order discussed and agreed upon earlier by the old people. They may decide to make last-minute changes, causing considerable stress for the person whose responsibility it is to record the order of dances, names of dancers, and new names to be given. When this happens, I think back to the days when nothing was written down, but somehow people kept everything straight without the writing system on which we have become totally dependent. If the dancer is new, his or her name will be announced, along with the history of the dance, its name, and how the family acquired the right to it.

Once in a while, a dancer will appear without the appropriate mask, which is probably in the collections of some distant museum. We are grateful to the British Columbia Provincial Museum (RBCM) for its enlightened policy which permits the loan of ceremonial gear from its collections for use in potlatches. This helps to fill the gaps, as do the contributions of contemporary carvers who produce replicas of those objects in foreign places. The important point is that the right to the dance remains, even though its mask may be gone.

When all of the specific dances are finished, women from various branches of the family are invited to dance in tribal groups. This is a chance for young children to demonstrate the skills they have learned in dance classes at school. There are so many dancers at this time that no new names are given. The speaker simply announces that their names will be the same as before.

At the end of the *tseka*, if the family has a right to it, a *hilikala* may be sung, indicating that everything has gone well. Everyone in the big house stands, holding their hands out with palms up, and moves in time to the song. They then take off their cedar bark headbands as the speaker says, *"La'man's lixaliltł"* (Now we are turning over in the house), meaning that

5.12 **Bee mask by Tony Hunt**. Wood, plastic, cougar pelt, H 45 cm, W 36 cm. 1967. *RBCM 12731*

THE DANCE OF THE BEES MAY HAVE AS MANY AS A dozen masks appearing together, the smallest ones worn by one or two young children. The dancers are called out one at a time by the mother bee, the youngest appearing last. As the dance comes to an end, the baby bees are "lost," hidden among the spectators, as the other bees go behind the curtain. The mother bee then comes out again, looking for her babies, and does not leave until she has found them. All the dancers reappear, holding their masks under one arm, as they dance around the floor again. GCW

we are changing to the *łła'sala*, sometimes called the peace dance. But before these dances begin, coffee, sandwiches, apples, and oranges are served.

Just as the *hamatsa* is the most important of the *tseka* dances, so is the *hoylikalał* the most important of the *łła'sala*. If the oldest son of the host is the *hamatsa*, his younger brother or a younger son will be the *hoylikalał*. This is the only serious dance of the *łła'sala*.

When the other dancers appear in groups, the attendants ridicule and mimic one of them. The dancer leaves, followed by the attendants, who return, carrying his frontlet, saying that there is a *długwe'* (treasure). If the *długwe'* is a creature from the sea, the dancer will appear through the front door, as a killer whale, sea eagle, man of the sea, chief of the undersea world, or the *gadaxanis*, who represent a Tlingit chief and his slaves. If the *długwe'* is from the land or the forest, the dancer will appear from the back of the house, in the form of a *bakwas* or *dzunukwa* (fig. 5.16).

The *długwe'* may be a pair of strangers or intruders, who appear in ragged clothing, carrying mops or brooms, and pretend not to speak Kwakwala when the attendants try to find out where they have come from. They exhibit a lot of curiosity about the people in the audience, pretend to fight, and generally clown around, causing much laughter. Another pair of dancers are the moon and half-moon, who argue about which of them is superior to the other. They try to involve the audience in their argument.

As in the *tseka*, in the *łła'sala*, most dancers wear a button blanket (fig. 5.21). Some of us wear a Chilkat blanket. Our family's right to the Chilkat blanket was inherited from my great-great-grandmother, Anisalaga, who came from Tongass, Alaska. Her oldest son was George Hunt, but that's another story.

Sometimes white people are invited to dance in the *łła'sala*. They are friends of the host family or have made some kind of contribution. The custom has become accepted in recent years and there are a number of politicians, bureaucrats, and others who take great pride in having names they can't pronounce and the meanings of which they don't know.

When the *łła'sala* dances are finished, it may be midnight or later, and it is time for the *am'lala*, the "fun" dances (5.17). These are also owned by families, and everyone participates. One such dance is called the *sudi* and was brought back by the Da'naxda'xw of New Vancouver, who went to the World's Fair in St. Louis in 1904. There, they met Sioux people who gave them the dance. If there are guests from the Nuu-chah-nulth

5.13 **Killer whale mask by Richard Hunt**. Wood, leather, metal, H 580 cm. 1980. *RBCM 16460*

THIS STRIKING MASK THAT REPRESENTS A KILLER whale has been worn during both the *tseka* and the *łła'sala* at recent potlatches. It has also appeared during the initial mourning ceremonies of a potlatch as an *imas* mask. During the *tseka*, it appears after the *hamatsa* dances. During the *łła'sala*, it is a *długwe'*, or treasure, from the sea. The dancer, usually wearing a button blanket and frontlet, disappears from the big house. Attendants, who enter the big house carrying his costume, inform the guests that the dancer has disappeared. Soon the dancer reappears, wearing this mask.

5.14 Sea monster mask by Tony Hunt, Jr. Wood, cedar bark, copper, quartz crystal, cord, H 69 cm, W 60 cm. 1987. *1987–0813, RBCM 18651*

THE GENERAL TERM FOR SEA MONSTER IS *'yagam̲* (bad), but this represents a specific monster, 'Na̲mx̱xelagiyu, one of the ancestors of the 'Na̲mgis. After the great flood, 'Na̲mx̱xelagiyu came out of the river Gwa'ni and became the man 'Namukusto'lis. He began to build a house but was unable to lift the heavy beams by himself. A thunderbird flew down and perched on a large rock nearby. 'Namukusto'lis saw the bird and wished that it could help him. Because the thunderbird was also a supernatural creature, it knew the wish in 'Na̲mukusto'lis' mind. The thunderbird lifted its bird face, revealing a human face underneath, saying, "I will help you," as it lifted the beams in its talons and put them into place. When the work was finished, the thunderbird assumed human form by removing his bird skin and throwing it into the air. As it flew away, he said, "You will only cause thunder and lightning when one of the people in this place dies."

Too heavy to be worn as a normal dance mask, the sea monster mask is held over the face of the dancer, who stands behind a low screen, moving from side to side and over the top of the screen during his performance. GCW

5.15 *Tła'sa̲la dancers*; potlatch given by Pa̲l'nakwa̲la Wa'kas (Douglas Cranmer), 1978. *RBCM*

5.16 Intruders, a *długwe'* of the *tła'sa̲la*; potlatch given by T'la̲kwagila (W. T. Cranmer), 1983. *Photo by Vickie Jensen*

tribes of the west coast of Vancouver Island, they will add their own fun dances. Everyone has been sitting for a very long time, so that getting up and joining in the fun dances is a welcome break.

Finally, it is time to bring out the goods to be given away. All family members help to carry cartons, boxes, and bags, which are emptied and spread out on the floor. While everything is being unpacked, the host and an older family member begin to distribute money, first to the chiefs and singers, then to the rest of the people (fig. 5.18). The chiefs and singers may receive up to one hundred dollars each; men and chief's wives or widows, twenty dollars each; then, for younger men and women, from two to ten dollars each.

Those who will give out the gifts are reminded that chiefs and their wives, chief's widows, and those who have come from far away must receive more than ordinary people. Even chiefs who are not present must be remembered and their gifts and money are sent home with a relative. Special gifts, such as silver bracelets, may be given to those who have contributed in a significant way (figs. 5.19–20).

If the potlatch has included the recognition of young girls who have reached the age of puberty, the gifts for children will include bars of soap, combs, and toys, symbolic of earlier purification rites and the fact that the girls are leaving their childhood behind them.

The distribution of gifts takes some time, and while it is going on, the speaker invites the chiefs to speak. They do so, in order of their rank, thanking the host for his generosity, praising him for walking in his forefathers' footsteps and for remaining strong. They often reiterate the remarks made earlier in the potlatch meeting about how little we have left and how we must work together. After each chief has spoken, the speaker thanks him by name, saying, "For your breath, chief, let this go to you," giving him money. Even those who have not spoken but occupy chief's positions will be thanked for their breath and given money.

Reading transcriptions and listening to tape recordings of earlier potlatches are reminders of another change from the past. Those eloquent speeches, with their flamboyance and high-flown praise, powerfully delivered, are rare today. In the past, young men learned to give speeches, and by the time they were in chief's positions, they were able to speak without the microphones on which speakers today are dependent. A few younger chiefs are able to offer their remarks only in English, because they can't speak Kwakwala.

It is all finished. All that needs to be done is to clean up the

5.17 *Am'lala*, fun dance; potlatch given by Pa̱l'nakwa̱la Wa̱'kas (Douglas Cranmer), 1978. *RBCM*

5.18 Distributing money; potlatch given by T'la̱kwagila (W. T. Cranmer), 1983. *Photo by Vickie Jensen*

5.19 Potlatch goods to be given away; potlatch given by T'la<u>k</u>wagila (W. T. Cranmer), 1983. *Photo by Vickie Jensen*

5.20 Giving out towels; potlatch given by P<u>a</u>l'nakw<u>a</u>la Wa'kas (Douglas Cranmer), 1974. *RBCM*

big house, but that will be left until tomorrow. People leave the big house slowly, stopping to congratulate the host and his family on the success of their potlatch, saying goodbye to those they will not see tomorrow. It may be two or three o'clock in the morning by now, but for some people, the levels of energy and excitement are still too high just to go home to bed, although it has been an exhausting day, so there may be a party at someone's house to help us unwind. The U'mista Cultural Centre produced a film in 1983, in which my mother, Agnes Cranmer, appears, welcoming guests in Kwakwala. At the end of her welcome, she says, "Now, I ask that we all enjoy ourselves tonight. What the white people call a good time. We will have a good time." Our good time continues for many hours after the potlatch has ended.

If my ancestors from two hundred years ago were able to be with us today, I often wonder what they would think of a contemporary potlatch. Would they be able to recognize what we do as being related to what they did? Would they pity us for having lost so much, or be proud that we are still here? I think that after recovering from the shock of seeing so many changes, not only in the potlatch but in all aspects of our lives, they would tell us that under the circumstances, we are not doing too badly. They would also urge us to keep on strengthening what we have, if we are to survive and continue having our good times.

5.21 **Button blanket by Shirley Ford**. Wood, cotton, plastic, H 168 cm, W 150 cm. 1980. *1980–27:U*, RBCM *16621*. *Photo by Andrew Niemann*

THE DESIGNS ON BUTTON BLANKETS REPRESENT THE crests of the owner. This design is the two-headed *sisiyutł*. Looking directly at a *sisiyutł* caused certain death. However, if a human being killed such a creature, he obtained superhuman strength, either by rubbing the blood of the *sisiyutł* over his body, which then turned to stone, or by dipping his hands in its blood, turning them to stone. He might also place scales from the *sisiyutł* on the tips of his arrows. When these were shot, their targets turned to stone.

The large rocks in front of the village of 'Mi'mkwamlis at Village Island are said to have been the enemies of Tłisalagi'lakw, who were turned to stone when the hero looked at them while wearing the skin of a *sisiyutł* he had killed.

The border on this blanket has copper and diamond designs. Other designs found on blanket borders may be mountains, arrows, or broken coppers. The earliest button blankets were made of Hudson's Bay Company blankets, with designs outlined in handmade shell buttons imported from China. Button blankets may also be decorated with pieces of abalone shell. GCW

6.1 (*pp. 252–53*) **Mask of Born-to-Be-Head-of-the-World**. Hopetown. Wood, red and undyed cedar bark, rope, L 75 cm, W 62 cm, D 23 cm. *Collected by George Hunt, 1901. 16/8410. AMNH 1901–32*

Here is the face of the hero Born-to-Be-Head-of-the-World in two aspects. An outer mask rigged to be flung open by the dancer reveals a second version of the same face on the inside. The features of this personage are those of a human being painted with a dark green masklike configuration and a black mustache and beard on a plain wooden ground. The mask shape terminates in two hooklike curves painted on the cheeks. Similar configurations may be seen on two other masks in this catalogue (figs. 6.11 and 6.15).

The entire head has been luxuriously adorned with a great many hairlike strands of cedar bark and a twisted headring. This slightly larger than life-sized face separates down the center. It opens like two doors to reveal two stylized black hands painted inside. Framed by a black scalloped border, the inner set of features clearly represents the same individual but is painted upon a bright white ground, creating the impression of some dazzling transformation.

Apparently the substantial powers of Born-to-be-Head-of-the-World were not limited to his ability to assume the forms of various animals. The gifts of Ḵumugwe' initiated a metamorphosis in this character's nature and appearance, which enabled him to leave behind his old name, Siwidi, and become 'Nalanukwame'gi'lakw, "Born-to-Be-Head-of-the-World." JO

6.2a (*pp. 254–55*) **Killer whale dish** (*front and back*). Hopetown. Wood, L 73 cm. *Collected by George Hunt, 1901. 16/8528. AMNH 1901–32*

6.2b (*pp. 256–57*) **Killer whale dish**. Hopetown. Wood, H 61 cm, W 34.4 cm. *Collected by George Hunt, 1901. 16/8527. AMNH 1901–32*

These killer whale feast dishes commemorate one of the adventures of Siwidi (Hunt, acc. 1901–32, AMNH). According to the legend, Chief Ḵumugwe' advised Siwidi to embark upon a voyage that would eventually lead him back again to the house of supernatural treasures. In the course of his travels, he was escorted by Born-to-Be-Head-Harpooner, the killer whale. Siwidi's supernatural benefactor Ḵumugwe' commanded the killer whale, "Go all round our world with Paddled-to [Siwidi], that he may go and watch my servants":

Then Born-to-be-Head-Harpooner started, and told his people to get ready. Then he loaned to Paddled-to a small canoe, and Born-to-be-Head-Harpooner asked Paddled-to to try to spout. Paddled-to went aboard the new little canoe. As soon as he went aboard, the small canoe became a killer-whale, and Paddled-to did well with his spouting. (Boas and Hunt 1906:63)

Accompanied by all the killer whales, Siwidi visited the tribes underneath the sea.

Both these feast dishes convey a distinct sense of the speed with which the killer whale canoe carried Siwidi through the water. The two dishes, however, are not identical. Fig. 6.2b is a bit smaller than the other, and the color of the wood has remained lighter in spite of the varnishlike coating of grease splattered here and there on its surface. More of the original paint, a rich vermilion, remains on this dish in the areas of the teeth, nostrils, and hands, and on the conventionalized design elements appearing on the fins.

Both dishes include a detachable dorsal fin, which may be inserted near the functional openings at the top of the vessels. A small face has been carved at the base of each. The personage depicted in fig. 6.2b displays a horizontal grimace filled with teeth. A furrowed brow contributes to its rather menacing appearance. On fig. 6.2a, however, the little being sticks out his tongue.

Fig. 6.2a is carved with a combination of killer whale and human attributes that functions as an extraordinary yet credible whole. The animal's powerful tail curls upward and around the back of its body, where the transformation from sea creature to man takes place. From the base of this tail emerges a carved human face, showing its teeth in an exaggerated grin. Its arms, clothed in the sleeves of a white man's jacket, grow convincingly from the back of the killer whale's body, and the two hands are placed at the man's temples. They appear to hold back those portions of the tail that might obscure the view of this being as it moves through the water, the human end leading the way.

The spout of the carved killer whale is articulated with a small tube, which may have been designed to dispense some liquid, probably oil, since the dish is darkened with a greasy residue. The spout strengthens the association of this feast dish with the First-Beaver story, because the act of spouting figures prominently in Siwidi's experiences beneath the waters. JO

6 / Postscript: The Treasures of Siwidi

Judith Ostrowitz and Aldona Jonaitis

ONE OF THE MOST REMARKABLE FEATURES OF THE research done for *Chiefly Feasts* emerged when we came to realize that an assortment of masks and ritual paraphernalia Hunt collected between 1901 and 1902, from the Gwawa'enuxw people of Hopetown, were all part of a single dance cycle, the Dance of the Undersea Kingdom, and that they represented the treasures of the hero Siwidi (fig. 6.1). The manner in which this realization came about demonstrates the way in which the ongoing vitality of Kwakiutl culture can have a major impact on our understanding of nineteenth century materials in museum collections.

In her initial selection of artworks for *Chiefly Feasts*, Jonaitis was drawn to some complex objects such as the triple transformation mask depicting a bullhead, a Raven of the Sea, and a man (fig. 6.3), a large whale mask with an eagle on its back (fig. 6.4), and an assemblage consisting of a sea otter head surrounded by four curving pieces of wood upon which birds sit; projecting from the top of that creature's head is a thin wooden slat with a movable figure (fig. 6.5).

While Jonaitis was selecting artworks in New York, Peter Macnair of the Royal British Columbia Museum was working on an exciting project. Chief Tom Willie of Hopetown owns the privilege to perform the dances that tell the story of Siwidi and his adventures in the undersea kingdom; in the past five years, he has demonstrated this privilege by having the dances performed at several potlatches. Since 1987, Macnair has commissioned for the Campbell River Museum a series of masks by contemporary Kwakiutl carvers that could be used in performances of this dance sequence; these masks are imaginative representations of a number of sea creatures from the story (fig. 6.6).

When Macnair came to New York in the fall of 1989 to serve as a consultant on *Chiefly Feasts*, he looked at the assortment of objects Hunt had acquired at the beginning of the century from the Gwawa'enuxw. Macnair was very familiar with the published versions of the Siwidi legend (Boas and Hunt 1906:63–76; Boas 1935a:175–90); when he visited the museum, he reread the Boas and Hunt version and reviewed the catalogue and accession records. He soon realized that he was looking at earlier depictions of sea creatures similar to those he was commissioning contemporary artists to create. He pointed this out to researchers Stacy Marcus and Judith Ostrowitz, requesting that they search for the original typescript of the Boas and Hunt version to determine if any additional information might be found. When Gloria Cranmer Webster and Wayne Suttles visited the museum during the winter of 1989, they scrutinized all the documentation in the archives, including the materials in Kwakwala (which Gloria Cranmer Webster translated). Their research clarified which carvings were part of the Siwidi story. By the end of this process, we were confident that we own a truly remarkable array of interrelated artworks which, although not all purchased at the same time, had been used in a single highly significant ceremonial.[1]

In May 1990, Chief Tom Willie and his wife, Elsie Williams, visited the American Museum of Natural History as members of the delegation of Kwakiutl old people who came to New York to advise us on *Chiefly Feasts*. At that visit, each mask was examined and its role in the Siwidi dance cycle was thoroughly and enthusiastically recounted in the course of discussion. In an oration that deeply impressed both Kwakiutl guests and museum personnel, Chief Willie rose from his seat and recited his own version of this compelling legend in Kwakwala. During the course of the afternoon, the greater part of the story line was translated into English as it became applicable to the individual works of art that were examined by the visitors. Chief Willie's version of the circumstances surrounding Siwidi's acquisition of supernatural treasures is quite definitely related to the story published by Boas and Hunt eighty-five years ago. This continuity, vividly disclosed as the full significance of the Siwidi material came to light, has served as an enlightening example of the enduring nature of many Kwakiutl traditions (fig. 6.7).

6.3 **Bullhead mask**. Hopetown. Wood, rope, L 89 cm, W 54.4 cm. *Collected by George Hunt, 1902. 16/8942, AMNH 1902–46*

The bull-head that was Born-to-be-Head-of-the-World spoke, and said, "O brother! Born-to-be-always-Chief! go and call our parents to come quick, that I may see them." (Boas and Hunt 1906:67)

I T WAS IN THE FORM OF THE BULLHEAD OR SCULPIN that Born-to-Be-Head-of-the-World first revealed himself to his younger brother, Born-to-Be-Always-Chief, upon his return from the undersea kingdom. At first their skeptical father would not believe that the bullhead was the long-lost Siwidi (see fig. 6.4). But eventually he saw that this fish had the face of his son, and soon the whole tribe knew that Siwidi had returned.

George Hunt recorded, on a label inscribed in his own hand, that the triple transformation mask illustrated here represented a bullhead on the outside, then a Raven-of-the-Sea, and finally the face of Born-to-be-Head-of-the-World on the inside (acc. 1902–46, AMNH). This exceptional combination of successive images is designed to articulate the manifold nature of this hero, now capable of any number of supernatural transformations.

The wall-eyed fish on the outside of the mask has been painted a deep gray-green, the color of the sea floor. Its wide mouth opens to reveal the dazzling white face of the Raven-of-the-Sea, its features articulated with strokes of red and green. At the core of this construction is the face of the hero, also on a white ground, his mouth turned down at the corners like the mouth of a fish.

When the mask is entirely open, some conventionalized characteristics of each of the three creatures may be seen simultaneously. The eyes of the bullhead are painted on the inner surface of the first section, the features of the raven are represented inside the second section, and the face of Born-to-be-Head-of-the-World stares out from the center of the mask with the penetrating expression of a most powerful being, master of many forms. JO

The Legend of Siwidi

6.4 **Whale mask**. Hopetown. Wood, hide, rope, L 213 cm, W 74 cm. *Collected by George Hunt, 1901. 16/8390.* AMNH 1901–32

Then Born-to-be-Head-of-the-World spoke to his father, and said, "O father! look at my house! Come and look at the dancing-paraphernalia of my great supernatural house!" (Boas and Hunt 1906:70)

We now know that among the various objectives that influenced George Hunt's collecting agenda between 1901 and 1902 was the desire to assemble a significant body of this same dancing paraphernalia—those masks, dishes, and other objects which were used by the Gwawaʾenuxw people in the dramatic celebration of their ancestor's adventures in the undersea kingdom. Hunt's field lists of those years frequently refer to a being known as Nāʾlanōkumēˑgᵉi lakwē (ʾNalanukwameˑgiʾlakw) or Born-to-Be-Head-of-the-World, the special name acquired by Siwidi (Paddled-to) after he had been transformed by his supernatural experiences (acc. 1901–32, AMNH). On one occasion, Hunt wrote to Boas: "I mean to get the sea otter mask from the ts!awadaeno [Dzawadaʾenuxw] tribe Belong to the Nalanokomigelakwe storie" (Hunt to Boas, 2/22/01, AMNH),[2] making explicit his motive to gather together these objects for the American Museum of Natural History.

Among these same records, Hunt also provided direct references to the version of the legend published as "First-Beaver" from the traditions of the Gwawaʾenuxw (Boas and Hunt 1906:60–79), along with every mask, dish, or figure that had been used for this dance performance. The objects linked with this family history were not acquired by Hunt all at once, as one cohesive set, but were accumulated a few at a time, and the styles in which they were carved and painted are not always consistent.

The Raven-of-the-Sea headdress mask (fig. 6.9), for instance, was executed in a manner favored by Bella Coola rather than Kwakiutl artists. The deeply carved eyes and the particular type of bulge that defines the cheek area are sculptural qualities that characterize Bella Coola works. The intense blue and vermilion paint also emphasize this origin (Holm 1987:124). Furthermore, the carefully carved killer whale feast dishes in this set of objects (fig. 6.2) may not have been executed by the same hand that produced the huge and impressive, but hardly refined, whale mask (fig. 6.4).

These factors, however, are not incompatible with the practices of the Kwakiutl, as they assemble masks from a variety of sources for an elaborate performance. An individual who owns so important a dance privilege might not have on hand all of

WHEN BORN-TO-BE-HEAD-OF-THE-WORLD ROSE from the water to return to the ancestors of the Gwawaʾenuxw people, he was elusive and appeared to them in the guise of various creatures. At first he revealed himself as a bullhead (sculpin) to his younger brother, Born-to-Be-Always-Chief. Next he assumed the shape of a huge whale with an eagle sitting on its dorsal fin, but he retained a double tail, one like the bullhead's and the other like the whale's. The people chased this great creature in their canoes but could not keep up with it. Born-to-Be-Always-Chief's father spoke to him of his older son's supernatural feats: "O son! look at the way your elder brother acts, that we may have this for our crest" (Boas and Hunt 1906:68).

This large and extremely heavy mask was apparently carved to depict Born-to-Be-Head-of-the-World as a whale. The sheer size of this creature and its exaggerated features are consistent with the significant power this hero acquired and demonstrated. The red nostrils resemble two enormous tubes divided by the curving extension of the septum. Fragments of mica on this section and the bulging eyeballs must have reflected light and looked like drops of water, as if this monstrous sea creature had just risen from the depths.

This entire sculpture was elaborately rigged so that parts of its body moved back and forth as the dancer, whose lower body might have been camouflaged with cedar bark, manipulated various strings. The dorsal fin moved up and back inside a slot, and the eagle, perched next to it, moved with it. The eagle's wings were made of soft hide and flapped slightly as the bird moved.

The lower tail, carved with the graceful flukes of a whale, is able to flap up and down beneath the curving upper sculpin tail. The oversized mouth was snapped open and shut as the lower jaw, square and filled with teeth, swung up and down. The dancer would glide into the house mimicking the swimming movements of a gigantic whale, in a dramatic display of great power. JO

the required masks and other items. Borrowing an object from a near friend or relative might have been possible in 1900 and is an acceptable practice today. A Bella Coola work, moreover, might find its way to a Kwakiutl village, far from its place of origin, as a function of the gift-giving practices of these groups carried out on the occasion of aristocratic marriages. Alternatively, such a work may have been acquired in war or possibly through trade. Even if it were not originally carved for a performance of the dance of the undersea kingdom, a mask might have been redefined as a part of this set, once it had been included in the dance.

Hunt recorded three distinct versions of the Siwidi legend (Boas and Hunt 1906:60–79; Boas 1935a:75–190). In each one, the circumstances that surround the acquisition of this hero's supernatural powers, his wonderful house, the works of art, and dance privileges are described in a different way. Only some of the masks and dishes actually resemble the characters that appear within these narratives; others do not. It is possible that those carvings which do not correspond to the characters in one of these stories fit more closely the characteristic features of beings described in other, unpublished versions of the Siwidi legend.

As the "First-Beaver" version of the legend goes (Boas and Hunt 1906), among the ancestors of the Gwawa'enux̱w was a youth called Siwidi, who aroused the anger of his father for his lack of initiative in matters of spiritual endeavor. His father abused him and said: "O Fool! don't think too much [only] of sleeping. Look at your elder brother! He is all the time rubbing his body with hemlock-branches" (Boas and Hunt 1906:60).

The young hero retreated to the woods, ashamed and contemplating suicide. He sat down beside a large lake and, mysteriously, the waters rose around him. A devilfish (octopus) appeared and grew until it completely engulfed Siwidi, dragging him down into the lake to the fantastic house of Ḵumugwe' (Wealthy), the chief of the undersea kingdom, also known as Copper-Maker. This great benefactor launched Siwidi on a series of adventures, visits to the various tribes beneath the sea in which he was accompanied by Ḵumugwe's attendants, the killer whales.

Although Siwidi calculated his absence from home as a period of four days, in fact four full years passed. When his voyages were finished, Siwidi returned to Ḵumugwe', and this richest of chiefs gave him his own house called Sea-Lions-All-Over. Ḵumugwe' also bestowed several new names upon Siwidi to commemorate his acquisition of great supernatural

THIS CARVING WAS PROBABLY THE SUPERSTRUCTURE of a mask that operated as an extraordinary device, designed so that its four curving arms whirled around and around at the dancer's command. Four birds, mounted at the tip of each of these extensions, revolve in a circle, flapping their cloth wings. The mechanical principle used to achieve this effect is like that of a child's top: a string wound around the midsection of the structure is pulled, initiating this circulating movement.

At the heart of this construction is the head of a sea otter, once painted a vibrant green in the eye area and at the nostrils. At the top of the head is a flat wooden extension, rigged to move forward and back and provided with a vertical slot, along which a little wooden man, possibly the brother of Siwidi, could be raised and lowered.

The characteristics of this fantastically constructed creature are clearly described, more than once, within the legend of Born-to-Be-Head-of-the-World. According to the story, one of the many forms the hero assumed upon his return to his tribe was that of a sea otter with many gulls flying around it (Boas and Hunt 1906:68–69). This same form was taken as well by Born-to-Be-Always-Chief, the youngest brother, after his mysterious disappearance from the Winter Dance. Born-to-Be-Head-Speaker discovered him floating on his back on the water like a large sea otter, with four white gulls flying over him. All the men, women, and children of the tribe went out to have a look and try to capture him. He was brought back to the house by this group and they were able to tame him, at least for a while, until his next transformation (ibid.:74–75). JO

6.6 **Raven-of-the-Sea mask by Tony Hunt**, with the assistance of John Livingstone. Victoria. Red cedar, acrylic paint, eagle feathers, copper, L 91 cm, W 27.55 cm, H 36.5 cm. 1989. *CRM 0989.0050*

CONTEMPORARY KWAKIUTL ARTISTS ARE STILL actively involved in creating masks used for dance performances at potlatches. This mask represents the creature known as Raven-of-the-Sea, carved by Tony Hunt, Sr., as part of a special project arranged by the Campbell River Museum.

The head of the bird is represented with a well-rounded beak supplied with a full set of teeth, flaring nostrils, and the wide, staring eyes typical of the raven. Its features are vividly painted in rich black and intense shades of red and green upon a plain wooden ground and then sealed with a protective layer of clear acrylic.

The brow area, surmounted by a carved wing, is covered by a piece of copper painted with black, crescentlike forms meant to represent scales. Copper, also appearing on the eyes and teeth, is a substance consistently associated with K̓umugwe', the undersea chief. The addition of this metal, as well as the fishlike scales, help to identify this bird as the Raven-of-the-Sea, an inhabitant of K̓umugwe's kingdom.

Chief Tom Willie of Hopetown claims the exclusive right to contemporary performances of the dance of the undersea kingdom, along with the authority to commission artists to carve masks of the numerous creatures from that realm, including the Raven-of-the-Sea. The Campbell River Museum has been able to establish a special partnership with Chief Willie concerning these masks. Both parties have come to a legal agreement that permits the museum to commission and exhibit a set of them. With the guidance of Peter Macnair, the museum has invited several major Kwakiutl artists to participate in this ongoing project.

In addition to the mask illustrated here, Tony Hunt, Jr., has created a representation of K̓umugwe'; Richard Hunt has carved a sculpin transformation mask that opens to reveal the face of Siwidi, the hero of the story; Henry Speck has carved a Grizzly-Bear-of-the-Sea; George Hunt, Jr., has produced a large halibut mask that is danced close to the floor to imitate the actual movements of this flat fish; Russell Smith has represented a sea anemone; and Calvin Hunt has made a complete Sea-eagle costume. Eventually, the Campbell River Museum hopes to commission a full set of about thirty masks for this particular dance performance. Chief Willie may borrow the masks when the dance of the undersea kingdom is to be performed.

When the performance begins, a sea eagle dancer appears first and functions as a "caller" who causes each successive creature to emerge in turn from behind a painted screen depicting the house-front of the undersea chief. The screen is appropriately decorated with images of marine life. His assistant, Raven-of-the-Sea, comes out to dance with the sea eagle, accompanied by the sound of a high-pitched whistle, the call of the sea eagle. After each character in turn has been escorted from behind the screen, the sea eagle and Raven-of-the-Sea guide the entire group of assembled creatures out of the ceremonial house (Macnair: personal communication, 1990). JO

6.7 Chief Tom Willie (standing) reciting the Siwidi legend at the American Museum of Natural History, May, 1990. Seated from left to right: Elsie Williams, Adam Dick, Peter Macnair, and Ethel Alfred. *Photo by D. Finnin*

6.8 **Mask of the madam dancer**. Hopetown. Wood, hide, rope (wolf fur added for exhibition), L 79 cm, H 46 cm. *Collected by George Hunt, 1901. 16/8531, AMNH 1901–32*

BOAS MAKES NO REFERENCE TO A MASK IN CONNEC-tion with the *madam* dancer, but specifies instead that this performer wore five pieces of wood covered in mica and cut to resemble hexagonal prisms or quartz crystals attached across the middle of his head. When the dancer sang his *madam* song he appeared naked on the roof of the house and then jumped down, first to the rear bedrooms and then to the floor (Boas 1897:483–84). This carving may represent some departure from this tradition, as George Hunt recorded that this particular mask was worn for the *madam* dance in the context of the performance commemorating the history of Born-to-Be-Head-of-the-World (Acc. file 1901–32, Dept. of Anthropology, AMNH).

The *madam* is the mythological bird whose abode is a high mountain. This creature may give quartz crystals as a gift that endows the recipient with the ability to fly (Boas 1897:395, 413). The *madam* is not specifically mentioned in the First-Beaver version of the Siwidi legend, but when Born-to-Be-Always-Chief, the hero's youngest brother, left his tribe to hunt mountain goats, he disappeared and later returned with various characteristics consistent with the *madam*'s nature. He was spotted that following winter perched high up on a mountain, wearing long pieces of quartz crystal on his head, which squeaked all the time. The ancestors of the Gwawaʼenuxw tried to bring him back, but without much luck. Later, he appeared to his father in yet another form. He was bald, had no nose, and his eyes were a frightening red. His father didn't recognize him, and Born-to-Be-Always-Chief flew off to the upper world, his head squeaking, presumably from the quartz crystals of the *madam* (Boas and Hunt 1906:77–79).

In other versions of the story, the *madam* plays a more explicit role. In *Kwakiutl Tales* (1935a) Boas published the Siwidi story as "Siʼwit." In this tale, the hero arrived back from the house of Ḳumugweʼ announcing that he was a *madam* dancer. When he sang his sacred song his head squeaked, and the quartz crystals in his hair caused it to shine, instilling fear among the ancestors of the Gwawaʼenuxw (1935a:187–88). Today, in the version of the Siwidi story claimed by Chief Tom Willie, a *madam* dancer is an important part of the performance.

This mask, which Hunt collected in 1901, represents a huge, wide-eyed creature with the same exaggerated snout and tubular red nostrils seen on the whale mask (fig. 6.4) also collected in association with this story. Its squared jaw may be raised and lowered to reveal a mouth full of teeth. A piece of hide on top of the mask had just a few hairs left on it to suggest the furry scalp as it might have appeared when the mask was new. Wolf fur was added for the *Chiefly Feasts* exhibition.

Five flat pieces of wood are attached across the middle of the head and perforated with a "pinched" triangular form. Joined by a network of strings, they would have moved back and forth during the dance. The sparkling white color remaining on some of these slats suggests that when they quivered, they dazzled the audience, appearing as rays of white light emitted from the crystal-like headgear. JO

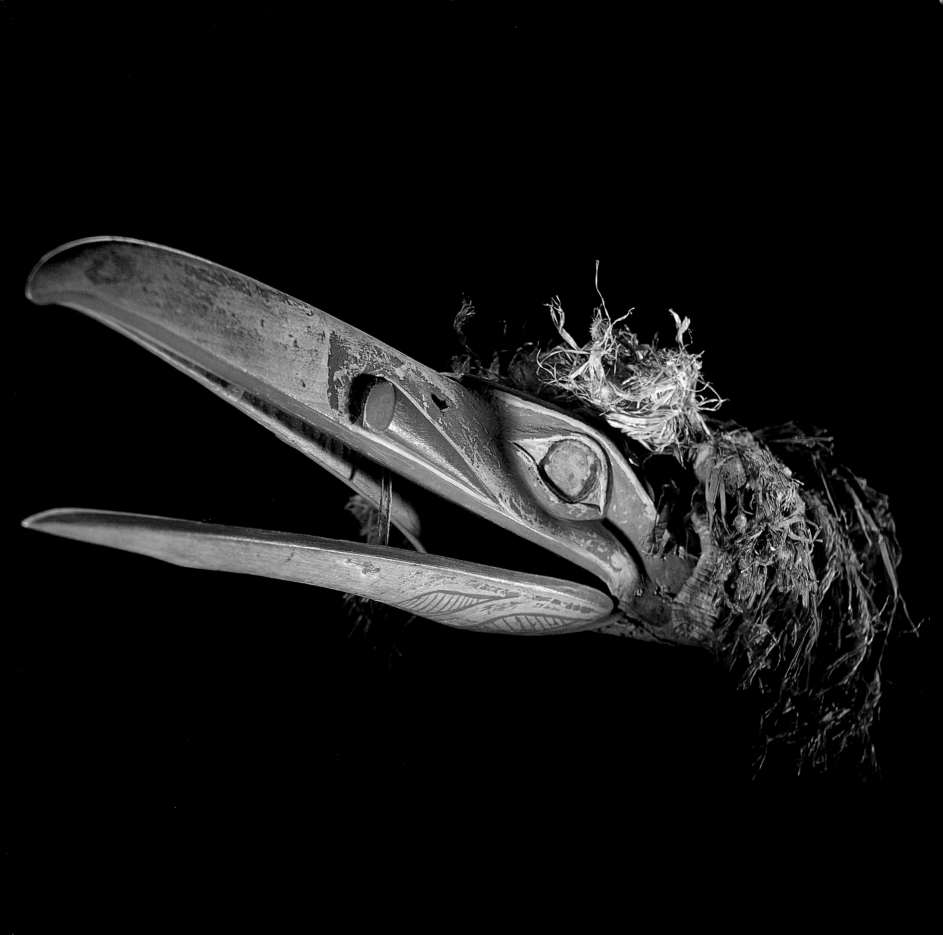

6.9 **Raven-of-the-Sea headdress**. Alder, red cedar bark, glass,
L 50 cm, H 20 cm, W 12 cm. *Collected by George Hunt, 1901.*
Burke 1–11389; 16/8403, AMNH 1901–32

AMONG THE DANCING PARAPHERNALIA IN Born-
to-Be-Head-of-the-World's supernatural house was the
mask of Raven-of-the-Sea, along with the bullhead and
whale combination, the sea otter mask, and the Grizzly-Bear-of-
the-Sea (Boas and Hunt 1906:70–71). This mask (see also fig. 6.11),
carved with the sharply protruding head typical of Raven-of-the-
Sea, is mounted on a headring and covered with shredded cedar
bark partially frayed into strands that cover the top of the headdress. Hunt recorded that this mask was used as a *gwawisaml*
hamsiwe' (acc. 1901–32, AMNH), a contradiction in terms that translates as both a face mask and a forehead mask that exposes the
masker's face (Gloria Cranmer Webster: personal communication,
1990). The term *hamsiwe'* suggests the type of forehead mask used
by attendants of the *hamatsa* initiate (ibid.).

This designation may contradict the assignment of the mask to
the Siwidi cycle. On the other hand, the disappearance of Siwidi
and his brothers at various times during the course of this narrative suggest the activities of those initiating spirits that are the mo-
tivating forces behind the various "secret societies," including that
of the *hamatsa* (Boas 1897:431).

The elongated face of the bird has been painted in ultramarine
blue, which contrasts sharply with the vermilion paint of the
tube-shaped nostrils and the line that functions as the "lips" of
the bird. The deeply set eyes have been covered over with glass
inserts, providing them with a fixed stare, further dramatized by
the black and angular brows.

This piece, a Bella Coola work (Holm 1987:124), and perhaps
other masks that Hunt included within the Siwidi set, are not of
Gwawa'enuxw origin. They may have been acquired as part of a
marriage payment, or perhaps they were acquired through trade
(Macnair: personal communication, 1990). JO

6.10 **Raven-of-the-Sea neckring**. Cedar bark, wood, L 54 cm.
Collected by George Hunt, 1901. 16/8404, AMNH 1901–32

THIS COSTUME ELEMENT WAS WORN BY THE Raven-
of-the-Sea dancer and, according to Hunt, is linked with
the headdress mask (fig. 6.9) assigned to the Siwidi dance
cycle (acc. 1901–32, AMNH).

Finely constructed of many tightly twisted cedar bark ropes
sewn to a red cloth lining, three dramatic sections drape,
fringelike, from the ring. These sections, which might have
swung and whirled around the neck of the dancer, are composed
of the same fine ropes, and two of them have been ornamented
with flat bird-wing shapes cut from thin pieces of wood. They
are painted with conventionalized design elements that probably
represent the feathers of Raven-of-the-Sea. JO

6.11 **Raven-of-the-Sea mask**. Hopetown. Wood, rope, L 83 cm, H 38.2 cm. *Collected by George Hunt, 1901. 16/8529, AMNH 1901–32*

WITH THE PRIDE AND ENTHUSIASM OF A HUMAN boy, Born-to-Be-Head-of-the-World called his parents into his house to see the treasures he had brought back from the undersea kingdom. Among the various dancing paraphernalia that Ḵumugwe' had bestowed upon him was a whale mask combined with the characteristics of a bullhead (see fig. 6.3), a sea-otter mask (see fig. 6.5), a Grizzly-Bear-of-the-Sea, and a mask like the one illustrated here, made to represent the being known as Raven-of-the-Sea (Boas and Hunt 1906:70–71).

This supernatural bird has been carved as a transformation mask. The external aspect of this creature is a darkly painted raven, its nostrils and mouth outlined with bright red paint. The masked dancer would swing his head from one side to the other as the raven's face was thrown open, then split into four segments to reveal the second mask within. This movement drew the audience's attention away from the mechanical process so completely that the dancer appeared transformed in the blink of an eye. The composite depicted inside this mask is carved with human features, except for the hooked bird's beak instead of a nose. When the mask is open, this inner face is dramatically framed by the four split segments, which are crisply painted with conventionalized design elements configured as facelike representations. JO

power, including the name 'Nalanukwamgila, Born-to-Be-Head-of-the-World.

Then up Born-to-Be-Head-of-the-World floated, house and all, to the place called Monster-Receptacle, near Gwamgwamliga, where his family lived. There he was first spotted by his elder brother, First-Beaver. In vain his family came near, but each time they approached, both house and hero disappeared beneath the waters. Next, the elusive Born-to-be-Head-of-the-World appeared to his brother in the form of a bullhead (sculpin). His parents and the entire tribe tried to capture him, but he eluded their grasp, changing himself into various creatures. After appearing as the bullhead, he became a whale that retained the tail of that fish in addition to a whale's characteristic flukes. An eagle flew down and settled on his back, and then he became a sea otter with many gulls flying around it. At last Born-to-Be-Head-of-the-World became a man again and instructed his tribe to bring gravel and fill the watery gap between the shore of Gwamgwamliga and Monster-Receptacle, creating a new village site as a suitable place for the supernatural house of Ḵumugwe'. Here Born-to-Be-Head-of-the-World held a Winter Dance for his people.

Born-to-Be-Head-of-the-World's two brothers disappeared just as the festivities began and were later transformed into powerful supernatural beings. One brother, First-Beaver, who assumed the forms of a whale and a bullhead, was eventually tamed and brought back to the people. The youngest however, Born-to-Be-Always-Chief, appeared at first as a sea otter and was later transformed into many different and unusual beings (figs. 6.5, 6.8). In time he became completely unrecognizable to his hot-headed father, the same man who had originally scorned his middle son, Siwidi. Then, when the father finally recognized his child, it was too late, and Born-to-Be-Always-Chief flew to the upper world and never returned.

This history, preserved to document the considerable supernatural power obtained by an ancestral hero, would have been commemorated by the performance of an elaborate dance sequence, owned as the privilege of a high-ranking chief. The type of story represented, a characteristic *tseka* tale in which a young man shamed into a quest for supernatural treasures eventually acquires a house, masks, and dance privileges for his tribe, may be celebrated by this kind of grand-scale performance in the course of a potlatch.

The Siwidi story has as its parallel the *atlaḵim* dance of the 'Nakwaxda'xw of Blunden Harbour. The *atlaḵim* represents another hero's adventures among the spirits of the woods (Boas

1921:1179–220), and the performance of this legend requires the similar sequential display of a great many masked dancers, appearing as the creatures of the forest realm.

The dance of the undersea kingdom, however, consistent with its origin in the watery habitat which was the domain of Ḵumugwe', featured performers who emerged from behind a painted screen that depicted the house of this chief, decorated with the appropriate images of sea creatures. One masked dancer, a sea eagle, functioned as the "caller," introducing each of the characters as they entered the house, one by one, from behind the screen. The various creatures described in the story were represented. Their gestures, appropriate to each particular animal's nature, were accompanied by a song, repeated for each dramatic entrance, varying only to accommodate the name of the individual character. Here the moving parts of the masks were brought into play in order to mimic the movements of these beings. Transformation masks snapped open and shut as these sea creatures turned into humans and then changed back into animals once again. This was a long performance, and in Hunt's day the speaker may have included the whole story of Siwidi in his address to the assembled audience.

Hunt's Siwidi Collection

Between 1901 and 1902, Hunt succeeded in collecting from the Gwawa'enuxw people an array of objects associated with the Siwidi story, some of which refer directly to episodes in the legend just recounted, and some of which, although part of this ceremonial complex, are not described in any published version of the story. In addition to those already described that depict the hero's various transformations, other anthropomorphic masks represent the hero in two aspects (fig. 6.1), as well as the hero's speaker (fig. 6.16). Additional carvings depict an assortment of other beings that according to Hunt's records are associated with Born-to-Be-Head-of-the-World.

In addition to an extraordinary assortment of masks, the Siwidi collection includes two carved bowls and a figure. The bowls (fig. 6.2) depict the killer whales directed by Ḵumugwe' to accompany Siwidi on his travels to the undersea kingdom. As Ḵumugwe' instructed the killer whale, Born-to-Be-Head-Harpooner, "Go all round our world with Paddled-to [Siwidi], that he may go and watch my servants" (Boas and Hunt 1906:63). Hunt identifies the carved figure (fig. 6.17) as Husagame', Born-to-Be-Head-of-the-World's "blanket counter." Presumably this figure depicts the attendant who counted

6.12 **Whistle**. Hopetown. Wood, rope, L 8.5 cm, W 6 cm, H 37.5 cm. *Collected by George Hunt, 1901. 16/8540, AMNH 1901–32*

WHEN THE OLD PEOPLE ENTERED THE HOUSE OF Born-to-Be-Head-of-the-World to see for themselves the supernatural treasures he had obtained from the under-sea kingdom, four great "wealth sounding" whistles were heard in a corner of the house (Boas and Hunt 1906:72). A "wealth sounding" whistle was again blown to herald the entrance of the great whale mask during the course of the Winter Dance, as it appeared in the rear of the house, spouting and transforming itself from whale to bullhead and making its way around the fire (ibid.:76). Whistles are frequently used to announce the presence of supernatural forces in the ceremonial house (Holm 1972:23).

Hunt recorded that this particular instrument was meant to be used along with a Raven-of-the-Sea mask when it was danced to commemorate Born-to-Be-Head-of-the-World's story. It is likely that he was referring to fig. 6.11, as that mask is listed on the same page of Hunt's ledger (acc. 1901–32, AMNH).

Carved as two sections, which are lashed together with string, the rectangular main body of the whistle is incised with a face in shallow relief. The mouth has been cut through to form a gaping hole, as if it is this open-mouthed being who emits the supernatural voice of Raven-of-the-Sea. A bird's head, perhaps that of a raven, emerges from the back of this boxlike construction, and its beak disappears again, penetrating the body of the whistle. JO

the wealth to be distributed at the *tseka* ceremony, during which the hero revealed to all his great supernatural wealth and power.

This discovery of the American Museum of Natural History's Siwidi masks and ritual paraphernalia is an excellent example of how careful analysis of all available information, published and unpublished, can lead to exciting discoveries within collections. We are extremely pleased that some of the most remarkable artworks the American Museum owns are part of a dance privilege, a version of which is still in the possession of a living Kwakiutl chief.

6.13 **Mask**. Hopetown. Wood, rope, copper, H 21.4 cm, W 36.7 cm, D 40 cm. *Collected by George Hunt, 1901. 16/8392, AMNH 1901–32*

THE TERM THAT GEORGE HUNT RECORDED FOR THIS mask, *ha'msiwe'*, translates as *"hamatsa* forehead mask," suggesting that it would have been worn as a headdress by a dancing attendant of this initiate of the Cannibal-of-the-North-End-of-the-World. No *hamatsa* is mentioned in the Siwidi story, but the hero's two brothers disappeared at the very outset of the Winter Dance, indicating that they had been abducted by some initiating spirit (Boas and Hunt 1906:74). Even Hunt notes in his objects-purchased list that the mask is rather large for this purpose, since forehead masks usually rest atop the head, allowing the dancer's face to show (acc. 1901–32, AMNH).

Boas later called this carving a grizzly bear mask (1909:521), and it is possible that it represents the Grizzly-Bear-of-the-Sea mask, which Born-to-Be-Head-of-the-World proudly showed off when his father entered the supernatural house (Boas and Hunt 1906:71).

This creature was carved with substantial emphasis on the area of the snout. The nostrils are fitted with movable hemispherical caps, rigged to open and shut, revealing a circular copper lining under each nostril cover. The globular eyeballs can wiggle in their sockets, and the square jaw can snap open and closed. JO

6.14 **Dogfish mask**. Hopetown. Wood, rope, leather, red, green, white, and brown paints, glass, iron nails, L 157 cm. *Collected by George Hunt, 1902. 16/8943AB, AMNH 1902–46*

GEORGE HUNT AFFIXED A LABEL TO THIS MASK before it was packed up and shipped to New York. To avoid any question about its identity, he recorded that it was a dogfish mask from the Born-to-Be-Head-of-the-World story belonging to the Gwawaʾenuxw, and he included the page number of the First-Beaver legend (acc. 1902–46, AMNH). It is fortunate that Hunt provided this information, because this particular creature (like others in the mask set) is not mentioned in any of the published versions of Siwidi's story. Such masks may have appeared as some of the many animals that Born-to-Be-Head-of-the-World was capable of becoming, or perhaps they signify, in a less direct way, the many creatures that populate the undersea kingdom.

This mask is carved with the unmistakable angular features of the dogfish, a small shark. Hunt, for the sake of convenience, called this creature a shark when he translated the word *xwalgwam* (ibid.). A pointed snout and a series of painted gills, along with a mouth characteristically positioned on the underside of the head, are consistent with this designation. The large round eyes are covered with glass inserts, which give them a fixed and distinctly "fishy" stare.

The dorsal fin has been carved in an unusual manner, as a series of curving forms, each with a drilled hole rimmed with white paint. Riding on the foremost fin is the small figure of a man, a simple polelike form wrapped in shredded cedar bark tied at the ends to form two tufts. Because of the cedar bark, the figure may be a representation of Siwidi himself, outfitted as a *hamatsa*. When the dancer pulled the string wound around the bottom of the figure, the little man would turn around. Its one remaining arm is also movable. There used to be cotton plain-weave cloth nailed to the wood from the lower edge of the head and mid-section. This would conceal the dancer wearing the mask.

Several tiny pieces of white down have been discovered in the crevices of this sculpture, perhaps indicating that its appearance in the performance was accompanied by a shower of down particles. JO

6.15 **Thunderbird mask**. Hopetown. Wood, fur, feathers, rope, L 44 cm, H 165 cm. *Collected by George Hunt, 1901. 16/8532, AMNH 1901–32*

Kwakiutl masks constructed with movable parts, or those meant to be flung open to reveal a second being carved inside of the first, afford impressive dramatic displays, which may only be fully appreciated within the context of the performance. In its outer aspect, this bird's head is surrounded by seven triangular rays. While the skillful masker swung his head from side to side, the bird's face separated into seven sections that radiate dramatically around the human mask, which was hidden within. This transformation might take place so rapidly that the performer appeared momentarily as a bird, and in the next instant as a human being.

The rays, or opened sections of the bird's head, that surround the inner face have been painted with abstract design elements in red, white, and blue, arranged in the forms of profile birds and animals. The topmost extension curves forward, and a small figure with arms of hide is carved at its base. Its face has been painted with the same blue, masklike configuration as that of the larger being whose face is visible at the heart of this construction.

Although Hunt recorded this mask as a representation of a thunderbird (acc. 1901–32, AMNH), this being does not specifically appear in any of the published versions of the Siwidi story. Perhaps it was one of the many forms the hero was capable of assuming. Or it may be that this mask, the treasured possession of the sponsoring family, was danced before the guests during the course of the same potlatch, and Hunt mistakenly included it among the masks used for the Siwidi dance.

We do know that a character called Stone Body, who inherited the woodworm blanket of Thunderbird, appears in the Kwikwasutinuxw story of Head-Winter-Dancer. With this cloak he could produce lightning. In the course of his adventures he visited the Gwawa'enuxw people and married the daughter of their chief (Boas and Hunt 1905:211–13). Perhaps this is how the image of the thunderbird came to the Gwawa'enuxw people. JO

6.16 **Mask of Born-to-Be-Head-Speaker**. Hopetown. Wood, H 35 cm, W 28.3 cm. *Collected by George Hunt, 1901. 16/8430, AMNH 1901–32*

Listen, O tribe! This house of Born-to-be-Head-of-the-World here has been entered by the supernatural powers. Now come in! (Boas and Hunt 1906:73)

These were the words of Born-to-Be-Head-Speaker, Born-to-Be-Head-of-the-World's attendant, charged to make some announcement about the most significant events to occur at the Winter Dance. He is represented by this ovoid mask carved with human features and surrounded by a simple framelike border. The area of the eyes and the "split U" design elements painted on the face were at one time colored a vibrant blue. Several holes around the outer edge of the mask suggest that cedar bark once covered the speaker's head.

When the ancestors of the Gwawaʼenux̱w entered Born-to-Be-Head-of-the-World's supernatural house, they passed through the mouth of a sea lion, which was the doorway to the fantastic masks and hereditary dance privileges that awaited them within. One of the old people even had the heel of his foot nipped at as he entered. At this point, Born-to-Be-Head-Speaker announced that Siwidi was their new chief. Then the animated but contentious speaking posts of this magical house announced the new names of Siwidi. They were henceforth to refer to him as "Born-to-Be-Head-of-the-World" and "Copper-Maker." The more belligerent of the two posts advocated an attack upon the visitors, but the other one, ever the calming influence, advised that they be treated well. Then the Winter Dance was announced by this speaker as he invited in the tribes. JO

6.17 **Blanket counter figure**. Hopetown. Wood, L 149 cm, W 44 cm. *Collected by George Hunt, 1901. 16/8406, AMNH 1901–32*

THE INFORMATION THAT HUNT COLLECTED WITH this figure associates this representation with the history of Siwidi. He recorded the figure's name as Husag̱ame'. When Siwidi returned to his village, he gave a Winter Ceremony in which he demonstrated the wealth and supernatural power he had received from K̓umugwe'. Husag̱ame' was an attendant at the back of Siwidi's house, helping him to count his wealth.

The specific attribution of this carving as a named character from a numaym history is of interest, because usually this type of figure is a means of making a public statement that either ridicules a rival or flatters oneself or one's family. If Hunt was correct, then this figure may have functioned as part of the performance relating to Siwidi and his adventures with the supernatural. SAM

Notes

1/ Chiefly Feasts: The Creation of an Exhibition

For their comments on earlier drafts of this essay and assistance in its research and writing, I wish to thank Janet Catherine Berlo, Douglas Cole, Stanley Freed, Bill Holm, Richard Inglis, Ira Jacknis, Peter Macnair, Wayne Suttles, and Gloria Cranmer Webster.

1. See, for example, Rosaldo (1989) and Riddington (1989).

2. In order to find the stories associated with individual artifacts, Stacy Marcus and Judith Ostrowitz, my research assistants on this exhibition, had to look at Hunt's field lists. Where Hunt collected additional textual information on a piece (and this was by no means always the case), he either noted the name of the being represented on the object, or referenced a page in his manuscript. The original manuscripts are in the Boas Archives in the American Philosophical Society in Philadelphia and in Columbia University's Manuscripts and Rare Books Collection. Many of these stories have been published in Boas and Hunt (1905, 1906).

3. Boas in particular was interested in using ethnographic information to dispute the unilineal evolutionism so prevalent at the end of the nineteenth century. See Stocking (1968) and Jonaitis (in press) for more on this.

4. For example, Lévi-Strauss (1982), Goldman (1975), Walens (1981) for books attempting to interpret Kwakiutl symbolism.

5. See Stocking (1985), Ames (1986), and Bennett (1988) for more analysis on the power relationships inherent in the displays of Native peoples in western museums. See Macnair et al. (1980) and Kasten (1990) for examples of exhibits that include "traditional" as well as contemporary Kwakiutl art. See Wright (1991) for a model of the creation of an exhibition by two co-curators, one Native, the other white, with the help of a Native advisory board. See also King (1989), Lavine (1989), Hoover and Inglis (1990), Jordanova (1989), Phillips (1988), Jonaitis (in press). For theoretical overviews of this theme, see Harvey (1989), Manganaro (1990).

6. See also Doxtoder (1988), Clifford (1988), Coe (1986), Durrans (1988), Greer (1989), Phillips (1988), Solomon-Godeau (1989), and Martin and Buchloh (1989).

7. As James Clifford (1987:126) puts it: "New definitions of authenticity (cultural, personal, artistic) are making themselves felt, definitions no longer centered on a salvaged past. Rather, authenticity is reconceived as a hybrid, creative activity in a local present-becoming-future. Non-western cultural and artistic works are implicated by an interconnected world cultural system without necessarily being swamped by it. Local structures produce *histories* rather than simply yielding to *History*."

8. Indeed, Native peoples experienced cultural changes from the moment of first contact with whites and in some cases even before the actual encounter. Thus there is virtually no "pristine" and "pure" Native culture that one has access to beyond the archaeological record.

9. Another issue being reconsidered today is that of tourist art, pieces made by Native peoples for sale, most often to whites. Although such pieces were once disregarded as inauthentic, scholars today are analyzing them as perfectly acceptable expressions of their originating cultures. See Graburn (1976), Coe (1986), Dominguez (1986).

10. The Hudson's Bay blanket as a central feature of the potlatch brings up the question of authenticity nicely. Although some may be of the opinion that the use of Hudson's Bay Company blankets indicated a less "Indian" aspect to the potlatch, this would certainly not have been the attitude of the nobles in whose social system these textiles displayed a significant and central role. Instead of questioning the authenticity of these blankets in Native culture, one ought to consider them a successful appropriation of a feature of white culture for a Kwakiutl purpose.

11. See Holm (1983) on Willie Seaweed and Duff (1981) on Martin.

12. See, for example, McGrane (1989) and Kuper (1988).

13. See, for example, Buckley and Gottlieb (1988), Rosaldo and Lamphere (1974), Harraway (1989), and Strathern (1988).

14. As Tyler (1986:132) points out, anthropologists themselves have begun to realize this, for no longer can they assume their own pure objectivity, for any ethnographer, conscious of this process or not, does have a voice that must be recognized and, if possible, shared with the voice of the peoples being represented. See also Crapazano (1990), Tyler (1990), Ridington (1990).

15. The term "elder" is frequently used to refer to old members of Native American communities. Both Gloria Cranmer Webster and Wayne Suttles argue (personal communication) that because this term is used only for Native peoples (and for the members of certain church groups), it is a subtle form of discriminatory language. Because of this, I have used the term "old people" to describe the visit of the senior members of the Kwakiutl community.

16. These people all come from the communities on the northern part of Vancouver Island from which Hunt acquired the Museum's Kwakiutl collections.

2/ *Streams of Property, Armor of Wealth*

1. I have used the portion of the whole history beginning at the bottom of p. 960 and ending at the bottom of p. 967. I have deleted Boas's technical apparatus (admirably designed to identify sentences in the translation with those in the text and to keep track of persons through multiple name changes); I have changed Boas's spelling and typography to conform to that used throughout this volume; I have changed his punctuation and paragraphing to conform to modern standards; I have changed a few words and rearranged a few phrases in the interest of clarity; and with help from Gloria Cranmer Webster, I have translated some of the names.

The family histories and other traditions recorded by Hunt, the product of Boas's principle of "letting the Indians speak for themselves," are an enormously rich resource on Kwakiutl culture, which has no parallel. But we cannot assume that they are wholly accurate accounts of Kwakiutl history. At the beginning of "Marriage with the Comox," three generations before the founding of Fort Rupert, the Comox are identified as living at Comox Harbour and the Ligwiłda'xw at Cape Mudge, but we know from historical documents (Taylor and Duff 1956) that the Comox were living at Cape Mudge and the Ligwiłda'xw farther north until about the time Fort Rupert was built. There are other family histories with the same anachronism. As may happen in all oral traditions, the narrators must have simply reinterpreted what they had heard about the past in the light of what they knew about the present.

2. The Kwakwala term is either 'na'mima (one-kind) or 'na'mimut (one-kind-fellowship). Boas himself earlier used "gens" and "clan" for the numaym, while others have used "lineage," all terms commonly used for some kind of exogamous unilinear kinship group. However, the numaym is non-unilinear (you can get membership from your father, your mother, or somebody else) and nonexogenous (you can marry another member or a nonmember, whichever is most expedient) and, in fact, because its members are not necessarily of common descent, the numaym seems not to have been a kinship group at all in the usual sense of the term. "Numaym" is an anglicization, in which the vowels are given their common English values, rather than a phonetic transcription; Boas must have intended it to be pronounced "numb aim" rather than "noo mime."

3. Also called by the plural *tsitseka*, or in today's English "red cedar bark dances." Boas (1966:172) reports that the term *tseka* means 'to be fraudulent, to cheat,' and relates this to the fact that the ceremonies were admittedly largely theater, not reality. Lincoln and Rath (1980:164) identify the root (in linguistic orthography) as *cas*—'to deceive, to impersonate (?)' In other Wakashan languages, related words suggest shamanism (Heiltsuk and Oowekyala *caiqa*, 'shaman, Winter dancer'; Nootka *caayiq*, the name of a curing ceremony), and Kwakwala participants in the Winter Dance address each other as

paxala, 'shaman.' For these and other reasons, Drucker (1940) identifies the *tseka* performances as the "shamans' series" within a wider category "dancing societies."

4. Boas (1935b:141) explains that the name means literally 'Having man eating at the mouth of the river,' and because north is 'downriver,' he translated the term 'Cannibal-of-the-North-End-of-the-World.' Goldman (1975:10) objects to "cannibal" on the grounds that the human-eating being is not human himself. Based on comparative work on North Wakashan, Hilton and Rath (1982) reject Boas's identification of components of the name with 'human-eating' and 'mouth of river' and see the name as meaning something like 'ever more perfect manifestation of the essence of humanity.' Speakers of Kwakwala, however, find Boas's translation altogether supportable (G.C. Webster: personal communication, 1990).

5. While I have generally followed Boas (1897), in describing the *hamatsa* performance I have relied on information from Bill Holm.

6. The term "potlatch" has been in use in English for well over a century. Its source is Chinook Jargon, the pidgin spread throughout most of the Northwest Coast by traders and missionaries and by increased contact among different Indian peoples employed in commercial fishing, logging, hop-picking, and berry-picking. The Chinook Jargon *pátač* means 'give' in a general sense of 'gift.' But it came to refer in English to the ceremonial giving of property that was practiced by Indians from southeastern Alaska to Puget Sound. This ceremonial giving is called by different terms in each of the languages of the people who practiced it. The Chinook Jargon term may itself be based on the Nootka *pačix* translated "to potlatch" by Sapir and Swadesh (1939:174–75).

One might reasonably question whether the term "potlatch" actually refers throughout the region to the same kind of event. However, descriptions of these events suggest that in fact from one end of the region to the other what are called potlatches do have a number of features in common. They involve the giving of property other than food, involve participants from two or more local groups, and serve to mark a change of status of one or more members of the host group. The guests witness ceremonial prerogatives of the hosts, and by accepting the gifts offered, they acknowledge the claims to status made by the hosts. Potlatch gifts are widely regarded as payments to witnesses. From one part of the Northwest Coast to another differences exist in who gives to whom, and to validate what claims. But the common features seem to justify identifying the potlatch as a single, region-wide institution. Explaining this institution has become a major concern in anthropological work in the region and a minor industry in anthropology generally (Suttles and Jonaitis 1990:84–86).

7. By identifying these as the potlatcher's purposes or conscious motives I do not mean to rule out possible unconscious motives, latent functions, useful consequences of which the potlatcher is unaware, etc. Addressing these issues is beyond the scope of this essay.

8. Boas's translation. The U'mista Cultural Centre translates Nakapankam, which was Mungo Martin's name, as Ten-Times-Chief.

9. Helen Codere (1950) first used the Boas-Hunt family histories, together with historical documents, to show these changes, and later (1961) divided Kwakiutl history into Pre-potlatch (before 1849), Potlatch (1849–1921), and Post-potlatch periods. I follow Codere on the

expansion of potlatching, but I cannot entirely agree with her emphasis on the potlatch itself as a late phenomenon.

In support of this position, Codere (1961:445) has said that before 1849 "the Kwakiutl 'potlatch' does not seem to be so developed or striking an institution that there is need for a distinctive term for it." It does indeed appear that in Kwakwala there is no generic term or at any rate no single term that appears in every context where the English "potlatch" appears in Boas's translations of Hunt. But in fact, the Kwakwala lexicon contains a good many terms that document the importance of the potlatch, and these give the possible absence of a generic term in Kwakwala for "potlatch" about the same significance as has the absence in Japanese of a generic word for "rice."

The term p̓asa, "to potlatch," seems to be the most general in meaning. The root p̓as- appears in p̓idze', 'number of potlatches,' and p̓asap, 'give potlatches to each other.' Like any verb, it can be used nominally, as in 'walas p̓asa, 'great potlatch' (Boas 1935a:43/1943:41). The term 'maxwa, 'to potlatch,' seems restricted to intertribal potlatches, as perhaps is yak̓wa, 'to distribute property.' All three occur fairly often in the Kwakwala texts of the family histories. They also appear as elements in a number of personal names that appear in genealogies going back well before 1849. These terms contrast with k̓wilas, 'a feast' (from the root k̓wił-, 'be a guest at a feast.' The potlatch-feast contrast is also evident in dzuxwa, 'to promise a potlatch' versus k̓asu, 'to promise a feast.' There are also several other terms for specific kinds of potlatches and several for specific kinds of feasts.

10. This description was given by Charles Nowell of Fort Rupert to Philip Drucker in 1947 or 1953. I have not found an abbreviated version of the Winter Dance described by Boas or mentioned in the Hunt texts. What Nowell described is clearly the prototype of the contemporary potlatch.

11. There are several sources on the events of these twenty days. In his 1897 monograph, "The Social Organization and Secret Societies of the Kwakiutl," Boas gave a running account of what he and Hunt saw (pp. 544–606), together with more detailed descriptions of specific dances, costumes, and paraphernalia (elsewhere in the volume). This monograph was supplemented by a part of one of the Jesup volumes (Boas and Hunt 1905:447–91), where there appear the Kwakwala texts of myths, speeches, and songs and a more extended account of a part of a ceremony described only briefly in the 1897 monograph. This supplement corrects many of the numerous inaccuracies that appear in the transcription of Kwakwala that Boas used in the 1897 work. The 1897 running account appears again in Boas's posthumous *Kwakiutl Ethnography* (1966:179–241), with revised transcriptions and a few terms and names translated but otherwise verbatim. Internal evidence (his use of "clan" for numaym, his retention of the 1897 translation of personal names that he corrected later, and his failure to incorporate the 1905 extension) suggest that this revision was done very early.

To these accounts we can add Boas's letters from the field (Rohner 1969:176–90), which give us glimpses of Boas himself (in headring and blanket, getting caught up with George Hunt in a procession surrounding a *tuxw'id* initiate, trying to eat berries and grease, and giving feasts) and give us a bit more information on the events. They include brief accounts of two events that do not appear at all in the 1897 running account, though the details of the performance appear else-

where in the volume. On November 29, he saw the return of a new k̓uminoga with skulls that a *hamatsa* licked and appeared to eat maggots from, and the next evening he saw her first dance.

It has been pointed out (White 1963:8) that there are discrepancies in the dates Boas gave for his field work. In the 1897 work, the running account has the heading "The Winter Ceremonial at Fort Rupert, 1895–96," though the dates within the account indicate that Boas was there during November and December only. In the 1966 volume, the heading is the same except it is dated 1895 only. But it is clear from the diary that Boas was there in 1894. My guess is that Boas was neither confused himself or trying to confuse his anthropological readers. By moving the date, omitting the maggoty skulls from the narrative, and identifying people by their Native names only, Boas may have been trying to protect George Hunt and the rest of his friends from any danger of prosecution for what were, after all, illegal activities.

3/ *The History of the Kwakiutl Potlatch*

1. The following is based upon a study of the application of the potlatch law in British Columbia and of the Indian reaction to it. See Cole and Chaiken 1990.

2. These modifications were not twentieth century scholarly discoveries. Everyone at all familiar with late nineteenth century Kwakiutl life recognized it, not least the Kwakiutl themselves. See, for example, Dawson 1887:79; Pidcock 1895.

3. The dates are sometimes confused in the literature. In June 1883 the Cabinet passed an order-in-council requesting the Indians to abandon the custom; on 7 July the Governor General issued a proclamation to "enjoin, recommend, and earnestly urge" Indians to abandon the potlatch. On 19 April 1884, an amendment to the Indian Act, effective 1 January 1885, made anyone engaging or assisting in a potlatch ceremony guilty of a misdemeanor.

4. There was a single prosecution, among the Salmon River Kwakiutl, which only confirms the point. Made at the instigation of the Cape Mudge missionary, who was disturbed by the empty schoolrooms of his mission, Agent Pidcock issued a warrant for the arrest of two Ligwiłda'wx. The special constables encountered resistance, during which one of the accused, Chief Harry, escaped. Johnny Moon was discharged by a Nanaimo court on the grounds that the depositions did not prove a potlatch had actually taken place. Vowell strongly disapproved of Pidcock's action (Pidcock 1897; Vowell 1897).

5. The letter's left edge is torn, thus the bracketed extrapolations.

6. This was probably true: there appears to have been only a handful of arrests of Native women for street prostitution in Victoria between 1880 and 1910, fewer than of white, Chinese, and Black women (Mitchell and Franklin 1988:59). Nanaimo's "Uclataw Camp," however, was composed of Kwawkewlth Agency women.

7. The arrests were not for potlatching but for trespassing on another reserve.

8. At the same time A-ki-ou-gu-luk (or Inguik), a Matilpi, was committed for trial for causing himself to be bitten. A-ki-ou-gu-luk went to

trial in the case of Regina vs. Kailukwirs (for Kalugwis, presumably), but left no record.

9. According to Provincial records, Hunt served as constable thirteen days (at two dollars per diem) during the 1 July 1899 to 30 June 1900 fiscal year. Another constable was simply enumerated as "Indian" (British Columbia, *Sessional Papers* 1900).

10. Hunt is the most frequent witness for the presence of such cannibalism on the coast. He is reported by Boas (Boas 1897: 439–40), by Sproat (Sproat 1879b) and, most importantly, by Edward S. Curtis, who, though Hunt spoke as a believer "in the recent existence of ceremonial cannibalism," had grave doubts whether the flesh was actually eaten (Curtis 1915, 10:222–42). The other central-coast practice, of "biting" witnesses on the arms and chest by the *hamatsa* novice, is indubitable because it left scars observed by many. Similarly, however, there is considerable doubt if the flesh was ever ingested.

11. The surrendered potlatch regalia and coppers from those accepting the agreement were gathered in Halliday's woodshed, then moved to the parish hall and put on exhibition. They numbered over 450 items, including twenty coppers, scores of *hamatsa* whistles, and dozens of masks. Halliday was directed to ship the material to the National Museum in Ottawa, but was delayed for several months. In the meantime, George Heye, founder of New York's Museum of the American Indian, called in and wanted to buy "a considerable amount of the stuff." Halliday, feeling that Heye's prices were exceptionally good, sold him thirty-five pieces for $291, an action which angered Ottawa. The remaining material, seventeen cases, went to Ottawa where museum anthropologist Edward Sapir appraised it at a value of $1,456, without the coppers. Checks were sent to Halliday in April to be given to the former owners. No compensation was ever paid for the coppers. The bulk of the collection was kept by the National Museum with a portion donated to the Royal Ontario Museum in Toronto. Both have since returned their portions to Native museums in Alert Bay and Cape Mudge where they are displayed with stunning appropriateness (see Carpenter 1981).

4/ *George Hunt, Collector of Indian Specimens*

This is a revised version of a paper originally presented at the October 1981 meeting of the B.C. Studies Conference, Simon Fraser University. It is a part of a larger work-in-progress on George Hunt as a native anthropologist, concentrating especially on his relationship with Franz Boas. Jacknis 1989 includes a more analytical discussion of Hunt's collecting.

I would like to thank the following institutions for permission to quote material from their collections (cited with the following abbreviations): the American Philosophical Society, Franz Boas Professional Papers (APS); the American Museum of Natural History, Department of Anthropology, departmental correspondence and accession records (AMNH); Harvard University Archives, Frederic W. Putnam Papers (HUA); British Columbia Archives and Records Service, Charles F. New-

combe Papers (BCARS). For assistance with the research and comments on the manuscript I would like to thank Marlene Dullabaun Block, Douglas Cole, Stanley Freed, James Glenn, Barry Gough, Curtis Hinsley, Richard Inglis, Aldona Jonaitis, Peter Macnair, Ronald Rohner, Janette Sacket, George Stocking, and Victoria Wyatt.

1. Other accounts of Hunt's collecting include Cole 1985:156–63 and Jonaitis 1988:171–84.

2. Annie Hunt married Stephen Allen Spencer, the founder of Alert Bay and owner of its cannery. Sarah's husband, Alexander Lyon, a merchant, founded the nearby town of Port Hardy. In this practice they were not alone, as Captain McNeil, the chief factor of Fort Rupert, had married a Haida, as did several other company employes.

3. Among them were an antique mahogany desk, a table once owned by Governor James Douglas, an organ which had come around the Horn, a Chinese chest, a Japanese figure, Haida argillite, as well as native Kwakiutl artifacts. In fact, once George got his collection mixed up with his sister's. In 1902 Boas unpacked one of Hunt's collections at the American Museum and came across parts of a mask that did not seem to be included, nor was it on the inventory. Hunt later explained that he had left his collection with his sister for safekeeping, and when it was sent on to him, she mistakenly sent some of her own collection (Hunt to Boas, 7/4/02, Acc. 1902–46, AMNH).

4. For another account, see Hunt, 10/20/21, "How I became first acquainted with Indian life," p. 245.10–246.14, vol. 14, "Manuscript in the Language of the Kwakiutl Indians of Vancouver Island," Special Collections, Columbia University Library.

5. I base the date of marriage on the names and ages of the Hunt family contained in the 1881 Federal Census for the Alert Bay district, compiled by Indian Agent George Blenkinsop, which was kindly supplied to me by Douglas Cole.

6. Now the Canadian Museum of Civilization.

7. I would like to thank Douglas Cole for the HBC, Reserve Commission Survey, and Powell references.

8. This collection (acc. 30,192), though listed under Boas's name, was actually made entirely by Hunt, and much of the earlier one (acc. 29,057) was gathered by Hunt before Boas's arrival in Fort Rupert.

9. These were Rivers Inlet, Blunden Harbour, Hope Island, Watson Island, Fort Rupert, Alert Bay, Nimpkish River and Lake, Quatsino, Village Island, Harbledown Island, Turnour Island, Gilford Island, Kingcome Inlet, Knight Inlet. This is a minimal list; some sites he planned to visit, but we do not know if he actually did, and he undoubtedly went to sites he did not mention in his letters.

10. In 1898 Hunt helped Harlan Smith, then working for the Jesup Expedition, search for skeletons. As Smith reported back to Boas: "George Hunt got permission to take these bones. We are doing it secretly however, leaving no traces behind us and will use the permission to cover a possible detection" (Smith to Boas, 6/13/98, acc. 1898–41, AMNH). In a later letter Smith added, "Although George Hunt told me I might have the skeletons I thought what the Indians did not know about would not hurt them" (Smith to Boas, 7/6/98, acc. 1898–41, AMNH). Hunt had probably secured permission from village elders and/or relatives. See Cannizzo 1983:51 for further Kwakiutl reactions to Smith's activities.

11. The "address episode," mentioned at the beginning of this essay, occurred when Hunt was sent his second check.

12. The second was made by Pliny Goddard in the summer of 1922. He filmed Hunt and his wife demonstrating the use of tools and craft techniques. Unfortunately this film does not seem to have survived. The third and fourth were made in 1930: *Totemland*, made by J.B. Scott for Associated Screen News of Montreal, and research footage filmed by Franz Boas on his last trip to Fort Rupert. In each, Hunt and his wife demonstrated crafts as well as dances.

13. As noted, this structural manipulation of artifacts was a common practice for Charles Nowell and his brother Tom in their collecting for C.F. Newcombe.

14. This discussion can be only a sketch of an analysis that will be considered in greater detail in my work-in-progress on the Boas-Hunt relationship.

15. Hunt was not the only Native collector at the turn of the century. William Benson, Eastern Pomo, was his contemporary, and he was soon followed on the Northwest Coast by Tlingit Louis Shotridge (Milburn 1986) and Tsimshian William Beynon (Halpin 1978), both of whom worked briefly with Boas. See Liberty 1978 on similar American Indian intellectuals.

16. George Hunt, September 1922, "Notes on the Anthropological Collections in the [B.C.] Provincial Museum," 20 pp., box 40, file 16, Newcombe Papers, BCARS.

6/ Postscript: The Treasures of Siwidi

1. Waite (1966) associated a few of these nineteenth-century masks with the Boas and Hunt (1906) story.

2. According to Wilson Duff's compilation of data on the movement of Kwakiutl tribes, the Gwawa'enux̱w lived at Hopetown earlier but by 1885 had joined the Dzawada'enux̱w and Ḵwiḵwasutinux̱w at Gwa'yasdᶻams on Gilford Island. It is not clear how long they were there, but by 1914 they were back at Hopetown (Duff n.d.). The co-residence of these tribes might explain Hunt's comment quoted here.

Bibliography

Abbreviations:

AMNH   American Museum of Natural History, New York.
        See Boas 1895–1905a; Hunt 1895–1905a.

APS   American Philosophical Society, Philadelphia.
        See Boas 1895–1905b; Hunt 1895–1905b.

DIA   Department of Indian Affairs.

Ames, Michael M.
   1986   *Museums, the Public and Anthropology: A Study in the Anthropology of Anthropology*, Vancouver: University of British Columbia Press.

Anfield, F. Earl
   1940   "Personal Report on Two Conferences," n.d. [April 1940], Department of Indian Affairs (DIA), vol. 8481, file 1/24–3.

Barnett, Homer G.
   1938   "The Nature of the Potlatch," *American Anthropologist* 40:349–58.

Benedict, Ruth
   1934   *Patterns of Culture*. Boston: Houghton Mifflin Co.

Bennett, Tony
   1988   "Museums and 'The People,' " pp. 63–86 in *The Museum Time-Machine: Putting Cultures on Display*, ed. R. Lumley. London: Routledge.

Blackman, Margaret B.
   1976   "Creativity in Acculturation: Art, Architecture and Ceremony from the Northwest Coast," *Ethnohistory* 23:387–413.

Boas, Franz
   1888a   "The Indians of British Columbia," *Popular Science Monthly* 32:628–36.
   1888b   "The Houses of the Kwakiutl Indians, British Columbia," *Proceedings of the United States National Museum* 11:197–213.
   1889   "Reisen in British-Columbien," *Verhandlungen der Gesellschaft für Erdkunde zu Berlin* 16:257–68.
   1890   "The Use of Masks and Head-ornaments on the Northwest Coast of America," *Internationales Archive für Ethnographie*, 3:7–15.
   1892   "The Indians of British Columbia: Seventh Report of the Committee on the North-Western Tribes of Canada; The Bilqula, Secret Societies and the Potlatch," *Report of the British Association for the Advancement of Science for 1891*, 408–17.
   1895–1905a Correspondence and collection notations, Anthropology Department Archives, American Museum of Natural History (AMNH).
   1895–1905b Correspondence and collection notations, Franz Boas Professional Papers, American Philosophical Society (APS).
   1896   "The Decorative Art of the Indians of the North Pacific Coast," *Science*, 4:101–103.
   1897   "The Social Organization and Secret Societies of the Kwakiutl Indians," *Report of the U.S. National Museum for 1895*, 311–738.
   1898   "The Jesup North Pacific Expedition," *Publications of the Jesup North Pacific Expedition* 1:1–11.
   1900   *Ethnological Collections from the North Pacific Coast of America: Being a Guide to Hall 108 in the American Museum of Natural History*. New York.
   1904   "Primitive Art," *American Museum Journal* (supplement), 4, no. 3, guide leaflet no. 15, 1–39.
   1909   "The Kwakiutl of Vancouver Island," *Publications of the Jesup North Pacific Expedition* 5:301–522.
   1910   *Kwakiutl Tales*. Columbia University Contributions to Anthropology, 2.
   1920   "The Social Organization of the Kwakiutl," *American Anthropologist* 22:111–26.
   1921   "Ethnology of the Kwakiutl," *Bureau of American Ethnology Thirty-fifth Annual Report*, parts 1 and 2.
   1925   "Contributions to the Ethnology of the Kwakiutl," Columbia University Contributions to Anthropology, 3.
   1926   "Remarks on Masks and Ceremonial Objects of the Kwakiutl," manuscript, APS.
   1927   *Primitive Art*. Oslo: Institutet for Sammenlignende Kulturforskning, ser. B., vol. 8.
   1930   "Religion of the Kwakiutl," Columbia University Contributions to Anthropology, 10, parts 1 and 2.
   1935a   *Kwakiutl Tales*, Part 1, Texts, Columbia University Contributions to Anthropology, 26.
   1935b   *Kwakiutl Culture as Reflected in Mythology*. American Folklore Society, Memoir 28.
   1940   *Race, Language and Culture*. New York: Macmillan Co.
   1943   *Kwakiutl Tales*, part 2, Translations, Columbia University Contributions to Anthropology, 26.
   1966   *Kwakiutl Ethnography*, ed. H. Codere. Chicago: University of Chicago Press.

Boas, Franz, and George Hunt
   1905   "Kwakiutl Texts," *Publications of the Jesup North Pacific Expedition* 3.
   1906   "Kwakiutl Texts, Second Series," *Publications of the Jesup North Pacific Expedition* 10.

Boyd, Robert T.

1990   "Demographic History, 1774–1874," pp. 135–48 in
        *Handbook of North American Indians, vol. 7, Northwest
        Coast*, ed. W. Suttles. Washington, D.C.: Smithsonian
        Institution.

Buckley, Thomas, and Alma Gottlieb, eds.

1988   *Blood Magic: The Anthropology of Menstruation*.
        Berkeley, Los Angeles, and London: University
        of California Press.

Cannizzo, Jeanne

1983   "George Hunt and the Invention of Kwakiutl
        Culture," *Canadian Review of Sociology and
        Anthropology* 20:44–58.

Carpenter, Carol Henderson

1981   *artscanada* 12:64–70.

Christmas, Rev. E.W.

1945   Archives of the Anglican Diocese of British
        Columbia, Christmas to Greene, [illeg.] April 1945.

Clark, George H.

1931   Clark to B.C. Police, 15 June 1931, DIA, Acc. 80–81/18,
        Box 10.

Clifford, James

1986   "On Ethnographic Analogy," pp. 98–121 in *Writing
        Culture: The Poetics and Politics of Ethnography*, ed. J.
        Clifford and G.E. Marcus. Berkeley: University of
        California Press.

1987   "Of Other Peoples: Beyond the 'Salvage' Paradigm,"
        pp. 121–30 in *Dia Art Foundation Discussions in
        Contemporary Culture*, no. 1, ed. H. Foster. Seattle:
        Bay Press.

1988   *The Predicament of Culture: Twentieth-Century
        Ethnography, Literature, and Art*. Cambridge: Harvard
        University Press.

Codere, Helen

1950   *Fighting with Property: A Study of Kwakiutl Potlatching
        and Warfare, 1792–1930*. American Ethnological
        Society Monograph 18. Reprint, Seattle: University of
        Washington Press.

1956   "The Amiable Side of Kwakiutl Life: The Potlatch and
        Play Potlatch," *American Anthropologist* 58:334–51.

1961   "Kwakiutl," pp. 431–516 in *Perspectives in American
        Indian Culture Change*, ed. E. Spicer. Chicago:
        University of Chicago Press.

1990   "Kwakiutl: Traditional Culture," pp. 171–89 in
        *Handbook of North American Indians, vol. 7, Northwest
        Coast*, ed. W. Suttles. Washington, D.C.: Smithsonian
        Institution.

Coe, Ralph T.

1986   *Lost and Found Traditions: Native American Art,
        1965–1985*. Seattle: University of Washington Press.

Cole, Douglas

1982   "Tricks of the Trade: Northwest Coast Artifact
        Collecting, 1875–1925," *Canadian Historical Review*
        63:439–60.

1985   *Captured Heritage: The Scramble for Northwest Coast
        Artifacts*. Seattle: University of Washington Press;
        Vancouver: Douglas and McIntyre.

Cole, Douglas, and Ira Chaikin

1990   *An Iron Hand upon the People: The Law against the
        Potlatch on the Northwest Coast*. Vancouver: Douglas &
        McIntyre; Seattle: University of Washington Press.

Colonist

1897   Victoria *Daily Colonist*, 13 April 1897.

1914   Victoria *Daily Colonist*, 7–9 May 1914.

Crapazano, Vincent

1990   "On Dialogue," pp. 269–91 in *The Interpretation of
        Dialogue*, ed. T. Maranhao. Chicago: University of
        Chicago Press.

Curtis, Edward S.

1915   *The North American Indian. Vol. 10, The Kwakiutl*.
        Reprinted, New York: Johnson Reprint, 1970.

Dawson, George Mercer

1885   "Nature and the effects of the so called Potlatch
        System among the Indians," Dawson Papers, McGill
        University Archives.

1887   "Notes and Observations on the Kwakiool People of
        the Northern Part of Vancouver Island and Adjacent
        Coasts, Made During the Summer of 1885,"
        Proceedings and Transactions, Royal Society of Canada
        5:2:63–98.

DeBeck, G.W.

1902   DeBeck to Vowell, 29 December 1902, DIA, vol. 1649.

Dominguez, Virginia R.

1986   "The Marketing of Heritage," *American Ethnologist*
        13:546–55.

1987   "Of Other Peoples: Beyond the 'Salvage' Paradigm,"
        pp. 131–37 in *Dia Art Foundation Discussions in
        Contemporary Culture*, no. 1, ed. H. Foster. Seattle:
        Bay Press.

Doxtoder, Deborah

1988   "The Home of Indian Culture and Other Stories for
        the Museum," *Muse* 6(6):26–31.

Drucker, Philip

1940   "Kwakiutl Dancing Societies," *Anthropological Records*
        2:201–30. Berkeley: University of California Press.

1951   "The Northern and Central Nootkan Tribes," Bureau
        of American Ethnology, Bulletin 144.

1965   *Cultures of the North Pacific Coast*. San Francisco:
        Chandler and Sharp.

Drucker, Philip, and Robert F. Heizer

1967   *To Make My Name Good: A Reexamination of the
        Southern Kwakiutl Potlatch*. Berkeley: University
        of California Press.

Duff, Wilson

1961   "The Killer Whale Copper (A Chief's Memorial to His
        Son)," Report, British Columbia Provincial Museum,
        Department of Education.

1967   *Arts of the Raven: Masterworks by the Northwest Coast Indian*. Vancouver: Vancouver Art Gallery.

1975   *Images, Stone, B.C.: Thirty Centuries of Northwest Coast Indian Sculpture*. Saanichton, B.C.: Hancock House; Seattle: University of Washington Press.

1981   "Mungo Martin, Carver of the Century," pp. 37–40 in *The World Is as Sharp as a Knife*, ed. D. Abbott. Victoria: British Columbia Provincial Museum.

n.d.   Field Notebook, no. 10. Archives, Royal British Columbia Museum.

Durrans, Brian

1988   "The Future of the Other: Changing Cultures on Display in Ethnographic Museums," pp. 144–69 in *The Museum Time Machine: Putting Cultures on Display*, ed. R. Lumley. London: Routledge.

Fabian, Johannes

1983   *Time and the Other: How Anthropology Makes its Object*. New York: Columbia University Press.

Ferguson, R. Brian

1983   "Warfare and Redistributive Exchange on the Northwest Coast," pp. 131–47 in *The Development of Political Organization in Native North America*, ed. E. Tooker. Proceedings of the American Ethnological Society for 1979.

1984   "A Reexamination of the Causes of Northwest Coast Warfare," pp. 267–328 in *Warfare, Culture, and Environment*, ed. R.B. Ferguson. Orlando: Academic Press.

Fitzhugh, William W., and Aaron Crowell, eds.

1988   *Crossroads of Continents: Cultures of Siberia and Alaska*. Washington, D.C.: Smithsonian Institution Press.

Ford, Clellan S., ed.

1941   *Smoke from Their Fires: The Life of a Kwakiutl Chief*. New Haven: Yale University Press.

Geertz, Clifford

1988   *Works and Lives: The Anthropologist as Author*. Stanford: Stanford University Press.

Goldman, Irving

1975   *The Mouth of Heaven: An Introduction to Kwakiutl Religious Thought*. New York: John Wiley & Sons.

Gough, Barry M.

1982   "A Priest versus the Potlatch: The Reverend Alfred James Hall and the Fort Rupert Kwakiutl, 1878–1880," *Journal of the Canadian Church Historical Society* 24:75–89.

1984   *Gunboat Frontier: British Maritime Authority and Northwest Coast Indians, 1846–1890*. Vancouver: University of British Columbia Press.

Graburn, Nelson H., ed.

1976   *Ethnic and Tourist Arts: Cultural Expressions from the Fourth World*. Berkeley: University of California Press.

Greer, Sandy

1989   "Stereotypes, Native Art and Art," *Art Views*, March, April, May, 18–23.

Hall, Rev. A.J.

1878   Hall to Wright, 30 March 1878, in Barry Gough, "A Priest versus the Potlatch: The Reverend Alfred James Hall and the Fort Rupert Kwakiutl, 1878–1880," *Journal of the Canadian Church History Society* 24:78.

1889   Hall to Superintendent General, 5 October 1889, DIA, vol. 3628, file 6244–2.

Halliday, William

1906   Halliday to Vowell, 5 September 1906, DIA, vol. 1652.

1907a   Halliday to Oliver, 1 February 1907, DIA, vol. 1652.

1907b   Halliday to Sloan, 7 November 1907, DIA, vol. 1652.

1913a   Halliday to McLean, 30 October 1913, DIA, vol. 1653.

1913b   Halliday to McLean, 2 and 24 November 1913, DIA, vol. 3629, file 6244–2.

1915   Halliday to McLean [?] May 1915, DIA, vol. 3629, file 6244–3.

1919   Halliday to Scott, March 1919 report, DIA, vol. 1646.

1922   Halliday to Scott, 10 April 1922, DIA, vol. 3630, file 6244–4, pt. 2.

1931   Halliday to Scott, 26 February 1931, DIA, vol. 3631, file 6244–5.

1932   Halliday to Ditchburn, 29 March 1932, DIA acc. 80–81/18, box 10.

1935   *Potlatch and Totem, and the Recollections of an Indian Agent*. London and Toronto: J.M. Dent & Sons.

Halpin, Marjorie

1978   "William Beynon, Tsimshian, 1883–1958," pp. 141–58 in *American Indian Intellectuals*, ed. M. Liberty. St. Paul: West Publishing Co.

Harraway, Donna

1989   *Primate Visions: Gender, Race, and Nature in the World of Modern Science*. New York and London: Routledge.

Harvey, David

1989   *The Condition of Postmodernity: An Inquiry into the Origins of Cultural Change*. Cambridge: Basil Blackwell Inc.

Hawthorn, Audrey

1979   *Kwakiutl Art*. Seattle: University of Washington Press.

Hill, Tom

1988   Transcript of address, "Preserving Our Heritage: A Working Conference for Museums and First Peoples; Outcomes and Recommendations. Executive Summary." Ottawa.

Hilton, Susanne, and John Rath

1982   "Objections to Franz Boas's Referring to Eating People in the Translation of the Kwakwala Terms $Bax^{u}bakwalanux^{u}siwe$ and hamats!a," pp. 98–106 in "Working Papers for the 17th International Conference on Salish and Neighboring Languages," August 1982, Portland State University.

Hinsley, Curtis M., Jr., and Bill Holm

1976   "A Cannibal in the National Museum: The Early Career of Franz Boas in America," *American Anthropologist* 78:306–16.

Holm, Bill

1972   *Crooked Beak of Heaven: Masks and Other Ceremonial Art of the Northwest Coast*. Seattle: University of Washington Press.

1977   "Traditional and Contemporary Kwakiutl Winter Dances," *Arctic Anthropology* 14:5–24.

1983   *Smoky-Top: The Art and Times of Willie Seaweed*. Seattle: University of Washington Press.

1984   *The Box of Daylight: Northwest Coast Indian Art*. Seattle: University of Washington Press.

1987   *Spirit and Ancestor: A Century of Northwest Coast Indian Art at the Burke Museum*. Seattle: University of Washington Press.

1990   "Kwakiutl Winter Ceremonies," pp. 190–98 in *Handbook of North American Indians, vol. 7, Northwest Coast*, ed. W. Suttles. Washington, D.C.: Smithsonian Institution.

Holm, Bill, and George Irving Quimby

1980   *Edward S. Curtis in the Land of the War Canoes: A Pioneer Cinematographer in the Pacific Northwest*. Seattle: University of Washington Press.

Hoover, Alan, and Richard Inglis

1990   "Acquiring and Exhibiting a Nuu-chah-nulth Ceremonial Curtain," *Curator* 33:272–88.

House of Commons

1936   Canada, House of Commons *Debates*, 20 March, 23 April.

Hunt, George

1895–1905   Correspondence and collection notes, American Museum of Natural History, Anthropology Department archives [AMNH].

1895–1905   Correspondence and collection notes, American Philosophical Society, Franz Boas Professional Papers [APS].

1900   Hunt to Boas, 27 March 1900, American Philosophical Society, Franz Boas Professional Papers.

1906   "The Rival Chiefs," pp. 108–36 in *Boas Anniversary Volume*, ed. B. Laufer. New York: G. Stechert.

Jacknis, Ira

1980   "Franz Boas and Photography," *Studies in Visual Communication* 10:2–60.

1985   "Franz Boas and Exhibits: On the Limitation of the Museum Method of Anthropology," pp. 75–111 in *Objects and Others: Essays on Museums and Material Culture*, ed. G. Stocking. Madison: University of Wisconsin Press.

1989   "The Storage Box of Tradition: Museums, Anthropologists, and Kwakiutl Art, 1881–1981." Ph.D. dissertation, Department of Anthropology, University of Chicago. Forthcoming from Smithsonian Institution Press.

1991   "Northwest Coast Indian Culture and the World's Columbian Exposition," in *The Spanish Borderlands in Pan-American Perspective, vol. 3, Columbian Consequences*, ed. D. H. Thomas. Washington D.C.: Smithsonian Institution Press.

In press   "George Hunt, Kwakiutl Photographer," in *Anthropology and the Camera*, ed. E. Edwards. New Haven: Yale University Press.

Jacobsen, Johan Adrian

1977   *Alaskan Voyage, 1881–1883: An Expedition to the Northwest Coast of America, from the German Text of Adrian Woldt*, trans. Erna Gunther. Chicago: University of Chicago Press.

Jonaitis, Aldona

1988   *From the Land of the Totem Poles: The Northwest Coast Indian Art Collection at the American Museum of Natural History*. New York and Seattle: American Museum of Natural History and University of Washington Press.

1990   "Die *hamatsa*-Zeremonie der Kwakiutl-Indianer einst und jetz," pp. 231–36 in *Männerbände/Männerbunde*. Cologne: Rautenstrauch-Joest-Museums für Völkerkunde.

In press   *A Wealth of Thought: Franz Boas on Native American Art*. Seattle: University of Washington Press.

In press   "Franz Boas, John Swanton, Charles Edenshaw, and the Creation of 'New' Haida Art at the American Museum of Natural History," in *The Early Years of Native American Art History*, ed. J. Berlo. Seattle: University of Washington Press.

In press   "Art and the Feminine in Museum Ideology," *European Review of Native American Studies*.

Jonaitis, Aldona, and Richard Inglis

In press   "Authenticity and Appropriation: The Mowachaht Whaler's Washing Shrine," *South Atlantic Quarterly*.

Jopling, Carol F.

1989   "The Coppers of the Northwest Coast Indians," *Transactions of the American Philosophical Society* 79.

Jordanova, Ludmilla

1989   "Objects of Knowledge: A Historical Perspective on Museums," pp. 22–40 in *The New Museology*, ed. P. Vergo. London: Reaktion Books.

Kasten, Erich

1990   *Maskentänze der Kwakiutl: Tradition und Wandel in Einem Indianischen Dorf*. Berlin: Staatliche Museen.

Keynes, Geoffrey, ed.

1968   *The Letters of Rupert Brooke*. New York: Harcourt, Brace & World.

King, J.C.H.

1986   "Tradition in Native American Art," pp. 65–92 in *The Arts of the North American Indian: Native Traditions in Evolution*, ed. E. Wade. New York: Hudson Hills Press.

1989   *Living Arctic: Hunters of the Canadian North*. London: The British Museum.

Kobrinsky, Vernon

1975   "Dynamics of the Fort Rupert Class Struggle:

Fighting with Property Vertically Revisited," pp. 32–59 in *Papers in Honor of Harry Hawthorn*, ed. V. Serl and H. Taylor. Bellingham: Western Washington State College Press.

Kuper, Adam
1988   *The Invention of Primitive Society*. London and New York: Routledge.

Kwawkewlth Indian Agency
1918   Indians of Kwawkewlth Agency to Scott, n.d. [26 December 1918] DIA, vol. 3629, file 6244–3.

La Violette, Forrest
1961   *The Struggle for Survival: Indian Cultures and the Protestant Ethic in British Columbia*. Toronto: University of Toronto Press.

Lavine, Steven D.
1989   "Museums and Multiculturalism: Who Is in Control?" *Museum News* 68(2):36–42.

Lévi-Strauss, Claude
1982   *The Way of the Masks*. Seattle: University of Washington Press. Translation of *La Voie des Masques* (1975) by Sylvia Modelski.

Liberty, Margot, ed.
1978   *American Indian Intellectuals*. Proceedings of the American Ethnological Society for 1976. St. Paul: West Publishing Co.

Lincoln, Neville J., and John C. Rath
1980   "Northern Wakashan Comparative Root List," National Museum of Man Mercury Series, Canadian Ethnology Service Paper No. 68.

Lomas, William H.
1885   Lomas to Powell, 17 January 1885, DIA, vol. 1353.

MacCannell, Dean
1989   *The Tourist: A New Theory of the Leisure Class*. New York: Schocken Books.

McGrane, Bernard
1989   *Beyond Anthropology: Society and the Other*. New York: Columbia University Press.

McIlwraith, Thomas F.
1948   *The Bella Coola Indians*. Toronto: University of Toronto Press.

Mackay, Donald M.
1938   Mackay to McGill, 4 March 1938, DIA, Acc. 80–81/18, Box 10.

MacLaren, Carol Sheehan
1978   "Moment of Death: Gift of Life: A Reinterpretation of the Northwest Coast Image 'Hawk,'" *Anthropologica* 20:65–90.

Macnair, Peter L.
1971   "Descriptive Notes of the Kwakiutl Manufacture of Eulachon Oil," *Syesis* 4:169–77.
1974   "Kwakiutl Winter Dances: A Reenactment," *Artscanada*, December/January, 94–111.

Macnair, Peter L., Alan L. Hoover, and Kevin Neary
1980   *The Legacy: Continuing Traditions of Canadian Northwest Coast Indian Art*. Victoria: British Columbia Provincial Museum.

Manganaro, Marc
1990   "Textual Play, Power, and Cultural Critique: An Orientation to Modernist Anthropology," pp. 3–47 in *Modernist Anthropology: From Fieldwork to Text*, ed. M. Manganaro. Princeton: Princeton University Press.

Marcus, George E.
1986   "Contemporary Problems of Ethnography in the Modern World System," pp. 165–93 in *Writing Culture: The Poetics and Politics of Ethnography*, ed. J. Clifford and G.E. Marcus. Berkeley: University of California Press.

Martin, Jean-Hubert, and Benjamin H.D. Buchloh
1989   "The Whole Earth Show: An Interview with Jean-Hubert Martin by Benjamin H.D. Buchloh," *Art in America*, May 1989, 150–59, 211–13.

Mason, Peter
1990   *Deconstructing America: Representations of the Other*. London and New York: Routledge.

Mauzé, Marie
1986   "Boas, les Kwagul et le potlatch: éléments pour une réévaluation," *L'Homme* 26:21–63.

Menzies, Archibald
1923   *Menzies' Journal of Vancouver's Voyage, April to October, 1792*, ed. C.F. Newcombe, Archives of British Columbia, Memoir no. 5.

Milburn, Maureen
1986   "Louis Shotridge and the Objects of Everlasting Esteem," pp. 54–77 in *Raven's Journey: The World of Alaska's Native People*, ed. Susan A. Kaplan and Kristin J. Barsness. Philadelphia: The University Museum.

Mitchell, Marjorie, and Anna Franklin
1988   "When You Don't Know the Language, Listen to the Silence: An Historical Overview of Native Women in British Columbia," pp. 49–68 in *A History of British Columbia: Selected Readings*, ed. P. Roy. Toronto: Copp Clark Pitman.

Mochon, Marion Johnson
1966   *Masks of the Northwest Coast*. Milwaukee: Milwaukee Public Museum.

Moffat, H.
1889   Moffat to Vankoughnet, 30 August 1889, DIA, vol. 3628, file 6244–1.

Nanaimo Free Press
1915   *Nanaimo Free Press*, 10 May 1915.

Native Brotherhood of B.C.
1947   Submission to Joint Parliamentary Committee, DIA, vol. 6811, file 470–3–6, pt. 2.

Newnham, E.G.
1933   Newnham to DIA, April 1933 report, DIA, vol. 3631, file 6244–5.

News Advertiser
   1897   Vancouver *News Advertiser*, 14 April 1897.

Olson, Ronald L.
   1954   "Social Life of the Owikeno Indians," *Anthropological Records* 14:213–59. Berkeley: University of California Press.

Perry, C.C.
   1934   Perry to DIA secretary, 3 December 1934, DIA, vol. 3631, file 6244–5.

Phillips, Ruth
   1988   "Indian Art: Where Do You Put It?" *Muse* 4(3):64–71.

Pidcock, R.H.
   1886   Pidcock to Powell, 13 September 1886, DIA, vol. 3628, file 6244–1.
   1887   Pidcock to Powell, 19 March 1887, DIA, vol. 3628, file 6244–1.
   n.d.   Pidcock to Vowell [1890?], DIA vol. 3282, file 64,535.
   1893   Pidcock to Vowell, 16 March 1893, DIA, vol. 1648.
   1894   Pidcock to Vowell, 28 April 1894, DIA, vol. 1648.
   1895   Pidcock to Vowell, 17 July 1895, DIA, vol. 3737.
   1897   Pidcock to Vowell, 15 January 1897, DIA, vol. 3628, file 6244–1.
   1900   Pidcock to Vowell, 7 March 1900, DIA, vol. 1649.
   1901   Pidcock to Vowell, 10 February 1901, DIA, vol. 1649.

Powell, I.W.
   1885   Powell to Macdonald, 20 April 1885, DIA, vol. 3628, file 6244–1.

Powell, Jay, Vickie Jensen, Vera Cranmer, and Agnes Cranmer
   n.d.   *Yaxwatłan's*. Learning Kwakwala Series, Book 12. Alert Bay: U'mista Cultural Society.

Province
   1900   Vancouver *Daily Province*, 11 March and 18 April 1900.
   1915   Vancouver *Daily Province*, 10 February 1915.

Riddington, Robin
   1989   *Trail to Heaven: Knowledge and Narrative in a Northern Native Community*. Iowa City: University of Iowa Press.
   1990   "Cultures in Conflict: The Problem of Discourse," pp. 186–205 in *Little Bit Know Something: Stories in a Language of Anthropology*. Vancouver and Toronto: Douglas & McIntyre.

Ritzenthaler, Robert, and Lee A. Parsons, eds.
   1966   *Masks of the Northwest Coast: The Samuel A. Barrett Collection*. Publications in Primitive Art, no. 2. Milwaukee: Milwaukee Public Museum.

Rohner, Ronald P.
   1967   *The People of Gilford: A Contemporary Kwakiutl Village*. National Museum of Canada, Bulletin 225.

Rohner, Ronald P., ed.
   1968   *The Ethnography of Franz Boas: Letters and Diaries of Franz Boas Written on the Northwest Coast from 1886 to 1931*. Chicago: University of Chicago Press.

Rohner, Ronald P., and Evelyn C. Rohner
   1970   *The Kwakiutl Indians of British Columbia*. New York: Holt, Rinehart and Winston.

Rosaldo, Michelle Z., and Louise Lamphere, eds.
   1974   *Women, Culture, and Society*. Palo Alto: Stanford University Press.

Rosaldo, Renato
   1989   *Culture and Truth: The Remaking of Social Analysis*. Boston: Beacon Press.

Ruyle, Eugene E.
   1973   "Slavery, Surplus, and Stratification on the Northwest Coast: The Ethnoenergetics of an Incipient Stratification System," *Current Anthropology* 14:603–31.

Sapir, Edward, and Morris Swadesh
   1939   *Nootka Texts: Tales and Ethnological Narratives with Grammatical Notes and Lexical Materials*, Philadelphia: Linguistic Society of America.

Sessional Papers
   1874–1910 Canada, Parliament, *Sessional Papers*, Annual Report of the Department of Indian Affairs, variously numbered.

Solomon-Godeau, Abigail
   1989   "Going Native," *Art in America* 77 (7): 118–28, 161.

Spradley, James P., ed.
   1969   *Guests Never Leave Hungry: the Autobiography of James Sewid, A Kwakiutl Indian*. New Haven: Yale University Press.

Sproat, Gilbert Malcolm
   1879a   Sproat to Macdonald, 27 October 1879, DIA, vol. 3669, file 10,691.
   1879b   Sproat to Macdonald, 11 November 1879, DIA, vol. 3699, file 1665.

Stocking, George W., Jr.
   1968   *Race, Culture, and Evolution: Essays in the History of Anthropology*. Chicago: University of Chicago Press.
   1974   *The Shaping of American Anthropology, 1883–1911: A Franz Boas Reader*. New York: Basic Books.
   1977   "The Aims of Boasian Ethnography: Creating the Materials for Traditional Humanistic Scholarship," *History of Anthropology Newsletter* 4(2):4–5.
   1985   "Essays on Museums and Material Culture," pp. 3–14 in *Objects and Others: Essays on Museums and Material Culture*, ed. G. Stocking. Madison: University of Wisconsin Press.

Strathern, Marilyn
   1988   *The Gender of the Gift*. Berkeley and Los Angeles: University of California Press.

Suttles, Wayne, and Aldona Jonaitis
   1990   "History of Research in Ethnology," pp. 73–87 in *Handbook of North American Indians, vol. 7, Northwest Coast*, ed. W. Suttles. Washington, D.C.: Smithsonian Institution.

Taylor, Herbert C., Jr., and Wilson Duff
  1956   "A Post-Contact Southward Movement of the
          Kwakiutl," *Washington State University Research
          Studies* 24:56–66.
Todd, Murray
  1936   Todd to Mackenzie, 11 February 1936, DIA, vol. 8481,
          file 24–3, pt. 1.
  1939   Todd to Superintendent General, February 1939
          report, DIA, vol. 3631, file 6244–5.
Torgovnick, Marianna
  1990   *Gone Primitive: Savage Intellects, Modern Lives.*
          Chicago: University of Chicago Press.
Tyler, Stephen A.
  1986   "Post-Modern Ethnography: From Document of
          Occult to Occult Document," pp. 122–40 in *Writing
          Culture: The Poetics and Politics of Ethnography*, ed. J.
          Clifford and G. Marcus. Berkeley and Los Angeles:
          University of California Press.
  1990   "Ode to Dialog on the Occasion of the Un-for-seen,"
          pp. 292–300 in *The Interpretation of Dialogue*, ed. T.
          Maranhao. Chicago: University of Chicago Press.
Vancouver, George
  1984   *A Voyage of Discovery to the North Pacific Ocean and
          Round the World, 1791–1795*, ed. W. Kaye Lamb. 4
          vols. London: The Hakluyt Society.
Vancouver World
  1915   *Vancouver World*, 10 February 1915.

Vowell, A.W.
  1891   Vowell to Vankoughnet, 25 February 1891, DIA,
          file 57,045–1.
  1897   Vowell to Deputy Superintendent General, 16
          January 1897, DIA, vol. 3628, file 6244–1.
Waite, Deborah
  1966   "Kwakiutl Transformation Masks," pp. 264–300 in
          Many Faces of Primitive Art: A Critical Anthology, ed. D.
          Fraser. Englewood Cliffs, N.J.: Prentice-Hall.
Walens, Stanley
  1981   *Feasting with Cannibals: An Essay on Kwakiutl
          Cosmology*. Princeton: Princeton University Press.
Webster, Gloria Cranmer
  1989   The 'R' Word," *Muse* 4(3):43–46.
  1990   "Kwakiutl Since 1980," pp. 199–202 in *Handbook of
          North American Indians, vol. 7, Northwest Coast*, ed. W.
          Suttles. Washington, D.C.: Smithsonian Institution.
White, Leslie A.
  1963   "The Ethnography and Ethnology of Franz Boas,"
          Bulletin of the Texas Memorial Museum, no. 6.
Williams, David R.
  1977   *". . . The Man for a New Country": Sir Matthew Baillie
          Begbie*. Sydney: Gray's.
Wolf, Eric
  1982   *Europe and the People Without History*. Berkeley:
          University of California Press.
Wright, Robin
  1991   "Introduction," *A Time of Gathering*. Seattle: Burke
          Museum and University of Washington Press.

Contributors

Aldona Jonaitis is an art historian who has written on Northwest Coast art. Her books include *Art of the Northern Tlingit* (1986), *From the Land of the Totem Poles: The Northwest Coast Indian Art Collection at the American Museum of Natural History* (1988), and *A Wealth of Thought: Franz Boas on Native American Art* (in press). She is currently the Vice President for Public Programs at the American Museum of Natural History.

Douglas Cole, a historian at Simon Fraser University, Burnaby, British Columbia, writes on the history of anthropology and Indian-white relations. His most recent books are *Captured Heritage: The Scramble for Northwest Coast Artifacts* (1985), an edition of *The Journals of George M. Dawson* (with Bradley Lockner, 1989), and *An Iron Hand Upon the People: The Law Against the Potlatch on the Northwest Coast* (with Ira Chaikin, 1990). He is currently writing a biography of Franz Boas.

Ira Jacknis is a curatorial consultant for the Department of African, Oceanic, and New World Art at The Brooklyn Museum. He is author of *The Storage Box of Tradition: Museums, Anthropologists, and Kwakiutl Art, 1881–1981* (Smithsonian Institution Press), and coauthor of *Objects of Myth and Memory*, an exhibition catalogue on Stewart Culin's American Indian collections at The Brooklyn Museum (copublished with University of Washington Press). His research interests include art and aesthetics, museums, the history of anthropology, visual anthropology, and American Indian (especially Northwest Coast) cultures.

Wayne Suttles has taught anthropology at the University of British Columbia, the University of Nevada, and Portland State University. He is author of *Coast Salish Essays* and editor of the Northwest Coast volume of the Smithsonian's *Handbook of North American Indians*.

Gloria Cranmer Webster was born in Alert Bay. Her interest in anthropology came from the work of her great-grandfather George Hunt with Franz Boas. Later, her father Dan Cranmer also worked with Boas. Until this year, she was curator of the U'mista Cultural Centre, where she had worked for over 10 years. U'mista Cultural projects in which she was involved include the production of two documentary films, a series of Kwak̓wala language books, and translation and transcription of Kwak̓wala material for use in local schools.

Stanley A. Freed, Curator in the Department of Anthropology at the American Museum of Natural History, is responsible for North American ethnography. He has been at AMNH since 1960.

Lynton Gardiner is an internationally published specialist in photographing works of art. He has worked as a staff photographer for both the Montreal Museum of Fine Arts and the Metropolitan Museum of Art, New York. In 1985, he opened his own studio.

Peter L. Macnair has worked as Curator of Anthropology at the Royal British Columbia Museum since 1965. His publications include *The Legacy* (1980, with Alan Hoover and Kevin Neary), and *The Magic Leaves* (1984, with Alan Hoover).

Stacy Alyn Marcus is a graduate student in the Department of Art History and Archaeology, Columbia University, concentrating in Northwest Coast art.

Judith Ostrowitz is a graduate student in the Department of Art History and Archaeology, Columbia University, concentrating in Northwest Coast art.

Index